Sous Vide Cookbook for Beginners:

Dessert Lover's Book, Everyday, Party, and Holiday Sweet Treat Recipes for Two Servings with Ingredients, Nutritional Information, and Clear Instructions

ADDISON J. MEDLIN

Copyright © 2025 Addison J. Medlin

All rights reserved. No part of this publication may be reproduced, distributed, or transmitted in any form or by any means, including photocopying, recording, or other electronic or mechanical methods, without the prior written permission of the author, except in the case of brief quotations embodied in critical reviews and certain other non-commercial uses permitted by copyright law.

Disclaimer

The information in *"Sous Vide Cookbook for Beginners: Dessert Lover's Book, Everyday, Party, and Holiday Sweet Treat Recipes for Two Servings with Ingredients, Nutritional Information, and Clear Instructions"* is provided for general informational and educational purposes only. While the author has made every effort to ensure the accuracy of the information contained in this book, the recipes, nutritional information, and cooking instructions are intended for guidance and should not be considered as an exact science.

The author and publisher are not responsible for any errors or omissions or for any results obtained from the use of this information. Any cooking times, temperatures, or instructions should be adjusted based on individual equipment and preferences. Additionally, readers should consult their healthcare professional before making significant changes to their diet or food preparation methods, especially in cases of food allergies or dietary restrictions.

The author and publisher disclaim any liability for any injury, loss, or damage incurred from using the content in this book. All food safety and storage recommendations should be followed according to the latest guidelines, and it is the reader's responsibility to ensure proper food handling practices are followed.

Table of Contents

Introduction
- What Is Sous Vide Cooking?...............10
- Why Sous Vide for Desserts?...............10
- Who This Book Is for...............10

How To Use This Book

Introducing Sous Vide Desserts
- What Makes Sous Vide Preferred for Dessert Preparation...............12
- Overview of Recipe Categories in This Book...............13

Technical Equipment for Cooking Sous Vide Desserts
- Essential Tools...............14
- Sous Vide Machine (Immersion Circulator)...............14
- Vacuum Sealer and Bags...............14
- Containers and Lids...............14
- Jars and Ramekins...............15
- Optional Tools...............15
- Ice Cream Maker (For Frozen Desserts)...............15
- Tips for Maintenance and Usage...............15

Introduction to Infused Fruit Desserts Using Sous Vide Technology
- General Principles of Sous Vide Infused Fruit Desserts...............17
- Proper Packing Techniques...............17
- Storage Before and After Cooking...............18
- Serving the Finished Dish...............18
- Common Mistakes and How To Avoid Them...............18
- Conclusion...............19
- Popular Alcoholic Infusions...............19
- Plating Fruit Desserts...............20

Apple Cinnamon Compote...............23
Apricots With Amaretto...............23
Baked Apples...............24
Berry Compote...............24
Berry Medley Compote...............25
Berry Smoothie Bowl...............25
Blackberry Coulis...............26
Blueberry Syrup...............26
Caramelized Bananas...............27
Caramelized Pineapple...............27
Cherries With Bourbon...............28
Cinnamon Apples...............28
Cinnamon Pears...............29
Cinnamon-Infused Peaches...............29
Citrus Bliss Compote...............30
Citrus Marmalade...............30
Cranberry Sauce...............31

Fig Compote 31
Fruit Compote 32
Fruit Salad 32
Grapefruit 33
Grapefruit Segments In Vanilla Syrup 33
Honeyed Pears 34
Mango Passionfruit Compote 34
Mango With Lime and Chili 35
Orange Segments With Honey 35
Peach and Cardamom Compote 36
Peach Compote 36
Pineapple With Rum and Brown Sugar 37
Poached Figs 37
Poached Pears 38
Poached Pears in Red Wine 38
Pomegranate Arils With Rose Water 39
Spiced Plums 39
Strawberry Compote 40
Strawberry Rhubarb Sauce 40
Vanilla-Infused Apples 41
Watermelon Infused With Mint 41

Introduction to Preparing Custards and Creams Desserts Using Sous Vide Technology

General Principles and Features of Sous Vide Custards and Creams 42
How To Pack Custards and Creams Correctly 42
Shaping Custards and Creams for Presentation 43
Storing Custards and Creams Before and After Cooking 43
Preparing the Finished Dish for Serving 43
Common Mistakes and How To Avoid Them 44
Conclusion 44
Toppings for Sous Vide Flan 44
Caramelizing Flan With a Torch 46

Almond Custard 48
Almond Milk Panna Cotta 48
Berry Parfait 49
Caramel Flan 49
Chai Spiced Custard 50
Cherry Clafoutis 50
Coconut Custard 51
Coffee Crème Brûlée 51
Crème Brûlée 52
Eggnog Custard 52
Espresso Custard 53
Honey Lavender Panna Cotta 53
Key Lime Pots de Crème 54
Lavender Panna Cotta 54
Lemon Curd 55

Lemon Yogurt Parfait 55
Mango Custard 56
Maple Custard 56
Matcha Green Tea Custard 57
Panna Cotta 57
Peanut Butter Custard 58
Pumpkin Custard 58
Salted Caramel Custard 59
Salted Caramel Pots de Crème 59
Strawberry Panna Cotta 60
Strawberry Parfait 60
Tiramisu 61
Vanilla Bean Panna Cotta 61
Vanilla Custard 62
Vanilla Flan 62

Introduction to Preparing Yogurt Desserts Using Sous Vide Technology

General Principles and Features of Sous Vide Yogurt Desserts 63
How To Pack Yogurt Mixtures Correctly 63
Shaping Yogurt Desserts for Presentation 64
Storing Yogurt Before and After Cooking 64
Preparing the Finished Dish for Serving 64
Common Mistakes and How To Avoid Them 65
Conclusion 65
How To Add Fruit Compote to Sous Vide Yogurt Desserts 65

Banana Cream Yogurt 67
Blackberry Honey Yogurt 67
Blueberry Lemon Yogurt 68
Blueberry Yogurt 68
Chai-Spiced Yogurt 69
Chocolate Almond Yogurt 69
Chocolate Yogurt 70
Coconut Milk Yogurt 70
Greek Yogurt 71
Honey-Sweetened Yogurt 71
Key Lime Yogurt 72
Mango Lassi Yogurt 72
Maple Cinnamon Yogurt 73
Matcha Green Tea Yogurt 73
Orange Blossom Yogurt 74
Peach Ginger Yogurt 74
Pineapple Coconut Yogurt 75
Pumpkin Spice Yogurt 75
Raspberry Swirl Yogurt 76
Strawberry Yogurt 76
Vanilla Bean and Lavender Yogurt 77
Vanilla Yogurt 77

Introduction to Preparing Cakes and Puddings Using Sous Vide Technology

General Principles and Features of Sous Vide Cakes and Puddings 78
How To Pack Cakes and Puddings Correctly 78
Shaping Cakes and Puddings for Presentation 79
Storing Cakes and Puddings Before and After Cooking 79
Preparing the Finished Dish for Serving 79
Common Mistakes and How To Avoid Them 80
Conclusion 80
Some of the Sauces To Pair With Pudding 80
The Perfect Sauce for Bread Pudding 82

Key Lime Pie 84
Lemon Bars 84
Lemon Cheesecake 85
Apricot Almond Cake 85
Gooseberry Cardamom Cake 86
Fig Honey Cake 86
Kiwi Lime Cake 87
Pear Ginger Cake 87
Blackberry Sage Cake 88
Cranberry Orange Cake 88
Pineapple Upside-Down Cake 89
Banana Walnut Cake 89
Mango Coconut Cake 90
Lemon Blueberry Bundt Cake 90
Black Forest Cake 91
Cherry Vanilla Cake 91
Raspberry Almond Cake 92
Peach Cobbler Cake 92
Mixed Berry Cheesecake 93
Strawberry Shortcake 93
Blueberry Lemon Cake 94
Apple Spice Cake 94
S'mores Cake 95
Raspberry Lemon Bars 95
Pumpkin Pie 96
Pumpkin Cheesecake 96
Lemon Pudding 97
Lemon Tart 97
Fruit Tart 98
Coconut Rice Pudding 98
Cinnamon Rolls 99
Sticky Toffee Pudding 99
Vanilla Bean Cheesecake 100
Rice Pudding With Cinnamon 100
Carrot Cake Cheesecake 101
Gingerbread Pudding 101

Butterscotch Bread Pudding 102
Tres Leches Cake 102
Peach Cobbler Bread Pudding 103
Maple Pecan Pudding Cake 103
Apple Cinnamon Pudding 104
Red Velvet Cheesecake 104
Coconut Rum Pudding Cake 105
Salted Caramel Pudding Cake 105
Almond Butter Brownies 106
Apple Crumble 106
Banana Bread Pudding 107
Blueberry Cheesecake 107
Blueberry Cobbler 108
Bread Pudding With Whiskey Sauce 108
Brownies 109
Cheesecake 109

Introduction to Preparing Jellies and Gels Using Sous Vide Technology

General Principles and Features of Sous Vide Jellies and Gels 110
How To Pack Jellies and Gels Correctly 110
Shaping Jellies and Gels for Presentation 111
Storing Jellies and Gels Before and After Cooking 111
Preparing the Finished Dish for Serving 111
Common Mistakes and How To Avoid Them 112
Conclusion 112
The Choice of Molds for Sous Vide Jellies and Gels 112
Some Tips To Achieve Flawless, Visually Striking Layers 114

Apple Cider Gelée 116
Blueberry Lavender Jelly 116
Cherry Amaretto Gelée 117
Classic Fruit Jelly 117
Coconut Lime Gelée 118
Cranberry Orange Gelatin 118
Elderflower and Pear Jelly 119
Grapefruit Campari Jelly 119
Honey Lemon Gelée 120
Kiwi Lime Jelly 120
Lemon Gelatin Squares 121
Mango Passionfruit Jelly 121
Peach Bellini Gelée 122
Pineapple Ginger Jelly 122
Raspberry Gelée 123
Strawberry Champagne Jelly 123
Vanilla Bean Gelatin 124
Watermelon Mint Jelly 124

Introduction to Preparing Chocolate Treats Using Sous Vide Technology

    General Principles and Features of Sous Vide Chocolate Desserts 125
    How To Pack Chocolate Desserts Correctly 125
    Shaping Chocolate Treats for Presentation 125
    Storing Chocolate Treats Before and After Cooking 126
    Preparing the Finished Dish for Serving 126
    Common Mistakes and How To Avoid Them 127
    Conclusion 127
    Some Topping Ideas for Your Chocolate Creations 127
    Some Sweet-Salty Combos for Chocolate 129

Chocolate Brownies 131
Chocolate Cake 131
Chocolate Cheesecake 132
Chocolate Chip Cookies 132
Chocolate Coconut Custard 133
Chocolate Espresso Custard 133
Chocolate Fudge Brownies 134
Chocolate Ganache Tart 134
Chocolate Gelatin Mousse 135
Chocolate Hazelnut Cheesecake 135
Chocolate Lava Cake 136
Chocolate Mousse 136
Chocolate Oat Pudding 137
Chocolate Peanut Butter Cheesecake 137
Chocolate Pots de Crème 138
Chocolate Pudding 138
Chocolate Soufflé 139
Chocolate Tart 139
Chocolate Truffle Filling 140
Dark Chocolate Crémeux 140
Dark Chocolate Fondant Cake 141
Dark Chocolate Mousse 141
Fudge Brownies 142
Hazelnut Chocolate Spread 142
Hot Chocolate Custard 143
Mint Chocolate Mousse 143
Pomegranate Chocolate Cake 144
Raspberry-Infused Chocolate Ganache 144
Triple Chocolate Pudding Cake 145
White Chocolate Panna Cotta 145

Introduction to Preparing Frozen Desserts Using Sous Vide Technology

    General Principles and Features of Sous Vide Frozen Desserts 146
    How To Pack Frozen Desserts Correctly 146
    Shaping Frozen Desserts for Presentation 146
    Storing Frozen Desserts Before and After Cooking 147
    Preparing the Finished Dish for Serving 147
    Common Mistakes and How To Avoid Them 147

- Conclusion 148
  - Few Methods on How To Make Ice Cream by Hand Without Using an Ice Cream Maker 148
  - Some Unusual Fruit Pairings for Sous Vide Frozen Desserts 149
- Vanilla Bean Ice Cream Base 151
- Chocolate Gelato Base 151
- Strawberry Sorbet 152
- Mango Coconut Ice Cream 152
- Matcha Green Tea Ice Cream 153
- Peach Frozen Yogurt 153
- Mint Chocolate Chip Ice Cream 154
- Salted Caramel Ice Cream Base 154
- Espresso Gelato 155
- Raspberry Lemon Sorbet 155
- Pistachio Ice Cream 156
- Coconut Lime Sorbet 156
- Cookies and Cream Ice Cream 157
- Banana Peanut Butter Ice Cream 157
- Blueberry Cheesecake Ice Cream 158
- Pumpkin Spice Ice Cream 158
- Blackberry Frozen Yogurt 159
- Passionfruit Sorbet 159
- Cherry Vanilla Ice Cream 160
- Tropical Pineapple Coconut Sorbet 160

Appendices

- Common Conversion Charts 161
- Ingredient Substitution Guide 162
- Troubleshooting Sous Vide Desserts 163

Index Recipes

Why Sous Vide? Why Now?

Final Treat: Heartfelt Thanks and an Invitation To Explore More

- Discover More With the "Cookbook for Beginners" Series 173

INTRODUCTION

WHAT IS SOUS VIDE COOKING?

Sous vide, a French term meaning "under vacuum," is a revolutionary cooking method that involves sealing food in airtight bags and cooking it in a precisely controlled water bath. This method ensures even cooking by maintaining a consistent temperature throughout the process. Sous vide originated in the 1970s as a technique primarily used in professional kitchens to achieve unparalleled precision and consistency. Today, thanks to advancements in technology and accessibility, sous vide has become a popular choice for home cooks worldwide.

> For those seeking an in-depth exploration of sous vide technology and equipment, including temperature ranges and cooking techniques for various dishes, you can refer to our previous book:
>
> "Sous Vide Cookbook for Beginners: Two Servings Recipes with Ingredients Nutritional Information and Clear Instructions, Includes Temperature Ranges for Joint Cooking Different Dishes."
>
> Scan the QR code on page 173 to go to it.

WHY SOUS VIDE FOR DESSERTS?

Desserts are all about precision. The slightest variation in temperature or time can mean the difference between a silky custard and a curdled mess. Sous vide cooking offers unparalleled control over these variables, making it the perfect method for creating delicate and sophisticated desserts. Here are some key benefits:

- **Precision**: Achieve exact temperatures for perfect custards, puddings, and mousse textures.
- **Consistency**: Every batch will taste and look the same, ensuring your results are reliable.
- **Unique Textures:** Sous vide cooking can produce velvety smooth ice creams, moist cakes, and flavorful fruit compotes that are difficult to replicate with traditional methods.

Whether you are making a simple chocolate mousse or a complex layered dessert, sous vide guarantees impressive and delicious results.

WHO THIS BOOK IS FOR

This book is designed for anyone who loves desserts and wants to explore the magic of sous vide cooking. Whether you are a beginner trying sous vide for the first time or a home cook looking to expand your culinary repertoire, this book has something for you. With straightforward instructions and detailed nutritional information, it's also perfect for health-conscious individuals who want to know exactly what goes into their sweet creations.

This book is your guide if you are looking for foolproof recipes that deliver consistent, high-quality results. Each recipe has been tailored for two servings, making it ideal for couples, small families, or those who enjoy portion-controlled treats.

HOW TO USE THIS BOOK

This book is designed to be user-friendly and accessible. Each recipe follows a clear and consistent format to make your cooking experience as enjoyable as possible:

Ingredients and Measurements:

Every recipe includes precise measurements suitable for two servings. Adjustments for scaling up or down are provided, ensuring you can cook for more if needed.

Step-by-Step Instructions:

Simple, clear, and concise directions guide you through the sous vide process from start to finish.

Nutritional Information:

Each recipe includes detailed nutritional breakdowns so you can make informed choices.

Sous Vide Tips:

Helpful notes and suggestions are included to enhance your understanding of the sous vide process and ensure success.

Index of Ingredients:

A handy reference at the book's end lets you quickly locate recipes based on key ingredients.

As you read this book, you'll discover the joys of creating sous vide desserts. From classic favorites to innovative treats, each recipe is crafted to help you master this technique and impress yourself and others with delicious results. Let's begin this exciting journey into the magic world of sous vide desserts!

INTRODUCING SOUS VIDE DESSERTS

Desserts are the crown jewel of any meal, bringing sweetness and satisfaction to the dining experience. Sous vide cooking, a technique that has revolutionized professional kitchens and is now making waves in home kitchens, allows desserts to reach a new level of precision and perfection. If you've ever struggled to achieve the perfect texture, flavor, or consistency in your desserts, sous vide might be the game-changer you've been looking for.

WHAT MAKES SOUS VIDE PREFERRED FOR DESSERT PREPARATION

Sous vide is a cooking method in which food is vacuum-sealed in a bag and cooked in a water bath at a precisely controlled temperature. While it's often associated with savory dishes like steaks or vegetables, this technique offers unique dessert advantages that other methods can't match.

Traditional dessert preparation often involves baking, steaming, or stovetop cooking, all of which expose ingredients to fluctuating temperatures. This variability can lead to overcooking or undercooking, especially for delicate recipes like custards or puddings. Sous vide eliminates this inconsistency by maintaining an exact temperature throughout cooking. The result? Desserts with perfect texture, flavor, and doneness every time.

For example, custards made in an oven can turn grainy or watery if slightly overcooked. With sous vide, the gentle and steady heat ensures that the proteins in the custard don't curdle, delivering a silky, smooth texture. Similarly, infusing fruits with flavors or poaching them becomes an art form as sous vide allows you to retain their natural juices and vibrant colors.

Key Advantages: Control, Creativity, and Convenience

Sous vide offers three major advantages that make it ideal for dessert preparation: control, creativity, and convenience.

Control

Precision is the hallmark of sous vide cooking. By controlling the exact temperature, you can cook desserts to their optimal state without guesswork. Whether tempering chocolate, setting yogurt cultures, or poaching fruits, sous vide ensures consistent and repeatable results.

Creativity

The sous vide method allows for endless creativity. It is much easier to infuse syrups and creams with unique flavors, create layered desserts with intricate textures, or experiment with unconventional ingredients. This technique allows you to try new things with minimal risk of ruining the dish.

Convenience

Once your ingredients are sealed and placed in the water bath, you can essentially "set it and forget it." There's no need to hover over the stove or constantly check the oven. This hands-off approach lets you focus on other parts of the meal or relax while your dessert cooks perfectly.

OVERVIEW OF RECIPE CATEGORIES IN THIS BOOK

This book is designed to guide you through a wide range of sous vide dessert recipes, perfect for beginners. Each category highlights the versatility of this cooking method, offering something for every sweet tooth.

Infused Fruits

Sous vide excels at gently cooking fruits while preserving their shape, color, and flavor. Infused fruits like spiced pears, vanilla strawberries, or citrus-poached apples are not only delicious on their own but also make stunning toppings for cakes and ice cream.

Custards and Creams

Classic desserts like crème brûlée, flan, and pots de crème are transformed with sous vide. These creamy, indulgent treats achieve a perfect consistency—never overcooked, always silky smooth. Plus, precise temperature control means you can cook multiple jars at once without worrying about uneven results.

Yogurts

Sous vide elevates homemade yogurt. The consistent low temperatures required for fermentation ensure creamy, tangy yogurt every time. Sous vide simplifies the process, whether you prefer it plain or infused with honey, vanilla, or fruit.

Cakes and Puddings

From molten chocolate cakes to bread puddings, sous vide guarantees moist and tender results. The controlled environment ensures cakes don't dry out and puddings set perfectly without a rubbery texture.

Jellies and Gels

Desserts like panna cotta or fruit jellies benefit greatly from sous vide's precision. Achieving the perfect set without over-gelling is effortless, leading to delicate melt-in-your-mouth textures.

Chocolate Treats

Tempering chocolate can be intimidating, but sous vide makes it foolproof. The even heat of the water bath ensures glossy, professional-quality chocolate that's perfect for candies, truffles, and coatings.

Frozen Desserts

While sous vide doesn't freeze, it is vital for creating the bases for frozen desserts like ice cream and sorbets. Pasteurizing ingredients like eggs or dairy at precise temperatures ensures safety and consistency in your frozen creations.

Each recipe in this book is crafted to be simple yet impressive, with step-by-step instructions and nutritional information tailored for two servings. By exploring these recipes, you'll understand sous vide's magic and feel confident creating restaurant-quality desserts at home.

TECHNICAL EQUIPMENT FOR COOKING SOUS VIDE DESSERTS

ESSENTIAL TOOLS

Cooking sous vide desserts requires precision, and having the right tools is essential to achieving professional-quality results. In this chapter, we build upon the foundation laid in the "Sous Vide Cookbook for Beginners: Two Servings Recipes with Ingredients Nutritional Information and Clear Instructions, Includes Temperature Ranges for Joint Cooking Different Dishes," tailoring our discussion specifically for desserts. Let's dive into the essential tools to make your sous vide dessert-making experience seamless.

SOUS VIDE MACHINE (IMMERSION CIRCULATOR)

The sous vide machine, or immersion circulator, is the cornerstone of sous vide cooking. It provides precise temperature control for desserts, ensuring that delicate custards, puddings, and yogurts are cooked evenly without curdling or overcooking. When choosing a sous vide machine for desserts:

Temperature Accuracy: Select a machine with accuracy up to 0.1°F (0.05°C). This precision is critical for desserts like creme brûlée or sous vide cheesecakes.

Size and Portability: A compact model is well-suited for smaller batches, such as the two-serving recipes in this book.

Ease of Use: Machines with intuitive controls and app integration can simplify your cooking process.

VACUUM SEALER AND BAGS

A vacuum sealer is vital for sealing ingredients to prevent water from entering during cooking. For desserts, this tool ensures airtight sealing for items like fruit compotes or spiced poached pears, keeping flavors intact. Key points to consider:

Bag Quality: Opt for food-safe, BPA-free vacuum bags that can withstand high temperatures.

Manual vs. Automatic Sealers: An automatic sealer simplifies the process for beginners, but a manual one provides more control for delicate items.

Reusable Options: Reusable silicone bags are eco-friendly and suitable for dessert ingredients like fruit slices or chocolate mixtures.

CONTAINERS AND LIDS

A heat-resistant container acts as the water bath for sous vide cooking. Specific containers ensure even heat distribution and securely accommodate jars or ramekins for desserts. Look for:

Insulated Containers: These help maintain temperature stability during long cooks, reducing energy usage.

Compatible Lids: Choose lids that minimize evaporation, especially for recipes requiring extended cooking times.

Custom Racks: If your desserts require jars or ramekins, racks keep them upright and prevent tipping.

JARS AND RAMEKINS

Heat-resistant jars and ramekins are indispensable for individual servings like custards, yogurts, and lava cakes.

Material: Use tempered glass jars or ceramic ramekins to withstand high temperatures without cracking.

Size: Opt for smaller sizes (4-6 oz) to ensure even cooking for two serving portions.

Lids: Jars with tight-fitting lids are ideal for preventing water from seeping into desserts like panna cotta.

OPTIONAL TOOLS

Blow Torch

A blow torch is the ultimate finishing tool for sous vide desserts. It's perfect for creating the crispy sugar crust on creme brûlée or caramelizing fruits. When choosing a blow torch, consider:

Adjustable Flame: This allows for precise control over browning.

Refillable Design: A torch that uses standard butane canisters is economical and convenient.

Safety Features: Models with a safety lock and a stable base minimize risks.

Ice Bath Setup

An ice bath is a simple yet critical addition for frozen or chilled desserts. After cooking, quickly submerging your dessert base in an ice bath halts the cooking process, preserving texture and flavor. For this setup:

Large Basin: Use a large enough basin to submerge your sealed bag or jar.

Plenty of Ice: Combine ice with cold water for maximum cooling efficiency.

Drainage: Ensure the basin has a spout for easy water removal after use.

ICE CREAM MAKER (FOR FROZEN DESSERTS)

A **home ice cream maker** is a kitchen appliance designed to churn and freeze ice cream, sorbet, or gelato, allowing you to create delicious frozen treats from scratch. These machines offer an easy way to make fresh, preservative-free desserts using your choice of ingredients.

TIPS FOR MAINTENANCE AND USAGE

Proper care of your sous vide equipment ensures longevity and consistent results. Follow these maintenance tips to keep your tools in top condition:

For the Sous Vide Machine

Regular Cleaning: To remove calcium buildup, regularly clean the immersion circulator's heating element and impeller. For buildup. use a vinegar solution (1 part vinegar to 1 part water).

Storage: Store the machine upright in a cool, dry place to avoid damaging internal components.

Inspect Before Use: Check the machine for wear or malfunction before starting a recipe.

For Vacuum Sealers and Bags

Seal Test: Run a test seal periodically to ensure the vacuum mechanism functions correctly.

Avoid Overfilling: Overfilled bags may not seal properly, leading to leaks.

Reusable Bag Care: Wash reusable bags with warm, soapy water and air dry them completely before storing them.

For Containers, Lids, and Accessories

Sanitization: Wash containers, lids, jars, and ramekins with hot, soapy water after each use. To prevent contamination, sterilize jars used with dairy-based desserts.

Inspect for Cracks: Regularly check jars and ramekins for cracks or chips that could cause breakage during cooking.

Organized Storage: Store lids and racks neatly to avoid losing small components.

General Tips

Monitor Water Levels: Always ensure the water level in your container remains above the minimum required by the sous vide machine.

Use Proper Tools: Silicone-coated tongs and jar lifters are gentle on delicate desserts and prevent container scratches.

Plan Ahead: Desserts often require cooling or chilling time after cooking, so factor this into your schedule.

By investing in and maintaining the right tools, you'll be well-equipped to create stunning sous vide desserts easily. This cooking method's precision and versatility will elevate your dessert game to a professional level, even as a beginner!

INTRODUCTION TO INFUSED FRUIT DESSERTS USING SOUS VIDE TECHNOLOGY

Infused fruit desserts made with sous vide technology celebrate vibrant flavors and textures, combining precision cooking with creative presentation. Sous vide is ideal for making infused fruit desserts, allowing delicate fruits to absorb flavors while maintaining their structure and natural sweetness. Let's dive into the principles, features, and techniques for crafting these delightful desserts.

GENERAL PRINCIPLES OF SOUS VIDE INFUSED FRUIT DESSERTS

Flavor Infusion: The sous vide method infuses fruits with herbs, spices, syrups, or liquors. By sealing the fruits and flavoring agents together, the flavors intensify without the need for additional cooking or reducing liquids.

Temperature Control: Sous vide ensures precise temperature regulation, which is crucial when working with delicate fruits that can overcook or break apart at high heat. Depending on their firmness and desired texture, most fruits are cooked between 130°F (54°C) and 180°F (82°C).

Retention of Nutrients and Vibrancy: Because sous vide cooking takes place in a sealed bag, nutrients, natural juices, and vibrant colors are preserved, leading to desserts that look as good as they taste.

Consistency: The low-and-slow method ensures that every piece of fruit is cooked evenly, with no risk of uneven heat distribution.

PROPER PACKING TECHNIQUES

Selecting the Bag: Use food-safe, high-quality vacuum-sealable or resealable bags. Avoid thin plastic bags that can tear under heat.

Preparing the Fruit:

- Wash and peel fruits as needed.
- Cut into uniform sizes to ensure even cooking.
- Pat the fruits dry to prevent excess water from diluting the flavor infusion.

Adding Flavor Components:

- Choose complementary flavors like cinnamon sticks, vanilla beans, citrus zests, fresh herbs, or liquors.
- Place these components evenly around the fruits for uniform infusion.

Vacuum Sealing:

- Arrange the fruits in a single layer inside the bag.
- Using a vacuum sealer or the water displacement method. This helps the bag stay submerged during cooking and ensures full contact with the water bath.

Shaping the Dish: If you want the fruits to take on a specific shape (e.g., perfect cubes or decorative slices), arrange them neatly in the bag before sealing. Using molds or frames inside the bag can help achieve a structured shape.

STORAGE BEFORE AND AFTER COOKING

Before Cooking:
- Keep the fruits refrigerated until ready to cook. If pre-sealing, ensure the bag is airtight and stored in the coldest part of the fridge.
- Do not add perishable ingredients (e.g., dairy or eggs) to the bag if it is to be stored for extended periods before cooking.

After Cooking:
- If the cooked fruits are not served immediately, they should be chilled in an ice water bath below 40°F (4°C).
- You can store the sealed bag in the refrigerator for up to 5 days or freeze it for longer storage (up to 3 months).

Reheating for Serving:
- Reheat gently in a sous vide bath at the original cooking temperature for 10–20 minutes.
- Alternatively, serve chilled or at room temperature, depending on the dessert type.

SERVING THE FINISHED DISH

Presentation:
- Infused fruits can be served or used as toppings for cakes, pancakes, waffles, or ice cream.
- Plate with garnishes like fresh herbs, edible flowers, or syrup drizzled from the cooking bag.

Additional Preparation:
- Reduce the juices from the sous vide bag into a glaze for extra flavor.
- Pair fruits with complementary elements like whipped cream, custards, or crème fraîche.

COMMON MISTAKES AND HOW TO AVOID THEM

Overcrowding the Bag:
Problem: Too many fruits in one bag can lead to uneven cooking and poor infusion.
Solution: Cook fruits in smaller batches or use multiple bags.

Insufficient Air Removal:
Problem: Air pockets can cause uneven cooking or make the bag float.
Solution: Use a vacuum sealer or the water displacement method carefully to ensure the bag is fully sealed and air-free.

Overcooking Delicate Fruits:
Problem: Fruits like berries can become mushy if cooked too long or at too high a temperature.
Solution: Cook delicate fruits at lower temperatures (130°F–140°F or 54°C–60°C) for a shorter time (30–60 minutes).

Improper Storage:
Problem: Storing cooked fruits without chilling can lead to spoilage.
Solution: Always chill fruits in an ice bath before refrigeration or freezing.

Not Balancing Flavors:
> **Problem**: Overpowering spices or syrups can mask the natural flavor of the fruits.
> **Solution**: Use flavoring agents sparingly and taste-test combinations beforehand.

CONCLUSION

With these principles, techniques, and tips, you can create delightful infused fruit desserts at home. The sous vide method enhances the flavors and textures of fruits and opens up endless possibilities for creativity in your dessert repertoire. Whether serving them fresh, pairing them with other elements, or saving them for later, sous vide fruits are a versatile and delicious addition to any meal.

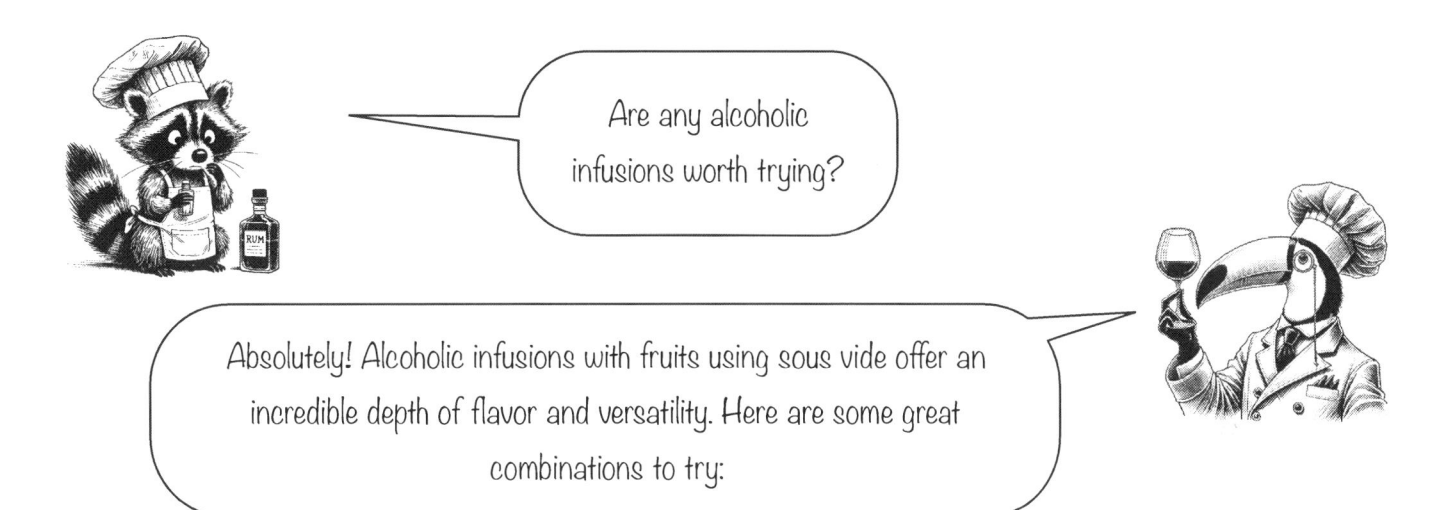

> Are any alcoholic infusions worth trying?

> Absolutely! Alcoholic infusions with fruits using sous vide offer an incredible depth of flavor and versatility. Here are some great combinations to try:

POPULAR ALCOHOLIC INFUSIONS

Bourbon-Infused Peaches
> **Ingredients**: Bourbon, sliced peaches, brown sugar, cinnamon stick.
> **Use**: Serve over vanilla ice cream, in cocktails, or as a dessert topping.

Rum-Infused Pineapple
> **Ingredients**: Dark rum, fresh pineapple chunks, brown sugar, and a pinch of nutmeg.
> **Use**: Add to tropical cocktails, serve with whipped cream, or caramelize for dessert.

Vodka-Infused Strawberries
> **Ingredients**: Vodka, halved strawberries, a splash of simple syrup.
> **Use**: Stir into sparkling water or champagne or drizzle over cakes.

Tequila-Infused Watermelon
> **Ingredients**: Tequila, watermelon cubes, lime zest, and a hint of chili powder.
> **Use:** Serve chilled as a refreshing adult snack or blend into Margaritas.

Brandy-Infused Cherries
> **Ingredients**: Brandy, pitted cherries, and a touch of sugar.
> **Use**: Use in cocktails like Manhattans or serve over cheesecake.

Limoncello-Infused Oranges
Ingredients: Limoncello, orange segments, and a hint of mint.
Use: Serve chilled as a palate cleanser or dessert.

Gin-Infused Blackberries
Ingredients: Gin, blackberries, a sprig of thyme, and a drizzle of honey.
Use: Muddle into gin cocktails or serve alongside dark chocolate.

Amaretto-Infused Apricots
Ingredients: Amaretto, apricot halves, and a pinch of vanilla.
Use: Perfect over panna cotta or as a topping for almond cake.

Whiskey-Infused Apples
Ingredients: Whiskey, sliced apples, maple syrup, and cinnamon.
Use: Serve warm with whipped cream or use in apple pie.

Cointreau-Infused Raspberries
Ingredients: Cointreau, raspberries, and a touch of sugar.
Use: Pair with chocolate desserts or use as a cocktail garnish.

Tips for Successful Alcoholic Infusions
- **Balance Flavors:** Use alcohol that complements the fruit's natural flavor. Add sweeteners, spices, or herbs for depth.
- **Vacuum-Sealing:** Ensure all ingredients are packed and sealed tightly to maximize infusion.
- **Temperature:** Cook sous vide at a low temperature (130°F…140°F / 55°C…60°C) to gently enhance the flavors without cooking off the alcohol.
- **Storage:** Cool and refrigerate the infusion immediately after cooking. Serve chilled or as needed.

> Suggest plating ideas for fruit desserts.

> Plating fruit desserts can elevate their visual appeal and enhance the dining experience. Here are some creative and approachable plating ideas for fruit desserts:

PLATING FRUIT DESSERTS

1. Layered Parfait Presentation
Example: Fruit compote, yogurt, and granola.

Plating Tip: Use a clear glass or jar to show off colorful layers. Add a sprig of mint or edible flowers on top for garnish.

2. Artistic Spread
Example: Mixed berries with sauces.
Plating Tip: Use a large white plate and spread fruit purees (e.g., raspberry or mango) in artistic swirls or dots. Arrange fruits symmetrically or in a crescent shape for elegance.

3. Tarts and Towers
Example: Mini fruit tarts or stacked fruit slices.
Plating Tip: Stack thinly sliced fruits like apples or mangoes into a tower. Place on a tart shell and drizzle with syrup or honey.

4. Rustic Charm
Example: Poached pears or baked apples.
Plating Tip: Serve on a wooden board or rustic ceramic plate. Sprinkle powdered sugar or cinnamon around the plate for a cozy touch.

5. Deconstructed Dessert
Example: Deconstructed pie or cobbler.
Plating Tip: Arrange the elements separately- a cream dollop, a crumbled crust line, and a portion of fruit filling. Use geometric arrangements for a modern look.

6. Elevated Skewers
Example: Fruit skewers with dipping sauces.
Plating Tip: Skewer assorted fruits upright in a glass or on a plate. On the side, add small bowls of chocolate or yogurt dipping sauce.

7. Minimalist Elegance
Example: Sous vide poached fruit with a sauce.
Plating Tip: Place one or two fruits (e.g., poached pear halves) on the plate. Add a small pool of sauce on the side and garnish with a sprig of fresh herbs.

8. Spiral Arrangements
Example: Thinly sliced fruits like mango or apple.
Plating Tip: Arrange the slices in a spiral pattern. Add a scoop of sorbet or ice cream in the center for balance.

9. Geometric Precision
Example: Cubed fruits or layered gelatin desserts.
Plating Tip: Cut fruits into uniform cubes and align them in a grid or tower. Use contrasting colors for visual interest.

10. Floral Inspiration
Example: Rosette-shaped fruits.
Plating Tip: Roll thin fruit slices, such as mangoes or strawberries, and arrange them with edible flowers or microgreens for a garden-inspired look.

11. Mirror Glaze Plate
Example: Fruit mousse or jelly.
Plating Tip: Use a glossy fruit glaze to cover the dessert and reflect light. Garnish minimally with fresh fruit slices.

12. Elevated Bowls
Example: Warm fruit compote with ice cream.
Plating Tip: Serve the compote in a shallow bowl with a scoop of ice cream in the center. Garnish with caramel drizzle or crumbled cookies.

13. Nature's Canvas
Example: Grilled or sous vide fruit.
Plating Tip: Serve the fruit on a banana leaf or slate board for a natural, earthy presentation.

14. Pairing with Textures
Example: Fruit paired with crunchy or creamy elements.
Plating Tip: Combine crunchy components (e.g., nuts or brittle) with smooth ones (e.g., panna cotta) and arrange them in contrasting patterns.

15. Individual Portions
Example: Mini fruit pavlova.
Plating Tip: Serve individual-sized desserts with small garnishes like mint leaves or fruit segments for a personalized touch.

16. Floating Elements
Example: Fruit served with a light sauce or broth.
Plating Tip: Place the fruit in a shallow dish and pour a small amount of liquid (e.g., citrus syrup or coconut milk) around it.

17. Interactive Platters
Example: Build-your-own fruit platter.
Plating Tip: Provide an assortment of fruits, sauces, and toppings (like nuts and chocolate chips) for guests to assemble themselves.

18. Contrast and Color Blocking
Example: Mango and berry coulis with fresh fruit.
Plating Tip: Use contrasting colors to create visual appeal. Plate bright-colored fruits on dark dishes or dark fruits on white plates.

19. Stack and Layer
Example: Fruit Napoleon.
Plating Tip: Layer fruit slices with pastry or cream. Alternate layers neatly and garnish the top layer with powdered sugar or edible gold.

20. Frozen Aesthetic
Example: Frozen fruit slices or sorbets.
Plating Tip: Plate chilled or frozen fruits on a frosted glass plate for an icy look. Add mint leaves for a pop of green.

General Plating Tips:
- **Clean Edges:** Wipe the plate's edges to avoid smudges for a professional finish.
- **Balance**: Combine different textures (smooth, crunchy, creamy) for contrast.
- **Height:** Add vertical elements (e.g., stacked fruits or tall garnishes) for drama.
- **Garnish Thoughtfully:** Use edible garnishes that enhance flavor and appearance.
- **Use Negative Space:** Leave some empty space on the plate for a minimalist, elegant look.

Apple Cinnamon Compote

Yield: 2 servings | Prep time: 10 minutes | Cook time: 1 hour

Warm your senses with our Sous Vide Apple Cinnamon Compote! Tender apple slices are infused with cinnamon's comforting aroma and a sweet touch. Sous vide precision preserves the fruit's texture and intensifies the flavors, making this compote a cozy topping for pancakes, desserts, or yogurt.

Ingredients:
- Apples (peeled, sliced) - 2 pieces
- Brown sugar - 2 tbsp
- Cinnamon (ground) - 0.5 tsp
- Butter (unsalted, melted) - 1 tbsp
- Lemon juice (freshly squeezed) - 1 tsp

Nutritional Information (for 2 servings):
calories 180 kcal, protein 1g, carbohydrates 38g, fat 4g, fiber 4g, cholesterol 10mg, sodium 30mg, potassium 200mg

Directions:
1. Preheat sous vide water bath to 185°F / 85°C
2. Mix apples, brown sugar, cinnamon, butter, and lemon juice (coat apples evenly for best flavor)
3. Transfer the mixture to a vacuum-sealed or zip-top bag (remove as much air as possible)
4. Sous vide for 60 minutes at 185°F / 85°C (fully submerge the bag in the water bath)
5. Serve warm as a topping or dessert (over pancakes, waffles, or ice cream)

Cooking Temperature Range:
Optimal 185°F / 85°C (permissible range 185°F / 85°C to 190°F / 88°C).

Apricots with Amaretto

Yield: 2 servings | Prep time: 10 minutes | Cook time: 45 minutes

Indulge in the luxurious harmony of our Sous Vide Apricots Amaretto. Juicy apricots are gently poached with amaretto's rich, nutty essence, creating a tender, flavor-infused treat. Sous vide precision ensures perfect texture and vibrant flavor, making it an elegant dessert or topping for any occasion.

Ingredients:
- Apricots (medium, halved, pitted) - 4 pieces
- Amaretto liqueur - 2 tbsp
- Honey - 1 tbsp
- Vanilla extract - 0.5 tsp
- Lemon zest (grated) - 1 tsp

Nutritional Information (for 2 servings):
calories 160 kcal, protein 1g, carbohydrates 28g, fat 3g, fiber 2g, cholesterol 0mg, sodium 10mg, potassium 310mg

Directions:
1. Preheat sous vide water bath to 175°F / 80°C
2. Halve and pit the apricots (ensure apricots are ripe but firm)
3. Combine all ingredients in a vacuum-seal bag (distribute liquids evenly)
4. Cook in a water bath for 45 minutes
5. Let cool and serve warm or chilled (garnish with fresh mint if desired)

Cooking Temperature Range:
Optimal 175°F / 80°C (permissible range 175°F / 80°C to 180°F / 82°C).

Baked Apples

Yield: 2 servings | Prep time: 15 minutes | Cook time: 1 hour

Sous vide baked apples are a delightful dessert, perfectly tender and infused with cinnamon and brown sugar. Cooking them sous vide ensures even cooking, preserving their natural sweetness while adding a rich, caramel-like flavor. Top with whipped cream or ice cream for an irresistible treat.

Ingredients:
- Apples (cored) - 2 pieces
- Brown sugar - 2 tbsp
- Cinnamon (ground) - 1 tsp
- Butter (unsalted, softened) - 1 tbsp
- Crushed walnuts (optional) - 2 tbsp

Nutritional Information (for 2 servings):
calories 230 kcal, protein 1g, carbohydrates 40g, fat 8g, fiber 4g, cholesterol 20mg, sodium 30mg, potassium 220mg

Directions:
1. Preheat sous vide water bath to 185°F / 85°C
2. Mix brown sugar, cinnamon, and butter in a bowl (ensure ingredients are well blended)
3. Fill cored apples with the mixture and add walnuts (pack filling evenly into apples)
4. Seal the apples in a bag and cook sous vide for 60 minutes (remove air from the bag completely)
5. Serve warm with whipped cream or ice cream if desired (customize with preferred toppings)

Cooking Temperature Range:
Optimal 185°F / 85°C (permissible range 183°F / 84°C to 190°F / 88°C).

Berry Compote

Yield: 2 servings | Prep time: 10 minutes | Cook time: 1 hour

Elevate your meals with our Sous Vide Berry Compote! A medley of ripe, juicy berries is gently cooked to create a rich, flavorful sauce bursting with natural sweetness and a hint of tartness. Sous vide precision ensures a perfectly smooth texture, making it a versatile topping for desserts, pancakes, or ice cream.

Ingredients:
- Mixed berries (fresh or frozen) - 1 cup
- White sugar - 0.25 cup
- Lemon juice (freshly squeezed) - 1 tbsp
- Vanilla extract - 0.5 tsp

Nutritional Information (for 2 servings):
calories 150 kcal, protein 1g, carbohydrates 37g, fat 0g, fiber 4g, cholesterol 0mg, sodium 5mg, potassium 180mg

Directions:
1. Preheat sous vide water bath to 185°F / 85°C
2. Combine ingredients in a bowl and mix (ensure sugar is evenly distributed)
3. Transfer mixture to a vacuum-seal or zip-top bag (remove air to ensure proper cooking)
4. Cook in the sous vide bath for 60 minutes (stir bag gently if using zip-top method)
5. Mash or blend and serve as desired (cool slightly before blending)

Cooking Temperature Range:
Optimal 185°F / 85°C (permissible range 185°F / 85°C to 190°F / 88°C).

Berry Medley Compote

Yield: 2 servings | Prep time: 10 minutes | Cook time: 45 minutes

This Sous Vide Berry Medley Compote combines a mixture of fresh berries with sugar and a touch of lemon juice. The gentle sous vide process preserves vibrant flavors and colors, resulting in a sweet and slightly tangy sauce perfect for topping desserts, pancakes, or yogurt.

Ingredients:
- Mixed berries (fresh, rinsed, drained) - 2 cups
- Sugar - 2 tbsp
- Water - 2 tbsp
- Lemon juice (freshly squeezed) - 1 tbsp

Nutritional Information (for 2 servings):
calories 200 kcal, protein 2g, carbohydrates 45g, fat 1g, fiber 5g, cholesterol 0mg, sodium 5mg, potassium 200mg

Directions:
1. Combine berries, sugar, water, and lemon juice in a bowl (gently stir to avoid crushing the berries too much)
2. Seal the mixture in jars or vacuum bags (leave some headspace in jars if using them)
3. Cook at 160°F / 71°C for 45 minutes in a sous vide water bath (ensure full submersion)
4. Remove from bath and cool briefly before serving or storing (carefully handle hot containers)

Cooking Temperature Range:
Optimal 160°F / 71°C (permissible range 155°F / 68°C to 165°F / 74°C).

Berry Smoothie Bowl

Yield: 2 servings | Prep time: 10 minutes | Cook time: 1 hour

Start your day with a burst of freshness with our Sous Vide Berry Smoothie Bowl! Packed with vibrant mixed berries, creamy yogurt, and a touch of natural sweetness, this bowl is a feast for the senses. Sous vide precision enhances flavor and texture, and it is topped with granola and fruits for a nutritious, colorful delight.

Ingredients:
- Mixed berries (fresh or frozen) - 1 cup
- Greek yogurt (plain) - 0.5 cup
- Honey - 2 tbsp
- Granola - 0.25 cup
- Chia seeds - 1 tbsp

Nutritional Information (for 2 servings):
calories 240 kcal, protein 6g, carbohydrates 40g, fat 6g, fiber 7g, cholesterol 0mg, sodium 45mg, potassium 150mg

Directions:
1. Preheat sous vide water bath to 135°F / 57°C
2. Combine berries, yogurt, and honey in a vacuum-sealed bag (avoid air pockets in the bag)
3. Submerge the bag in the water bath and cook for 60 minutes (ensure the bag remains fully submerged)
4. Remove and blend the mixture until smooth (blend for an even texture)
5. Pour into bowls, top with granola and chia seeds, and serve (serve immediately for best freshness)

Cooking Temperature Range:
Optimal 135°F / 57°C (permissible range 135°F / 57°C to 135°F / 57°C).

Blackberry Coulis

Yield: 2 servings | Prep time: 10 minutes | Cook time: 30 minutes

Elevate your desserts with our Sous Vide Blackberry Coulis! Bursting with the bold, tangy sweetness of ripe blackberries, this silky, vibrant sauce is a feast for the senses. Sous vide precision ensures a perfectly smooth texture, making it the ultimate topping for cakes, ice cream, or pancakes.

Ingredients:
- Blackberries (fresh) - 1 cup
- Sugar - 2 tbsp
- Lemon juice (freshly squeezed) - 1 tbsp
- Water - 2 tbsp

Nutritional Information (for 2 servings):
calories 80 kcal, protein 1g, carbohydrates 20g, fat 0g, fiber 4g, cholesterol 0mg, sodium 0mg, potassium 200mg

Directions:
1. Preheat sous vide water bath to 185°F / 85°C
2. Combine all ingredients in a vacuum-seal bag (ensure the bag is sealed tightly)
3. Cook in a water bath for 30 minutes
4. Blend the contents until smooth (use caution when handling hot contents)
5. Strain through a fine-mesh sieve and serve (discard seeds after straining)

Cooking Temperature Range:
Optimal 185°F / 85°C (permissible range 185°F / 85°C to 190°F / 88°C).

Blueberry Syrup

Yield: 2 servings | Prep time: 5 minutes | Cook time: 45 minutes

Elevate your breakfasts and desserts with our Sous Vide Blueberry Syrup! Bursting with fresh blueberries' natural sweetness and vibrant flavor, this silky syrup is perfectly balanced and irresistibly smooth. Sous vide precision ensures the pure essence of blueberries in every luscious drizzle.

Ingredients:
- Blueberries (fresh or frozen) - 1 cup
- White sugar - 0.25 cup
- Lemon juice (freshly squeezed) - 1 tbsp
- Water - 2 tbsp

Nutritional Information (for 2 servings):
calories 120 kcal, protein 0g, carbohydrates 31g, fat 0g, fiber 2g, cholesterol 0mg, sodium 5mg, potassium 50mg

Directions:
1. Preheat sous vide water bath to 185°F / 85°C
2. Combine blueberries, sugar, lemon juice, and water (mix thoroughly for even flavor)
3. Seal the mixture in a vacuum or zip-top bag (ensure proper sealing to prevent leaks)
4. Cook in a water bath for 45 minutes (occasionally agitate for better mixing)
5. Strain solids and serve warm or chilled (refrigerate for up to a week)

Cooking Temperature Range:
Optimal 185°F / 85°C (permissible range 185°F / 85°C to 190°F / 88°C).

Caramelized Bananas

Yield: 2 servings | Prep time: 5 minutes | Cook time: 45 minutes

Indulge in the golden sweetness of our Sous Vide Caramelized Bananas! Tender, perfectly ripe bananas are gently cooked with a touch of sugar and warm spices, creating a rich, caramelized flavor. Sous vide precision ensures a luscious texture, making this treat irresistible as a dessert or topping.

Ingredients:
- Banana (medium, ripe) - 2 pieces
- Brown sugar - 0.25 cup
- Butter (unsalted) - 2 tbsp
- Cinnamon (ground) - 0.25 tsp
- Vanilla extract - 0.5 tsp

Nutritional Information (for 2 servings):
calories 250 kcal, protein 2g, carbohydrates 40g, fat 9g, fiber 2g, cholesterol 20mg, sodium 30mg, potassium 300mg

Directions:
1. Preheat sous vide water bath to 185°F / 85°C
2. Peel and slice bananas into halves lengthwise (use ripe bananas for the best flavor)
3. Combine brown sugar, butter, cinnamon, and vanilla (mix thoroughly to avoid lumps)
4. Seal the bananas and caramel mixture in a vacuum bag (ensure no air remains in the bag)
5. Cook in the water bath for 45 minutes. Serve warm with caramel sauce (agitate the bag halfway for an even coating)

Cooking Temperature Range:
Optimal 185°F / 85°C (permissible range 185°F / 85°C to 190°F / 88°C).

Caramelized Pineapple

Yield: 2 servings | Prep time: 10 minutes | Cook time: 45 minutes

Elevate your dessert game with our Sous Vide Caramelized Pineapple! Juicy pineapple slices are gently cooked with a touch of sugar and spices, transforming into a golden, tender delight. Sous vide precision enhances the natural sweetness and ensures every bite bursts with tropical, caramelized flavor.

Ingredients:
- Pineapple (peeled, cored, sliced) - 1 piece
- Butter (unsalted, melted) - 2 tbsp
- Brown sugar - 3 tbsp
- Cinnamon (ground) - 0.5 tsp
- Vanilla extract - 1 tsp

Nutritional Information (for 2 servings):
calories 220 kcal, protein 1g, carbohydrates 45g, fat 7g, fiber 2g, cholesterol 15mg, sodium 60mg, potassium 200mg

Directions:
1. Preheat sous vide water bath to 183°F / 84°C
2. Combine pineapple, butter, sugar, cinnamon, and vanilla in a bag. Seal tightly (ensure proper sealing)
3. Cook in sous vide water bath (ensure the bag is fully submerged)
4. Sear pineapple in a hot skillet for caramelization /optional/ (which adds a golden crust for extra flavor)
5. Serve warm as a dessert or topping (best served fresh)

Cooking Temperature Range:
Optimal 183°F / 84°C (permissible range 183°F / 84°C to 185°F / 85°C).

Cherries with Bourbon

Yield: 2 servings | Prep time: 10 minutes | Cook time: 1 hour

Indulge in the bold flavors of our Sous Vide Cherries with Bourbon! Juicy cherries are gently poached with a bourbon splash and a touch of sweetness, creating a rich, aromatic treat. Sous vide precision enhances the fruit's natural juiciness, making this a perfect dessert or decadent topping.

Ingredients:
- Cherries (pitted, fresh) - 1 cup
- Bourbon - 2 tbsp
- Brown sugar - 2 tbsp
- Vanilla extract - 0.5 tsp
- Cinnamon (ground) - 1 pinch

Nutritional Information (for 2 servings):
calories 170 kcal, protein 1g, carbohydrates 30g, fat 0.5g, fiber 3g, cholesterol 0mg, sodium 5mg, potassium 190mg

Directions:
1. Preheat sous vide water bath to 185°F / 85°C
2. Combine cherries, bourbon, sugar, vanilla, and cinnamon (mix thoroughly)
3. Seal in a vacuum or zip-top bag, removing air (ensure proper sealing)
4. Cook in a water bath for 60 minutes (stir gently if needed)
5. Cool slightly before serving (use warm or chilled as desired)

Cooking Temperature Range:
Optimal 185°F / 85°C (permissible range 185°F / 85°C to 190°F / 88°C).

Cinnamon Apples

Yield: 2 servings | Prep time: 10 minutes | Cook time: 1 hour

Experience the warm, nostalgic flavors of our Sous Vide Cinnamon Apples! Tender apple slices are gently cooked with a touch of cinnamon and sugar, enhancing their natural sweetness and spice. Sous vide precision ensures perfect texture and flavor, making this a comforting treat for any occasion.

Ingredients:
- Apples (peeled, cored, sliced) - 2 pieces
- Cinnamon (ground) - 1 tsp
- Brown sugar - 2 tbsp
- Butter (unsalted) - 1 tbsp
- Lemon juice (freshly squeezed) - 1 tbsp

Nutritional Information (for 2 servings):
calories 200 kcal, protein 1g, carbohydrates 45g, fat 4g, fiber 4g, cholesterol 10mg, sodium 20mg, potassium 180mg

Directions:
1. Preheat sous vide water bath to 185°F / 85°C
2. Peel, core, and slice apples. Rub with lemon juice (to prevent browning)
3. Place ingredients into a sealed bag (ensure airtight sealing)
4. Cook in sous vide bath for 60 minutes (keep bag fully submerged)
5. Serve apples warm with sauce from the bag (garnish with nuts or cream if desired)

Cooking Temperature Range:
Optimal 185°F / 85°C (permissible range 185°F / 85°C to 190°F / 88°C).

Cinnamon Pears

Yield: 2 servings | Prep time: 10 minutes | Cook time: 1 hour

Delight in the cozy flavors of our Sous Vide Cinnamon Pears! Juicy pears are gently infused with the warm cinnamon spice and a sweet touch, creating a tender and flavorful treat. Sous vide precision preserves their natural texture, making every bite a comforting and elegant dessert.

Ingredients:
- Pears (peeled, cored) - 2 pieces
- Cinnamon (ground) - 1 tsp
- Brown sugar - 2 tbsp
- Lemon juice (freshly squeezed) - 1 tbsp
- Butter (unsalted) - 1 tbsp

Nutritional Information (for 2 servings):

calories 210 kcal, protein 1g, carbohydrates 45g, fat 4g, fiber 4g, cholesterol 10mg, sodium 30mg, potassium 200mg

Directions:
1. Preheat sous vide water bath to 185°F / 85°C
2. Peel, core, and slice pears. Rub with lemon juice (to prevent browning)
3. Place pears, cinnamon, sugar, and butter in a sealed bag (ensure airtight sealing)
4. Cook in sous vide bath for 60 minutes (keep bag fully submerged)
5. Serve warm, drizzled with sauce from the bag (garnish with nuts, if desired)

Cooking Temperature Range:

Optimal 185°F / 85°C (permissible range 185°F / 85°C to 190°F / 88°C).

Cinnamon-Infused Peaches

Yield: 2 servings | Prep time: 10 minutes | Cook time: 1 hour

Delight in the warm, comforting flavors of Cinnamon-Infused Sous Vide Peaches! Juicy peaches are gently cooked with a hint of cinnamon, enhancing their natural sweetness and creating a perfectly tender texture. Sous vide precision ensures a flavorful, aromatic treat that's cozy and delicious.

Ingredients:
- Peaches (halved, pitted) - 2 pieces
- Cinnamon stick (whole) - 1 piece
- Honey - 2 tbsp
- Butter (unsalted, melted) - 1 tbsp
- Lemon juice (freshly squeezed) - 1 tsp

Nutritional Information (for 2 servings):

calories 160 kcal, protein 1g, carbohydrates 25g, fat 5g, fiber 2g, cholesterol 10mg, sodium 20mg, potassium 200mg

Directions:
1. Preheat sous vide water bath to 180°F / 82°C
2. Mix honey, butter, and lemon juice (ensure the butter is fully melted)
3. Place the peaches, cinnamon sticks, and honey mixture in a bag (remove as much air as possible)
4. Cook in water bath for 60 minutes (keep bag fully submerged)
5. Serve the peaches warm with cooking liquid or garnish (optional: garnish with whipped cream)

Cooking Temperature Range:

Optimal 180°F / 82°C (permissible range 180°F / 82°C to 185°F / 85°C).

Citrus Bliss Compote

Yield: 2 servings | Prep time: 15 minutes | Cook time: 45 minutes

This Sous Vide Citrus Bliss Compote combines oranges, grapefruits, and lemons in a sweet-tart sauce, gently cooked to preserve bright flavors. The low sous vide temperature helps prevent bitterness and keeps the fruit segments intact, creating a vibrant topping for desserts or breakfast dishes.

Ingredients:
- Orange (small. peeled, segmented, seeds removed) - 1 piece
- Grapefruit (small. peeled, segmented, seeds removed) - 1 piece
- Sugar - 2 tbsp
- Water - 2 tbsp

Nutritional Information (for 2 servings):
calories 150 kcal, protein 2g, carbohydrates 36g, fat 0g, fiber 4g, cholesterol 0mg, sodium 10mg, potassium 300mg

Directions:
1. Peel and segment citrus fruits, remove seeds and pith (aim for clean, pith-free segments)
2. Combine fruit segments, sugar, and water in jars or bags, then seal (leave some headspace in jars if using them)
3. Cook at 160°F / 71°C for 45 minutes in a sous vide bath (ensure full submersion during cooking)
4. Remove from bath and let cool a few minutes before serving or refrigerating (carefully handle hot containers)

Cooking Temperature Range:
Optimal 160°F / 71°C (permissible range 155°F / 68°C to 165°F / 74°C).

Citrus Marmalade

Yield: 2 servings | Prep time: 15 minutes | Cook time: 2 hours

Brighten your mornings with our Sous Vide Citrus Marmalade! A vibrant blend of oranges, lemons, and grapefruits is gently cooked to preserve their natural zest and sweetness. Sous vide precision ensures a perfectly smooth, spreadable texture, making every spoonful a burst of sunshine on your toast or pastries.

Ingredients:
- Oranges (peeled, sliced) - 2 pieces
- Lemon (peeled, sliced) - 1 piece
- Sugar - 0.5 cup
- Water - 0.25 cup
- Orange zest (grated) - 1 tsp

Nutritional Information (for 2 servings):
calories 160 kcal, protein 0g, carbohydrates 42g, fat 0g, fiber 3g, cholesterol 0mg, sodium 10mg, potassium 200mg

Directions:
1. Preheat sous vide water bath to 185°F / 85°C
2. Combine ingredients in a bowl and mix well (ensure sugar dissolves evenly)
3. Transfer the mixture to a bag and vacuum seal (remove as much air as possible)
4. Cook in a water bath for 120 minutes (bag should stay fully submerged)
5. Blend the mixture until smooth (cool before serving or storing)

Cooking Temperature Range:
Optimal 185°F / 85°C (permissible range 185°F / 85°C to 190°F / 88°C).

Cranberry Sauce

Yield: 2 servings | Prep time: 5 minutes | Cook time: 45 minutes

Add a festive touch to your table with our Sous Vide Cranberry Sauce! Tart cranberries are gently cooked with a hint of sweetness and spices, creating a perfectly balanced, vibrant sauce. Sous vide precision enhances the flavors and ensures a luscious texture, making it the ultimate holiday side or topping.

Ingredients:
- Cranberries (fresh) - 1 cup
- Sugar - 0.25 cup
- Orange juice (freshly squeezed) - 2 tbsp
- Water - 2 tbsp
- Orange zest (grated) - 0.5 tsp

Nutritional Information (for 2 servings):
calories 100 kcal, protein 0g, carbohydrates 26g, fat 0g, fiber 2g, cholesterol 0mg, sodium 5mg, potassium 60mg

Directions:
1. Preheat sous vide water bath to 185°F / 85°C
2. Combine all ingredients in a vacuum-seal or zip-top bag (ensure even distribution)
3. Submerge the bag and cook in the water bath for 45 minutes
4. Transfer to a bowl, mash, and chill before serving (adjust consistency as desired)

Cooking Temperature Range:
Optimal 185°F / 85°C (permissible range 185°F / 85°C to 190°F / 88°C).

Fig Compote

Yield: 2 servings | Prep time: 10 minutes | Cook time: 1 hour

Indulge in the rich, earthy sweetness of our Sous Vide Fig Compote! Tender figs are gently cooked to perfection, creating a luscious spread bursting with natural flavor and a hint of warmth. Sous vide precision enhances the figs' texture and sweetness, making this compote a versatile topping or a standalone treat.

Ingredients:
- Figs (fresh) - 1 cup
- Brown sugar - 2 tbsp
- Water - 2 tbsp
- Lemon juice (freshly squeezed) - 1 tbsp
- Cinnamon stick (small) - 1 piece

Nutritional Information (for 2 servings):
calories 130 kcal, protein 1g, carbohydrates 34g, fat 0g, fiber 4g, cholesterol 0mg, sodium 10mg, potassium 300mg

Directions:
1. Preheat sous vide water bath to 185°F / 85°C
2. Combine ingredients in a vacuum-seal bag and seal (seal bag tightly to avoid leaks)
3. Submerge in a water bath and cook for 60 minutes (ensure the bag is fully submerged)
4. Remove and discard cinnamon stick, and mash slightly (mash to desired consistency)
5. Serve warm or chilled (great with cheese or desserts)

Cooking Temperature Range:
Optimal 185°F / 85°C (permissible range 185°F / 85°C to 190°F / 88°C).

Fruit Compote

Yield: 2 servings | Prep time: 10 minutes | Cook time: 1 hour

Transform fresh fruits into a vibrant delight with our Sous Vide Fruit Compote! Gently cooked to preserve its natural sweetness and texture, this luscious blend of fruits is infused with subtle spices. Sous vide precision ensures perfect consistency, making it a versatile topping or stand-alone treat.

Ingredients:
- Mixed fruits (cut into uniform pieces) - 1 cup
- Sugar - 2 tbsp
- Lemon juice (freshly squeezed) - 1 tbsp
- Cinnamon stick (whole) - 1 piece
- Vanilla extract - 0.5 tsp

Nutritional Information (for 2 servings):
calories 100 kcal, protein 1g, carbohydrates 25g, fat 0g, fiber 3g, cholesterol 0mg, sodium 5mg, potassium 200mg

Directions:
1. Combine ingredients in a sous vide bag and seal tightly (ensure no air remains in the bag)
2. Preheat sous vide water bath to 175°F / 79°C
3. Cook in a water bath for 60 minutes (keep the bag fully submerged)
4. Remove and discard the cinnamon stick (be careful when opening the bag)
5. Serve warm or chilled as desired (adjust sweetness if needed)

Cooking Temperature Range:
Optimal 175°F / 79°C (permissible range 175°F / 79°C to 180°F / 82°C).

Fruit Salad

Yield: 2 servings | Prep time: 10 minutes | Cook time: 30 minutes

Refresh your palate with our Sous Vide Fruit Salad! A vibrant medley of perfectly tender fruits, gently cooked to enhance their natural sweetness and preserve their juiciness. Each bite bursts with flavor and color, making this dish a delightful, healthy treat for any time of the day.

Ingredients:
- Strawberries (halved) - 0.5 cup
- Pineapple chunks (cut into bite-sized pieces) - 0.5 cup
- Blueberries (whole) - 0.33 cup
- Orange juice (freshly squeezed) - 0.33 cup
- Honey - 1 tbsp
- Mint leaves (optional) - to taste

Nutritional Information (for 2 servings):
calories 120 kcal, protein 1g, carbohydrates 30g, fat 0.5g, fiber 3g, cholesterol 0mg, sodium 10mg, potassium 150mg

Directions:
1. Preheat sous vide water bath to 140°F / 60°C
2. Combine fruits, juice, and honey in a bag. Seal tightly (ensure proper vacuum sealing)
3. Cook the sealed bag for 30 minutes in the water bath
4. Remove the bag, cool, and transfer to a serving bowl (handle with care when opening)
5. Garnish with mint leaves before serving, if desired (adds a fresh flavor)

Cooking Temperature Range:
Optimal 140°F / 60°C (permissible range 140°F / 60°C to 150°F / 65°C).

Grapefruit

Yield: 2 servings | Prep time: 10 minutes | Cook time: 1 hour

Transform tart into tender with our Sous Vide Grapefruit! This vibrant citrus treat is gently cooked to enhance its natural sweetness and soften its texture. Sous vide precision preserves the fruit's bright color and bold flavor, making it a refreshing and elegant addition to breakfasts or desserts.

Ingredients:
- Grapefruit (sliced, segmented) - 2 pieces
- Honey - 2 tbsp
- Vanilla extract - 1 tsp
- Cinnamon (ground) - 0.25 tsp

Nutritional Information (for 2 servings):
calories 120 kcal, protein 1g, carbohydrates 30g, fat 0g, fiber 2g, cholesterol 0mg, sodium 5mg, potassium 350mg

Directions:
1. Slice grapefruits and segment the flesh (use a sharp knife for clean cuts)
2. Mix honey, vanilla, and cinnamon, then spread on top (ensure an even coating)
3. Place grapefruits in vacuum or resealable bags (use the water displacement method if needed)
4. Cook in sous vide water bath at 140°F / 60°C for 60 minutes (maintain temperature accuracy)
5. Serve warm or chilled as desired (chilling enhances sweetness)

Cooking Temperature Range:
Optimal 140°F / 60°C (permissible range 122°F / 50°C to 149°F / 65°C).

Grapefruit Segments in Vanilla Syrup

Yield: 2 servings | Prep time: 10 minutes | Cook time: 30 minutes

Delight in the elegant simplicity of our Sous Vide Grapefruit Segments in Vanilla Syrup! Juicy, tangy grapefruit is gently poached in a fragrant vanilla-infused syrup, creating a tender and flavorful treat. Sous vide precision preserves the fruit's vibrant color and enhances its natural sweetness.

Ingredients:
- Grapefruit (peeled, segmented) - 1 piece
- Sugar - 2 tbsp
- Water - 3 tbsp
- Vanilla bean (split lengthwise) - 1 piece

Nutritional Information (for 2 servings):
calories 120 kcal, protein 1g, carbohydrates 30g, fat 0g, fiber 2g, cholesterol 0mg, sodium 0mg, potassium 200mg

Directions:
1. Preheat sous vide water bath to 185°F / 85°C
2. Combine all ingredients in a vacuum-seal bag (seal bag tightly to prevent leaks)
3. Submerge in a water bath and cook for 30 minutes
4. Remove and discard the vanilla bean, and serve (be careful when handling the hot bag)

Cooking Temperature Range:
Optimal 185°F / 85°C (permissible range 185°F / 85°C to 190°F / 88°C).

Honeyed Pears

Yield: 2 servings | Prep time: 10 minutes | Cook time: 1 hour

Savor the elegance of our Sous Vide Honeyed Pears! Tender, juicy pears are infused with golden honey and warm spices, creating a simple and luxurious dessert. Sous vide precision enhances their natural sweetness and ensures a perfectly soft texture, making every bite a delightful indulgence.

Ingredients:
- Pears (medium, peeled, halved, cored) - 2 pieces
- Honey - 2 tbsp
- Lemon juice (freshly squeezed) - 1 tbsp
- Cinnamon stick (whole) - 1 piece

Nutritional Information (for 2 servings):
calories 150 kcal, protein 0g, carbohydrates 40g, fat 0g, fiber 4g, cholesterol 0mg, sodium 10mg, potassium 220mg

Directions:
1. Peel and halve the pears, remove the core, and sprinkle with lemon juice (use ripe pears for the best flavor)
2. Combine all ingredients in a vacuum-seal bag and seal tightly (ensure no air remains in the bag)
3. Submerge the bag in a sous vide bath at 185°F / 85°C and cook for 60 minutes
4. Serve warm or chilled, optionally paired with yogurt or ice cream (let the pears cool slightly before serving)

Cooking Temperature Range:
Optimal 185°F / 85°C (permissible range 185°F / 85°C to 190°F / 88°C).

Mango Passionfruit Compote

Yield: 2 servings | Prep time: 10 minutes | Cook time: 45 minutes

Transport your taste buds to the tropics with our Sous Vide Mango Passionfruit Compote! Juicy mangoes meet the tangy sweetness of passionfruit in this vibrant, golden-hued delight. Sous vide precision preserves the fruits' natural flavors and textures, creating a luscious topping or a standalone treat that bursts with sunshine.

Ingredients:
- Mango (medium, peeled, diced) - 1 cup
- Passionfruit pulp (fresh. scoop pulp from the shell) - 2 pieces
- Sugar - 2 tbsp
- Water - 2 tbsp

Nutritional Information (for 2 servings):
calories 230 kcal, protein 2g, carbohydrates 58g, fat 1g, fiber 6g, cholesterol 0mg, sodium 5mg, potassium 400mg

Directions:
1. Dice the mango and scoop the passionfruit pulp into a bowl (ensure the mango is cut into even chunks)
2. Mix with sugar and water, then seal in jars or bags (leave some headspace if using jars)
3. Cook at 165°F / 74°C for 45 minutes in a sous vide water bath (keep jars/bags fully submerged)
4. Remove and let cool briefly before serving or chilling (carefully handle hot containers)

Cooking Temperature Range:
Optimal 165°F / 74°C (permissible range 160°F / 71°C to 170°F / 77°C).

Mango with Lime and Chili

Yield: 2 servings | Prep time: 10 minutes | Cook time: 45 minutes

Spice up your taste buds with our Sous Vide Mango with Lime and Chili! Sweet, juicy mango is perfectly paired with zesty lime and a hint of chili heat, creating a bold and refreshing flavor combination. Sous vide precision ensures tender, vibrant fruit, making this dish an exotic and irresistible treat.

Ingredients:
- Mango (peeled, sliced) - 1 cup
- Lime juice (freshly squeezed) - 1 tbsp
- Honey - 1 tbsp
- Chili powder - 0.25 tsp
- Salt - 1 pinch

Nutritional Information (for 2 servings):
calories 100 kcal, protein 1g, carbohydrates 25g, fat 0g, fiber 2g, cholesterol 0mg, sodium 20mg, potassium 200mg

Directions:
1. Preheat sous vide water bath to 170°F / 77°C
2. Mix mango, lime juice, honey, chili powder, and salt (coat the mango evenly)
3. Seal the mixture in a vacuum or zip-top bag, removing air (ensure the bag is properly sealed)
4. Cook in a water bath for 45 minutes (stir gently if needed)
5. Cool slightly before serving (serve warm or chilled)

Cooking Temperature Range:
Optimal 170°F / 77°C (permissible range 170°F / 77°C to 175°F / 80°C).

Orange Segments with Honey

Yield: 2 servings | Prep time: 5 minutes | Cook time: 30 minutes

Delight in the natural sweetness of our Sous Vide Orange Segments with Honey! Juicy orange slices gently infuse golden honey, creating a tender, flavor-packed treat. Sous vide precision preserves their vibrant color and texture, making this a versatile addition to desserts, breakfasts, or salads.

Ingredients:
- Oranges (medium, peeled, segmented) - 2 pieces
- Honey - 2 tbsp
- Vanilla extract - 0.5 tsp
- Mint leaves (fresh, optional) - 4 pieces

Nutritional Information (for 2 servings):
calories 120 kcal, protein 1g, carbohydrates 31g, fat 0g, fiber 3g, cholesterol 0mg, sodium 5mg, potassium 250mg

Directions:
1. Preheat sous vide water bath to 185°F / 85°C
2. Peel, segment, and remove pith from oranges (ensure segments are clean and intact)
3. Combine ingredients in a vacuum-seal or zip-top bag (distribute honey evenly)
4. Cook in a water bath for 30 minutes
5. Cool and serve or chill for later use (adjust sweetness if needed)

Cooking Temperature Range:
Optimal 185°F / 85°C (permissible range 185°F / 85°C to 190°F / 88°C).

Peach and Cardamom Compote

Yield: 2 servings | Prep time: 10 minutes | Cook time: 45 minutes

This Sous Vide Peach and Cardamom Compote highlights the natural sweetness of peaches with a subtle hint of cardamom. The sous vide method gently cooks the fruit, preserving its vibrant flavor and texture, resulting in a versatile topping for desserts, pancakes, or yogurt.

Ingredients:
- Peaches (medium, washed, pitted, sliced) - 2 pieces
- Sugar - 2 tbsp
- Water - 2 tbsp
- Cardamom (ground) - 1 pinch

Nutritional Information (for 2 servings):
calories 200 kcal, protein 2g, carbohydrates 48g, fat 2g, fiber 3g, cholesterol 0mg, sodium 0mg, potassium 250mg

Directions:
1. Slice peaches into bite-sized pieces (ensure peaches are evenly cut)
2. Mix peaches, sugar, water, and cardamom, then seal in jars or bags (leave a little headspace if using canning jars)
3. Cook at 160°F / 71°C for 45 minutes in a sous vide water bath (keep jars/bags fully submerged)
4. Remove and let cool briefly before serving or chilling (carefully handle hot containers)

Cooking Temperature Range:
Optimal 160°F / 71°C (permissible range 155°F / 68°C to 165°F / 74°C).

Peach Compote

Yield: 2 servings | Prep time: 10 minutes | Cook time: 45 minutes

Capture summer's sweetness with our Sous Vide Peach Compote. Juicy, ripe peaches are gently cooked to perfection, creating a luscious, golden sauce with just the right balance of natural sweetness and vibrant flavor. Perfect as a topping for desserts or breakfasts or enjoyed on its own!

Ingredients:
- Peaches (fresh, peeled, sliced) - 3 pieces
- Sugar - 2 tbsp
- Lemon juice (freshly squeezed) - 1 tbsp
- Vanilla extract - 1 tsp

Nutritional Information (for 2 servings):
calories 120 kcal, protein 1g, carbohydrates 30g, fat 0g, fiber 3g, cholesterol 0mg, sodium 5mg, potassium 280mg

Directions:
1. Combine all ingredients in a bowl and mix (use ripe peaches for best flavor)
2. Transfer to a sealed bag for sous vide cooking (remove as much air as possible)
3. Cook in water bath at 185°F / 85°C for 45 minutes
4. Cool slightly and serve warm or chilled (tastes best when fresh)
5. Use as a topping or enjoy on its own (pairs well with yogurt or pancakes)

Cooking Temperature Range:
Optimal 185°F / 85°C (permissible range 185°F / 85°C to 190°F / 88°C).

Pineapple with Rum and Brown Sugar

Yield: 2 servings | Prep time: 10 minutes | Cook time: 1 hour

Transport yourself to the tropics with our Sous Vide Pineapple with Rum and Brown Sugar! Juicy pineapple is gently infused with the rich sweetness of brown sugar and a hint of rum, creating a caramelized, tender delight. Sous vide precision ensures bold, vibrant flavors in every bite of this exotic treat.

Ingredients:
- Pineapple (peeled, cored, sliced) - 0.5 pieces
- Dark rum - 2 tbsp
- Brown sugar - 2 tbsp
- Vanilla extract - 0.5 tsp
- Butter (unsalted, melted) - 1 tbsp

Nutritional Information (for 2 servings):
calories 190 kcal, protein 0g, carbohydrates 30g, fat 5g, fiber 1g, cholesterol 10mg, sodium 10mg, potassium 150mg

Directions:
1. Preheat sous vide water bath to 185°F / 85°C
2. Mix rum, brown sugar, vanilla, and butter (ensure sugar is fully dissolved)
3. Place the pineapple and liquid in a sealed bag (remove as much air as possible)
4. Cook in the water bath for 60 minutes (keep the bag fully submerged)
5. Serve the pineapple warm or chilled with an optional garnish (optional: garnish with whipped cream)

Cooking Temperature Range:
Optimal 185°F / 85°C (permissible range 185°F / 85°C to 190°F / 88°C).

Poached Figs

Yield: 2 servings | Prep time: 10 minutes | Cook time: 1 hour

Indulge in the luxurious simplicity of our Sous Vide Poached Figs! These tender, honey-infused delights are gently cooked with warm spices, creating a soft texture and a rich, natural sweetness. Sous vide precision enhances the flavor, making every bite a sophisticated treat.

Ingredients:
- Figs (wash and trim if needed) - 4 pieces
- Honey - 3 tbsp
- Water - 0.5 cup
- Lemon zest (grated) - 1 tsp
- Cinnamon stick (whole) - 1 piece

Nutritional Information (for 2 servings):
calories 150 kcal, protein 1g, carbohydrates 35g, fat 0g, fiber 5g, cholesterol 0mg, sodium 15mg, potassium 210mg

Directions:
1. Wash figs and trim stems if needed (use fresh figs for best results)
2. Combine ingredients in a sous vide bag and seal tightly (ensure no air remains in the bag)
3. Preheat sous vide bath to 175°F / 79°C
4. Cook in water bath for 60 minutes (keep bag fully submerged)
5. Serve warm or chilled with syrup (reduce syrup for extra flavor)

Cooking Temperature Range:
Optimal 175°F / 79°C (permissible range 175°F / 79°C to 180°F / 82°C).

Poached Pears

Yield: 2 servings | Prep time: 15 minutes | Cook time: 1 hour

Elevate your dessert game with our Sous Vide Poached Pears! Perfectly tender and infused with a delicate blend of spices and sweetness, these pears boast a luscious texture and vibrant flavor. Sous vide precision ensures consistent cooking, making this elegant treat a feast for the senses.

Ingredients:
- Pears (peeled, cored) - 2 pieces
- White sugar - 0.25 cup
- Water - 1 cup
- Vanilla extract - 1 tsp
- Cinnamon stick (whole) - 1 piece

Nutritional Information (for 2 servings):
calories 150 kcal, protein 0g, carbohydrates 40g, fat 0g, fiber 4g, cholesterol 0mg, sodium 10mg, potassium 200mg

Directions:
1. Prepare the pears by peeling and coring them (use a corer for even results)
2. Combine ingredients in a sous vide bag and seal tightly (ensure no air remains in the bag)
3. Preheat sous vide bath to 175°F / 79°C
4. Cook for 60 minutes in the water bath (keep the bag fully submerged)
5. Serve warm or chilled with infused liquid (reduce liquid for a syrup)

Cooking Temperature Range:
Optimal 175°F / 79°C (permissible range 175°F / 79°C to 180°F / 82°C).

Poached Pears in Red Wine

Yield: 2 servings | Prep time: 10 minutes | Cook time: 1 hour 30 minutes

Elevate your dessert game with our Sous Vide Poached Pears in Red Wine! Tender, juicy pears are infused with the rich flavors of red wine, warm spices, and a touch of sweetness. Sous vide precision enhances their natural texture and creates a stunning, elegant treat perfect for any occasion.

Ingredients:
- Pears (medium, peeled, cored) - 2 pieces
- Red wine - 1 cup
- White sugar - 0.25 cup
- Cinnamon stick (whole) - 1 piece
- Orange zest (thin strips) - 1 tsp
- Cloves (whole) - 2 pieces

Nutritional Information (for 2 servings):
calories 220 kcal, protein 1g, carbohydrates 38g, fat 0g, fiber 4g, cholesterol 0mg, sodium 10mg, potassium 180mg

Directions:
1. Preheat sous vide water bath to 176°F / 80°C
2. Heat wine, sugar, and spices until sugar dissolves (do not boil the mixture)
3. Combine pears with wine mixture in a sealed bag (remove excess air from the bag)
4. Cook in the water bath for 90 minutes (keep the bag fully submerged)
5. Strain and reduce liquid; serve pears with sauce (chill or serve warm, as desired)

Cooking Temperature Range:
Optimal 176°F / 80°C (permissible range 176°F / 80°C to 185°F / 85°C).

Pomegranate Arils with Rose Water

Yield: 2 servings | Prep time: 10 minutes | Cook time: 30 minutes

Experience the exotic allure of our Sous Vide Pomegranate Arils with Rose Water! Juicy, jewel-like pomegranate seeds are delicately infused with the floral essence of rose water, creating a fragrant and refreshing treat. Sous vide precision ensures vibrant flavors and a perfect burst of sweetness in every bite.

Ingredients:
- Pomegranate arils (fresh) - 1 cup
- Rose water - 1 tbsp
- Sugar - 2 tbsp
- Water - 2 tbsp

Nutritional Information (for 2 servings):
calories 120 kcal, protein 1g, carbohydrates 31g, fat 0g, fiber 3g, cholesterol 0mg, sodium 0mg, potassium 300mg

Directions:
1. Preheat sous vide water bath to 190°F / 88°C
2. Combine ingredients in a vacuum-seal bag and seal (seal bag tightly to avoid leaks)
3. Submerge in a water bath and cook for 30 minutes (ensure the bag is fully submerged)
4. Remove, cool, and serve as desired (handle bag carefully when hot)

Cooking Temperature Range:
Optimal 190°F / 88°C (permissible range 190°F / 88°C to 195°F / 90°C).

Spiced Plums

Yield: 2 servings | Prep time: 10 minutes | Cook time: 1 hour 30 minutes

Savor the cozy flavors of our Sous Vide Spiced Plums! Juicy plums are gently poached with warm spices like cinnamon and star anise, creating a tender, aromatic treat. Sous vide precision enhances their natural sweetness and ensures a perfect texture, making this dessert a delightful and elegant indulgence.

Ingredients:
- Plums (halved, pitted) - 4 pieces
- Brown sugar - 2 tbsp
- Cinnamon stick (whole) - 1 piece
- Star anise (whole) - 1 piece
- Water - 0.25 cup
- Vanilla extract - 0.5 tsp

Nutritional Information (for 2 servings):
calories 120 kcal, protein 1g, carbohydrates 30g, fat 0g, fiber 2g, cholesterol 0mg, sodium 10mg, potassium 250mg

Directions:
1. Preheat sous vide water bath to 175°F / 80°C
2. Mix plums, sugar, and vanilla in a bowl (ensure sugar coats the plums evenly)
3. Place mixture and spices in a vacuum-seal bag (remove as much air as possible)
4. Cook in the sous vide bath for 90 min (ensure the bag is fully submerged)
5. Remove and serve warm or chilled (cool completely if storing for later use)

Cooking Temperature Range:
Optimal 175°F / 80°C (permissible range 175°F / 80°C to 180°F / 82°C).

Strawberry Compote

Yield: 2 servings | Prep time: 10 minutes | Cook time: 1 hour

Unlock the essence of strawberries with our Sous Vide Strawberry Compote. This vibrant, ruby-red topping combines the natural sweetness of strawberries with a hint of sugar and lemon, creating a silky, perfectly textured compote that is ideal for desserts, breakfast, or snacking.

Ingredients:
- Strawberries (fresh, medium, hulled) - 8 oz
- White sugar - 2 tbsp
- Lemon juice (freshly squeezed) - 1 tbsp
- Water - 2 tbsp

Nutritional Information (for 2 servings):
calories 90 kcal, protein 1g, carbohydrates 22g, fat 0g, fiber 2g, cholesterol 0mg, sodium 1mg, potassium 120mg

Directions:
1. Mix strawberries, sugar, lemon juice, and water (ensure sugar is fully dissolved)
2. Seal the mixture in a vacuum or zip-top bag (use the water displacement method if needed)
3. Cook in sous vide bath at 180°F / 82°C for 60 minutes (fully submerge bag in water)
4. Cool slightly and serve (serve warm or chilled)

Cooking Temperature Range:
Optimal 180°F / 82°C (permissible range 176°F / 80°C to 185°F / 85°C).

Strawberry Rhubarb Sauce

Yield: 2 servings | Prep time: 10 minutes | Cook time: 1 hour

Brighten your dishes with our Sous Vide Strawberry Rhubarb Sauce! Sweet strawberries and tangy rhubarb blend into a luscious, perfectly balanced sauce. Sous vide precision preserves vibrant flavors and ensures a silky texture, making it an ideal topping for desserts, pancakes, or yogurt.

Ingredients:
- Strawberries (hulled, halved) - 1 cup
- Rhubarb (chopped into 1-inch pieces) - 1 cup
- White sugar - 0.25 cup
- Lemon juice (freshly squeezed) - 1 tbsp
- Vanilla extract - 0.5 tsp

Nutritional Information (for 2 servings):
calories 120 kcal, protein 1g, carbohydrates 30g, fat 0g, fiber 2g, cholesterol 0mg, sodium 5mg, potassium 200mg

Directions:
1. Preheat sous vide water bath to 185°F / 85°C
2. Combine ingredients in a bowl and mix (ensure sugar dissolves evenly)
3. Place the mixture in a vacuum-seal or zip-top bag (remove air to ensure full submersion)
4. Cook in the sous vide bath for 60 minutes (stir bag gently if using zip-top method)
5. Blend or mash and serve as desired (cool slightly before blending)

Cooking Temperature Range:
Optimal 185°F / 85°C (permissible range 185°F / 85°C to 190°F / 88°C).

Vanilla-Infused Apples

Yield: 2 servings | Prep time: 10 minutes | Cook time: 1 hour

Savor the delicate sweetness of our Vanilla-Infused Sous Vide Apples! Tender apple slices are gently cooked with the warm essence of vanilla, creating a perfectly soft and flavorful treat. Sous vide precision enhances their natural juiciness, making this dessert a comforting and elegant delight.

Ingredients:
- Apples (medium, peeled, cored) - 2 pieces
- White sugar - 2 tbsp
- Vanilla extract - 1 tsp
- Water - 0.25 cup
- Lemon juice (freshly squeezed) - 1 tsp

Nutritional Information (for 2 servings):
calories 120 kcal, protein 0g, carbohydrates 32g, fat 0g, fiber 3g, cholesterol 0mg, sodium 5mg, potassium 150mg

Directions:
1. Preheat sous vide water bath to 185°F / 85°C
2. Mix water, sugar, vanilla, and lemon juice (ensure sugar is fully dissolved)
3. Combine apples and liquid in a sealed bag (remove as much air as possible)
4. Cook in the water bath for 60 minutes (keep the bag fully submerged)
5. Serve the apples warm or chilled with the liquid (optional: garnish with whipped cream)

Cooking Temperature Range:
Optimal 185°F / 85°C (permissible range 185°F / 85°C to 190°F / 88°C).

Watermelon Infused with Mint

Yield: 2 servings | Prep time: 5 minutes | Cook time: 30 minutes

Refresh your palate with our Sous Vide Watermelon Infused with Mint! Juicy watermelon is delicately infused with fresh mint's cool, aromatic essence, creating a vibrant and hydrating treat. Sous vide precision enhances the natural sweetness and ensures every bite bursts with a bright, refreshing flavor.

Ingredients:
- Watermelon (seedless, medium cubes) - 2 cup
- Mint leaves (fresh) - 5 pieces
- Honey - 2 tbsp
- Lime juice (freshly squeezed) - 1 tbsp

Nutritional Information (for 2 servings):
calories 90 kcal, protein 1g, carbohydrates 23g, fat 0g, fiber 1g, cholesterol 0mg, sodium 5mg, potassium 280mg

Directions:
1. Preheat sous vide water bath to 145°F / 63°C
2. Combine watermelon, mint, honey, and lime juice in a bag (ensure ingredients are evenly distributed)
3. Cook the sealed bag in the water bath for 30 minutes (check the seal to prevent leaks)
4. Serve infused watermelon chilled or at room temperature (ideal for salads or as a refreshing snack)

Cooking Temperature Range:
Optimal 145°F / 63°C (permissible range 145°F / 63°C to 150°F / 65°C).

INTRODUCTION TO PREPARING CUSTARDS AND CREAMS DESSERTS USING SOUS VIDE TECHNOLOGY

Custards and creams are among the most beloved desserts due to their smooth texture, rich flavors, and comforting nature. Sous vide cooking, with its precise temperature control, is a game-changer in preparing these desserts. It ensures flawless consistency, eliminates the risk of curdling, and allows even beginners to achieve professional-quality results. This guide will introduce you to the principles, techniques, and best practices for making custards and creams at home using sous vide technology.

GENERAL PRINCIPLES AND FEATURES OF SOUS VIDE CUSTARDS AND CREAMS

Custards and creams, such as crème brûlée, flan, and pots de crème, rely on a delicate balance of eggs, dairy, and sugar. Sous vide cooking provides gentle, even heat to set these mixtures perfectly without overcooking or creating lumps.

Key features of sous vide custards and creams include:

Temperature Precision: Sous vide ensures exact temperature control, typically between 176°F–185°F (80°C–85°C), which is crucial for setting custards without overcooking.

Elimination of Hot Spots: Traditional methods can result in uneven cooking; sous vide eliminates this problem by immersing the mixture in a water bath.

Consistent Texture: The controlled environment ensures a silky, uniform texture throughout the dessert.

Hands-Free Cooking: Once prepared, the custards do not require stirring or monitoring, freeing you up for other tasks.

HOW TO PACK CUSTARDS AND CREAMS CORRECTLY

Packing custards and creams for sous vide involves attention to detail to ensure even cooking and easy serving.

Choose the Right Containers:
- Use small, heat-resistant jars with lids, such as mason jars. They are convenient and aesthetically pleasing serving options.
- Avoid plastic bags for custards; their liquid consistency makes jars a more practical choice.

Fill Evenly:
- Pour the custard mixture into the jars, leaving about ½ inch of space at the top to allow for expansion during cooking.
- Use a funnel or spouted measuring cup for precision and to avoid spills.

Seal Loosely:
- Screw the lids onto the jars until just finger-tight. This allows air to escape during cooking while preventing water from entering.

Preheat the Water Bath:
- Always preheat the sous vide water bath to ensure accurate cooking times to the desired temperature before adding the jars.

SHAPING CUSTARDS AND CREAMS FOR PRESENTATION

Sous vide allows creative shaping and presentation of custards and creams:

Layered Custards:
- Create layered desserts by cooking one layer at a time, cooling it, and then adding the next layer before cooking again to create layered desserts.

Molded Shapes:
- Once cooked and cooled, custards can be unmolded from jars or ramekins for plating. If necessary, they can be loosened with a hot water dip.

Garnishing:
- Garnish with fresh fruit, caramel sauce, or edible flowers for an elegant finish.

STORING CUSTARDS AND CREAMS BEFORE AND AFTER COOKING

Before Cooking:
- **Refrigeration**: If you are not cooking immediately, cover and refrigerate the prepared custard mixture in jars. It can be stored for up to 24 hours before cooking.

After Cooking:
- **Cooling**: Once cooked, cool the jars in an ice bath to stop the cooking process. This also helps set the custard properly.
- **Refrigeration**: Cooled custards can be stored in the refrigerator for up to 5 days. To maintain freshness, keep the lids tightly sealed.
- **Freezing**: While custards generally don't freeze well due to texture changes, some dense varieties, like pots de crème, can be frozen for up to two months. Thaw slowly in the refrigerator before serving.

PREPARING THE FINISHED DISH FOR SERVING

Serve Chilled or Warm:
- Most custards, like crème brûlée or flan, are served chilled. Warm gently in a water bath if serving warm is preferred.

Caramelize:
- For desserts like crème brûlée, sprinkle an even layer of sugar on top and caramelize with a kitchen torch before serving.

Garnish Thoughtfully:
- Add a dollop of whipped cream, a drizzle of sauce, or a sprinkle of grated chocolate for extra flair.

Unmold with Care:

- To serve custards like flan, gently run a knife around the edge of the jar and invert it onto a plate. If necessary, shake lightly to release the custard.

COMMON MISTAKES AND HOW TO AVOID THEM

Overtightening Jar Lids:
  Mistake: Tight lids can trap air, causing jars to float and uneven cooking.
  Solution: Seal lids are just finger-tight.

Incorrect Temperature:
  Mistake: Cooking at too high a temperature can cause the custard to curdle.
  Solution: Always double-check the temperature settings on your sous vide device.

Uneven Filling:
  Mistake: Inconsistent jar filling leads to uneven cooking.
  Solution: Measure the custard mixture precisely for uniform results.

Skipping the Ice Bath:
  Mistake: Failing to cool the custards quickly can result in overcooking and texture changes.
  Solution: Always use an ice bath immediately after cooking.

Overcooking:
  Mistake: Leaving custards in the water bath for too long can make them overly firm.
  Solution: Remove jars promptly at the end of the cooking time.

CONCLUSION

Sous vide cooking opens up a world of possibilities for custards and creams, allowing even beginners to create desserts with unparalleled texture and flavor. You can easily craft various classic and creative desserts by mastering the basics of packing, temperature control, and storage.

> What are the best toppings for sous vide flan?

> Toppings can enhance the flavor and presentation of sous vide flan, making it even more appealing. Here are some of the best toppings to consider:

TOPPINGS FOR SOUS VIDE FLAN

1. Classic Caramel Sauce
- Caramel sauce is a rich, sweet, and slightly bitter sauce that is a must-have for flan. You can use the caramel layer from cooking or make a fresh batch to drizzle over the flan.

2. Fresh Fruits
- **Berries**: Raspberries, blueberries, or sliced strawberries add a burst of color and a tangy contrast to the creamy flan.
- **Citrus Slices:** Thin orange, mandarin, or grapefruit slices complement the flan's richness.

3. Whipped Cream
- A dollop of lightly sweetened whipped cream adds a fluffy, creamy contrast.

4. Toasted Nuts
- **Almonds, Pecans, or Hazelnuts:** Finely chopped and lightly toasted nuts add crunch and a nutty depth to the dessert.

5. Shredded Coconut
- Toasted coconut flakes bring a tropical flavor and a pleasant texture.

6. Chocolate
- **Chocolate Sauce:** A drizzle of melted dark chocolate pairs beautifully with flan.
- **Shaved Chocolate:** Use milk, dark, or white chocolate shavings for a subtle garnish.

7. Spices
- **Cinnamon or Nutmeg**: A light dusting adds warmth and complements the vanilla in flan.
- **Cardamom or Clove:** For an exotic twist, sprinkle a tiny amount of these spices.

8. Edible Flowers
- Delicate flowers like pansies or violets can elevate the presentation of your flan, making it visually stunning.

9. Fruit Sauces
- **Berry Coulis:** A smooth puree of raspberries, strawberries, or blueberries.
- **Mango or Passionfruit Sauce:** Bright and tropical flavors that perfectly balance sweetness.

10. Salted Caramel
- Enhance the caramel flavor with a sprinkle of flaky sea salt on top of the caramel layer.

11. Crumbled Cookies or Biscotti
- Add texture with crumbled shortbread, biscotti, or graham crackers sprinkled over the flan.

12. Honey or Maple Syrup
- A drizzle of honey or maple syrup brings a unique sweetness to the dessert.

13. Alcohol-Infused Toppings
- **Rum-Infused Whipped Cream:** A hint of rum in whipped cream complements the custard.
- **Brandy-Soaked Fruits:** Marinate fruits like cherries or figs in brandy for a luxurious topping.

14. Coffee-Based Toppings
- **Espresso Drizzle:** A light espresso or coffee syrup drizzle adds bold flavor.
- **Coffee Beans**: Crushed or whole, coffee beans provide a crunchy garnish.

15. Pistachio Dust
- Finely ground pistachios add a pop of green color and a subtle nutty flavor.

Pro Tip for Presentation:
- Use a small spoon or squeeze bottle for precise drizzling.
- Always garnish just before serving to maintain the freshness and texture of the toppings.

> Explain how I can caramelize flan with a torch.

> Caramelizing flan with a torch is a quick and efficient way to achieve a beautiful, glassy caramel layer that enhances the flavor and presentation of this classic dessert. Here's how to do it step by step:

CARAMELIZING FLAN WITH A TORCH

What You'll Need
Prepared Flan: Ensure your flan is chilled and set for caramelization.
Granulated Sugar: White sugar works best for even caramelization.
Torch: A culinary torch designed for kitchen use (butane-powered).
Optional: A small, fine-mesh sieve for evenly sprinkling the sugar.

Step-by-Step Guide

1. Prepare the Flan for Caramelizing
- If the flan already has a caramel layer (from baking or sous vide cooking), ensure it's smooth and even.
- If adding a fresh caramel topping:
  - Gently unmold the flan onto a serving plate by running a knife around the edges of the mold and inverting it onto the plate.
  - Sprinkle a thin, even layer of granulated sugar across the surface.

2. Sprinkle the Sugar
- Use about 1–2 teaspoons of sugar per flan, depending on its size.
- Tilt the plate slightly while sprinkling to ensure an even coating of sugar.
- Avoid adding too much sugar, which can melt unevenly and form clumps.

3. Torch the Sugar
- Hold the torch about 2–3 inches above the sugar surface.
- Turn on the torch and adjust it to a medium flame.
- Move the flame in small circular motions, focusing on one area until the sugar melts and turns golden brown.
- Keep the torch moving to avoid burning one spot.

4. Cool the Caramel
- Let the caramelized sugar cool for 1–2 minutes. As it cools, it will harden into a glassy, crisp layer.

Tips for Success
- Control the Flame: A medium flame gives better control and prevents scorching.

- Use Even Sugar Layers: Uneven sugar distribution can lead to patchy caramelization.
- Avoid Over-Torching: Too much heat can burn the sugar and create a bitter taste.
- Practice on a Test Surface: If you're new to using a torch, practice caramelizing sugar on a separate plate or test dessert.

Serving Suggestions
- Caramelize the flan just before serving to maintain the crisp texture of the caramel layer.
- Garnish the flan with fresh fruit, whipped cream, or edible flowers for a polished look.

Common Mistakes and How to Avoid Them

Uneven Caramelization:
Mistake: Holding the torch too close or staying too long in one spot.
Solution: Keep the flame moving and maintain a consistent distance.

Clumpy Sugar:
Mistake: Using uneven or damp sugar.
Solution: Use dry, fine granulated sugar and sprinkle it evenly.

Melting the Flan:
Mistake: Holding the torch too close or for too long, causing the custard to melt.
Solution: Focus only on the sugar layer and work quickly.

Almond Custard

Yield: 2 servings | Prep time: 15 minutes | Cook time: 1 hour

Indulge in the smooth elegance of our Sous Vide Almond Custard! This velvety dessert is infused with almonds' subtle, nutty flavor, creating a perfect balance of richness and sweetness. Sous vide precision ensures a flawless, creamy texture, making every spoonful a luxurious treat.

Ingredients:
- Almond milk (unsweetened) - 1 cup
- White sugar - 0.33 cup
- Egg yolk (large) - 2 pieces
- Almond extract (pure almond) - 0.5 tsp
- Salt - 1 pinch

Nutritional Information (for 2 servings):
calories 180 kcal, protein 5g, carbohydrates 25g, fat 7g, fiber 0g, cholesterol 100mg, sodium 70mg, potassium 50mg

Directions:
1. Preheat sous vide water bath to 176°F / 80°C
2. Mix all ingredients until smooth (use a whisk for even blending)
3. Pour mixture into a resealable bag, remove air, and seal (use water displacement method)
4. Cook in the sous vide bath for 60 minutes (submerge bag fully)
5. Chill in ramekins before serving (chill for optimal texture)

Cooking Temperature Range:
Optimal 176°F / 80°C (permissible range 175°F / 79°C to 179°F / 81°C).

Almond Milk Panna Cotta

Yield: 2 servings | Prep time: 10 minutes | Cook time: 1 hour

Delight in the light elegance of our Sous Vide Almond Milk Panna Cotta! This silky, dairy-free dessert combines almond milk's subtle nutty flavor with sweetness, creating a perfectly balanced treat. Sous vide precision ensures a smooth texture, making every spoonful pure indulgence.

Ingredients:
- Almond milk (unsweetened) - 1 cup
- White sugar - 3 tbsp
- Gelatin (unflavored) - 1 tsp
- Vanilla extract (pure) - 0.5 tsp

Nutritional Information (for 2 servings):
calories 120 kcal, protein 3g, carbohydrates 22g, fat 3g, fiber 1g, cholesterol 0mg, sodium 10mg, potassium 120mg

Directions:
1. Preheat sous vide water bath to 185°F / 85°C
2. Warm almond milk and sugar until sugar dissolves (avoid boiling the mixture)
3. Whisk in gelatin until fully dissolved. Add vanilla (stir continuously to prevent lumps)
4. Pour into jars, seal, and cook in a water bath for 60 minutes (ensure jars are fully submerged)
5. Cool and refrigerate for 2 hours before serving (serve chilled for best texture)

Cooking Temperature Range:
Optimal 185°F / 85°C (permissible range 185°F / 85°C to 190°F / 88°C).

Berry Parfait

Yield: 2 servings | Prep time: 15 minutes | Cook time: 1 hour 30 minutes

Sous Wide Berry Parfait is a delightful blend of fresh berries and creamy custard. This dish combines the sweetness of fruit and the richness of yogurt for a perfect dessert or breakfast treat. It's easy to prepare, with sous vide ensuring the custard's smooth texture.

Ingredients:
- Mixed berries (fresh, cleaned) - 1 cup
- Greek yogurt (plain or vanilla) - 1 cup
- Honey - 2 tbsp
- Vanilla extract - 1 tsp
- Granola (optional) - 0.5 cup

Nutritional Information (for 2 servings):
calories 250 kcal, protein 8g, carbohydrates 40g, fat 6g, fiber 3g, cholesterol 10mg, sodium 50mg, potassium 150mg

Directions:
1. Preheat sous vide water bath to 176°F / 80°C
2. Mix yogurt, honey, and vanilla in a bowl (blend until smooth)
3. Place the mixture in a bag or jar and sous vide for 90 minutes (ensure the bag is air-tight)
4. Layer cooked yogurt, berries, and granola in glasses (chill before serving if desired)
5. Serve immediately or refrigerate (enjoy fresh or chilled)

Cooking Temperature Range:
Optimal 176°F / 80°C (permissible range 175°F / 79°C to 179°F / 81°C).

Caramel Flan

Yield: 2 servings | Prep time: 15 minutes | Cook time: 1 hour 30 minutes

Indulge in the silky luxury of our Sous Vide Caramel Flan! This creamy custard dessert is topped with a golden layer of rich, caramelized sugar. Sous vide precision ensures a flawless, velvety texture and perfectly balanced sweetness, making every bite a decadent delight.

Ingredients:
- White sugar (for caramel) - 2 tbsp
- Egg (large) - 2 pieces
- Whole milk - 0.5 cup
- Heavy cream - 0.5 cup
- White sugar (for custard) - 4 tbsp
- Vanilla extract - 1 tsp

Nutritional Information (for 2 servings):
calories 320 kcal, protein 7g, carbohydrates 28g, fat 20g, fiber 0g, cholesterol 150mg, sodium 50mg, potassium 100mg

Directions:
1. Preheat sous vide water bath to 176°F / 80°C
2. Make caramel and pour into ramekins (work quickly to prevent hardening)
3. Mix custard ingredients and pour into ramekins (avoid overmixing to prevent bubbles)
4. Seal ramekins with foil and sous vide for 90 minutes (ensure ramekins are fully submerged)
5. Chill, unmold, and serve (chill for at least 2 hours for best texture)

Cooking Temperature Range:
Optimal 176°F / 80°C (permissible range 175°F / 79°C to 180°F / 82°C).

Chai Spiced Custard

Yield: 2 servings | Prep time: 10 minutes | Cook time: 1 hour

Warm your senses with our Sous Vide Chai Spiced Custard! This creamy, velvety dessert is infused with the aromatic blend of cinnamon, cardamom, ginger, and cloves, delivering the cozy essence of chai tea in every bite. Sous vide precision ensures a perfectly smooth texture for an indulgent, spiced treat.

Ingredients:
- Heavy cream - 0.5 cup
- White sugar - 3 tbsp
- Egg yolk (large) - 2 pieces
- Chai spice blend (pre-mixed) - 1 tsp
- Vanilla extract (pure) - 0.5 tsp

Nutritional Information (for 2 servings):
calories 310 kcal, protein 5g, carbohydrates 22g, fat 24g, fiber 0g, cholesterol 100mg, sodium 30mg, potassium 140mg

Directions:
1. Preheat sous vide water bath to 176°F / 80°C
2. Whisk all ingredients in a mixing bowl until smooth (ensure sugar is fully dissolved)
3. Divide the mixture into jars and seal or cover ramekins (leave some space for expansion)
4. Cook jars in a water bath for 60 minutes (fully submerge jars in the bath)
5. Cool, then refrigerate for 2 hours before serving (chill thoroughly for proper texture)

Cooking Temperature Range:
Optimal 176°F / 80°C (permissible range 176°F / 80°C to 180°F / 82°C).

Cherry Clafoutis

Yield: 2 servings | Prep time: 10 minutes | Cook time: 1 hour

Savor the elegance of our Sous Vide Cherry Clafoutis! Juicy cherries are nestled in a custard-like batter that's perfectly creamy and lightly sweet. Sous vide precision ensures a flawless texture and even cooking, transforming this French classic into a luxurious dessert bursting with fruity charm.

Ingredients:
- Whole milk - 0.5 cup
- Egg (large) - 2 pieces
- White sugar - 0.33 cup
- All-purpose flour (sifted) - 0.25 cup
- Cherries (pitted) - 1 cup
- Salt - 1 pinch

Nutritional Information (for 2 servings):
calories 250 kcal, protein 8g, carbohydrates 40g, fat 6g, fiber 1g, cholesterol 120mg, sodium 60mg, potassium 150mg

Directions:
1. Preheat sous vide water bath to 185°F / 85°C
2. Whisk milk, eggs, sugar, flour, and salt until smooth (ensure the batter is lump-free)
3. Divide cherries into jars and pour batter over them (use 6 oz mason jars for even cooking)
4. Submerge jars in the sous vide bath and cook (make sure jars are fully submerged)
5. Cool, chill, and serve with powdered sugar (chill for at least 1 hour before serving)

Cooking Temperature Range:
Optimal 185°F / 85°C (permissible range 183°F / 84°C to 190°F / 88°C).

Coconut Custard

Yield: 2 servings | Prep time: 10 minutes | Cook time: 45 minutes

Escape to paradise with our Sous Vide Coconut Custard! This creamy, silky dessert is infused with the tropical sweetness of coconut, delivering a rich and indulgent flavor. Sous vide precision ensures a flawless texture, making every spoonful a luxurious and refreshing treat.

Ingredients:
- Coconut Milk (unsweetened) - 1 cup
- Egg (large) - 2 pieces
- Sugar - 2 tbsp
- Vanilla Extract - 1 tsp
- Salt - 1 pinch

Nutritional Information (for 2 servings):
calories 300 kcal, protein 6g, carbohydrates 25g, fat 20g, fiber 2g, cholesterol 70mg, sodium 150mg, potassium 400mg

Directions:
1. Whisk coconut milk, eggs, sugar, vanilla, and salt until smooth (aim for a uniform consistency)
2. Pour into jars or vacuum bags and seal properly (leave some space at the top of jars)
3. Cook at 180°F / 82°C in a sous vide water bath for 45 minutes (ensure jars/bags are fully submerged)
4. Remove from bath and cool for about 2 minutes before serving or chilling (carefully handle hot containers)

Cooking Temperature Range:
Optimal 180°F / 82°C (permissible range 175°F / 79°C to 185°F / 85°C).

Coffee Crème Brûlée

Yield: 2 servings | Prep time: 15 minutes | Cook time: 1 hour

Awaken your senses with our Sous Vide Coffee Crème Brûlée! This velvety custard is infused with the bold, rich flavor of coffee and crowned with a crisp, caramelized sugar crust. Sous vide precision ensures a flawlessly smooth texture, making each spoonful a luxurious blend of sweetness and java bliss.

Ingredients:
- Heavy cream - 1 cup
- White sugar - 2 tbsp
- Egg yolk (whisked) - 2 pieces
- Espresso (brewed and cooled) - 2 tbsp
- Sugar (torch to caramelize for topping) - 2 tsp

Nutritional Information (for 2 servings):
calories 360 kcal, protein 5g, carbohydrates 25g, fat 29g, fiber 0g, cholesterol 170mg, sodium 30mg, potassium 80mg

Directions:
1. Preheat sous vide water bath to 176°F / 80°C
2. Whisk together cream, sugar, yolks, and espresso until smooth (do not over-whisk)
3. Pour into jars, seal tightly, and cook for 60 minutes (ensure jars are fully submerged)
4. Cool jars refrigerate for 4 hours (refrigerate for best results)
5. Sprinkle sugar, torch to caramelize, and serve (serve immediately)

Cooking Temperature Range:
Optimal 176°F / 80°C (permissible range 176°F / 80°C to 185°F / 85°C).

Crème Brûlée

Yield: 2 servings | Prep time: 15 minutes | Cook time: 1 hour

Indulge in the luxurious charm of our Sous Vide Crème Brûlée! This silky, creamy custard is infused with rich vanilla and topped with a perfectly caramelized sugar crust. Sous vide precision ensures flawless texture and even cooking, making every spoonful a decadent masterpiece of sweetness and crunch.

Ingredients:
- Heavy cream - 1 cup
- White sugar - 2 tbsp
- Egg yolk (whisked) - 2 pieces
- Vanilla extract - 1 tsp
- Sugar (torch to caramelize for topping) - 2 tsp

Nutritional Information (for 2 servings):
calories 350 kcal, protein 5g, carbohydrates 24g, fat 28g, fiber 0g, cholesterol 160mg, sodium 25mg, potassium 70mg

Directions:
1. Preheat sous vide water bath to 176°F / 80°C
2. Whisk together cream, sugar, yolks, and vanilla until smooth (do not over-whisk)
3. Pour into jars, seal tightly, and cook for 60 minutes (ensure jars are fully submerged)
4. Cool jars refrigerate for 4 hours (refrigerate for best results)
5. Sprinkle sugar, torch to caramelize, and serve (serve immediately)

Cooking Temperature Range:
Optimal 176°F / 80°C (permissible range 176°F / 80°C to 185°F / 85°C).

Eggnog Custard

Yield: 2 servings | Prep time: 15 minutes | Cook time: 1 hour

Celebrate the holiday spirit with our Sous Vide Eggnog Custard! This rich, creamy dessert blends the warm flavors of nutmeg, cinnamon, and a hint of vanilla with the classic taste of eggnog. Sous vide precision ensures a luxuriously smooth texture, making every spoonful a festive delight.

Ingredients:
- Eggnog (shake or stir well before using) - 1 cup
- Egg (large) - 2 pieces
- Sugar - 2 tbsp
- Nutmeg (ground) - 1 pinch

Nutritional Information (for 2 servings):
calories 300 kcal, protein 10g, carbohydrates 28g, fat 18g, fiber 0g, cholesterol 160mg, sodium 180mg, potassium 250mg

Directions:
1. Whisk eggnog, eggs, sugar, and nutmeg until well combined (aim for a smooth, fully integrated mixture)
2. Pour into canning jars or vacuum-sealed bags and seal (leave a little space for expansion)
3. Cook in a sous vide bath at 180°F / 82°C for 60 minutes (make sure jars/bags are fully submerged)
4. Remove from bath and let rest 5 minutes before serving or cooling (carefully handle hot jars/bags)

Cooking Temperature Range:
Optimal 180°F / 82°C (permissible range 175°F / 79°C to 185°F / 85°C).

Espresso Custard

Yield: 2 servings | Prep time: 10 minutes | Cook time: 45 minutes

Awaken your senses with our Sous Vide Espresso Custard! This silky, creamy dessert infuses espresso's bold, rich flavor, creating a perfect balance of sweetness and coffee intensity. Sous vide precision ensures a flawlessly smooth texture, making every spoonful an energizing indulgence.

Ingredients:
- Heavy Cream - 1 cup
- Espresso (brewed and cooled) - 1 oz
- Egg (large) - 2 pieces
- Sugar - 2 tbsp
- Salt - 1 pinch

Nutritional Information (for 2 servings):
calories 250 kcal, protein 8g, carbohydrates 15g, fat 16g, fiber 0g, cholesterol 90mg, sodium 120mg, potassium 150mg

Directions:
1. Whisk cream, espresso, eggs, sugar, and salt until smooth (aim for a fully combined, lump-free mixture)
2. Transfer to jars or bags and seal properly (leave a little space at the top for expansion)
3. Cook in a water bath at 180°F / 82°C for 45 minutes (ensure jars/bags are fully submerged)
4. Remove from bath rest 2 minutes before serving or chilling (carefully handle hot containers)

Cooking Temperature Range:
Optimal 180°F / 82°C (permissible range 175°F / 79°C to 185°F / 85°C).

Honey Lavender Panna Cotta

Yield: 2 servings | Prep time: 10 minutes | Cook time: 1 hour

Indulge in the delicate harmony of our Sous Vide Honey Lavender Panna Cotta! This silky, luxurious dessert is infused with the floral notes of lavender and the golden sweetness of honey. Sous vide precision ensures a flawless texture, creating an elegant, soothing, and delicious treat.

Ingredients:
- Heavy Cream - 1 cup
- Honey - 2 tbsp
- Culinary Lavender (dried) - 1 pinch
- Gelatin (unflavored) - 1 tsp
- Water (room temperature) - 2 tbsp

Nutritional Information (for 2 servings):
calories 400 kcal, protein 6g, carbohydrates 30g, fat 30g, fiber 0g, cholesterol 100mg, sodium 50mg, potassium 150mg

Directions:
1. Bloom gelatin with cold water (ensure gelatin is fully hydrated before adding it to the mixture)
2. Warm cream, honey, and lavender, then stir in bloomed gelatin until dissolved (be sure the gelatin dissolves completely)
3. Pour mixture into jars/bags and seal (leave a bit of space at the top if using jars)
4. Sous vide at 185°F / 85°C for 60 minutes (make sure jars/bags are fully submerged)
5. Cool for 5 minutes before chilling or serving (carefully handle hot jars/bags; allow some rest time to set)

Cooking Temperature Range:
Optimal 185°F / 85°C (permissible range 180°F / 82°C to 190°F / 88°C).

Key Lime Pots de Crème

Yield: 2 servings | Prep time: 10 minutes | Cook time: 1 hour

Savor the zesty elegance of our Sous Vide Key Lime Pots de Crème! This luscious custard is infused with the bright tang of key lime, perfectly balanced with a creamy richness. Topped with a hint of whipped cream, sous vide precision ensures a silky-smooth texture, making every spoonful a refreshing tropical indulgence.

Ingredients:
- Heavy cream - 0.5 cup
- Key lime juice (fresh or bottled) - 3 tbsp
- Egg yolk (large) - 2 pieces
- White sugar - 2 tbsp
- Lime zest (grated) - 1 tsp
- Vanilla extract (pure) - 0.5 tsp

Nutritional Information (for 2 servings):
calories 320 kcal, protein 5g, carbohydrates 25g, fat 22g, fiber 0g, cholesterol 110mg, sodium 25mg, potassium 150mg

Directions:
1. Preheat sous vide water bath to 176°F / 80°C
2. Whisk all ingredients in a mixing bowl until smooth (ensure no lumps remain)
3. Divide the mixture into jars and seal or cover the ramekins (leave space for expansion)
4. Cook jars in a water bath for 60 minutes (fully submerge containers)
5. Cool, then refrigerate for 2 hours before serving (allows custards to set properly)

Cooking Temperature Range:
Optimal 176°F / 80°C (permissible range 176°F / 80°C to 180°F / 82°C).

Lavender Panna Cotta

Yield: 2 servings | Prep time: 10 minutes | Cook time: 1 hour

Experience the delicate elegance of our Sous Vide Lavender Panna Cotta! Silky and creamy, this luxurious dessert is infused with the subtle floral notes of lavender, creating a perfectly balanced treat. Sous vide precision ensures a flawless texture, making every spoonful a soothing, aromatic delight.

Ingredients:
- Heavy cream - 8 oz
- White sugar - 2 tbsp
- Culinary Lavender (dried) - 1 tsp
- Gelatin (unflavored) - 1 tsp
- Vanilla extract - 1 tsp

Nutritional Information (for 2 servings):
calories 280 kcal, protein 3g, carbohydrates 20g, fat 22g, fiber 0g, cholesterol 60mg, sodium 35mg, potassium 50mg

Directions:
1. Heat cream, sugar, and lavender. Strain the lavender buds (do not boil the cream to prevent separation)
2. Bloom gelatin in cold water and add vanilla (ensure gelatin is fully bloomed)
3. Combine cream mixture with gelatin. Pour into jars and seal (use airtight jars for best results)
4. Cook in sous vide bath at 176°F / 80°C for 60 minutes (fully submerge containers)
5. Chill for 2 hours. Garnish and serve (refrigeration ensures firm panna cotta)

Cooking Temperature Range:
Optimal 176°F / 80°C (permissible range 176°F / 80°C to 180°F / 82°C).

Lemon Curd

Yield: 2 servings | Prep time: 10 minutes | Cook time: 1 hour 30 minutes

Elevate your desserts with our Sous Vide Lemon Curd! This luscious, tangy-sweet spread boasts a silky-smooth texture and vibrant citrus flavor. Perfectly balanced and cooked with sous vide precision, it's ideal for spreading, layering, or spooning straight from the jar for a burst of sunshine.

Ingredients:
- Lemon juice (freshly squeezed) - 0.25 cup
- Lemon zest (grated) - 1 tsp
- White sugar - 0.33 cup
- Egg yolk (whisked) - 4 pieces
- Butter (unsalted, cubed and softened) - 4 tbsp

Nutritional Information (for 2 servings):
calories 320 kcal, protein 4g, carbohydrates 25g, fat 24g, fiber 0g, cholesterol 200mg, sodium 50mg, potassium 40mg

Directions:
1. Whisk lemon juice, zest, sugar, and yolks until smooth (ensure the mixture is lump-free)
2. Transfer mixture to a sealed sous vide bag or jar (seal tightly to prevent water entry)
3. Preheat the water bath to 176°F / 80°C and cook for 90 minutes (use a rack to stabilize jars if needed)
4. Whisk in softened butter until creamy, then chill (chill for a smooth, thick texture)

Cooking Temperature Range:
Optimal 176°F / 80°C (permissible range 176°F / 80°C to 180°F / 82°C).

Lemon Yogurt Parfait

Yield: 2 servings | Prep time: 15 minutes | Cook time: 2 hours

Brighten your day with our Sous Vide Lemon Yogurt Parfait! Layers of creamy lemon-infused yogurt, fresh berries, and crunchy granola create a delightful balance of tart, sweet, and crunchy. Sous vide precision ensures the yogurt is silky smooth and packed with vibrant citrus flavor in every bite.

Ingredients:
- Plain yogurt (live cultures) - 1 cup
- Lemon juice (freshly squeezed) - 2 tbsp
- Honey - 2 tbsp
- Lemon zest (grated) - 1 tsp
- Granola - 0.5 cup
- Berries (fresh) - 0.5 cup

Nutritional Information (for 2 servings):
calories 250 kcal, protein 8g, carbohydrates 35g, fat 8g, fiber 2g, cholesterol 10mg, sodium 50mg, potassium 150mg

Directions:
1. Whisk yogurt, lemon juice, honey, and lemon zest until smooth (use a whisk to avoid lumps)
2. Transfer the mixture to jars and seal loosely (leave room for expansion)
3. Cook jars in a water bath at 130°F / 54°C for 120 minutes (ensure jars are fully submerged)
4. Chill jars for 2 hours in the refrigerator before serving (cool completely for best texture)
5. Layer yogurt with granola and berries in serving glasses (be creative with layering)

Cooking Temperature Range:
Optimal 130°F / 54°C (permissible range 130°F / 54°C to 135°F / 57°C).

Mango Custard

Yield: 2 servings | Prep time: 10 minutes | Cook time: 1 hour

Dive into tropical bliss with our Sous Vide Mango Custard! This silky, creamy dessert is infused with the vibrant sweetness of ripe mangoes, delivering a perfect balance of fruity brightness and velvety richness. Sous vide precision ensures a flawlessly smooth texture, making every spoonful a sunny delight.

Ingredients:
- Mango puree (fresh or canned) - 1 cup
- Heavy cream - 0.5 cup
- Egg yolk (large) - 2 pieces
- White sugar - 2 tbsp
- Vanilla extract (pure) - 0.5 tsp

Nutritional Information (for 2 servings):
calories 270 kcal, protein 5g, carbohydrates 28g, fat 16g, fiber 1g, cholesterol 100mg, sodium 20mg, potassium 200mg

Directions:
1. Preheat sous vide water bath to 176°F / 80°C
2. Mix mango puree, cream, yolks, sugar, and vanilla (whisk until smooth)
3. Pour mixture into jars and seal tightly (leave space for expansion)
4. Cook jars in a water bath for 60 minutes (ensure jars are fully submerged)
5. Cool and refrigerate for at least 2 hours (this enhances the flavor and sets the texture)

Cooking Temperature Range:
Optimal 176°F / 80°C (permissible range 176°F / 80°C to 180°F / 82°C).

Maple Custard

Yield: 2 servings | Prep time: 10 minutes | Cook time: 1 hour

Savor the comforting richness of our Sous Vide Maple Custard! This creamy, velvety dessert is infused with pure maple syrup's deep, caramel-like sweetness. Sous vide precision ensures a flawlessly smooth texture, making every spoonful a luxurious and cozy indulgence.

Ingredients:
- Heavy cream - 1 cup
- Pure maple syrup - 0.25 cup
- Egg yolk (large) - 3 pieces
- Vanilla extract (pure) - 0.5 tsp
- Salt - 1 pinch

Nutritional Information (for 2 servings):
calories 320 kcal, protein 5g, carbohydrates 28g, fat 23g, fiber 0g, cholesterol 220mg, sodium 35mg, potassium 70mg

Directions:
1. Preheat sous vide water bath to 180°F / 82°C
2. Whisk cream, maple syrup, egg yolks, vanilla, and salt until smooth (whisk gently to avoid air bubbles)
3. Strain the mixture into a measuring cup (to ensure a smooth texture)
4. Pour into jars, seal, and cook in a water bath for 60 minutes (ensure jars are fully submerged)
5. Cool and refrigerate for at least 2 hours (serve chilled for best texture)

Cooking Temperature Range:
Optimal 180°F / 82°C (permissible range 180°F / 82°C to 185°F / 85°C).

Matcha Green Tea Custard

Yield: 2 servings | Prep time: 10 minutes | Cook time: 1 hour

Experience the earthy elegance of our Sous Vide Matcha Green Tea Custard! This creamy, velvety dessert is infused with matcha's bold, antioxidant-rich flavor, delivering a perfect balance of sweetness and tea's natural bitterness. Sous vide precision ensures a flawlessly smooth texture in every vibrant bite.

Ingredients:
- Heavy cream - 0.5 cup
- White sugar - 3 tbsp
- Egg yolk (large) - 2 pieces
- Matcha green tea powder - 1 tsp
- Vanilla extract (pure) - 0.5 tsp

Nutritional Information (for 2 servings):
calories 310 kcal, protein 7g, carbohydrates 18g, fat 25g, fiber 1g, cholesterol 110mg, sodium 40mg, potassium 150mg

Directions:
1. Preheat sous vide water bath to 176°F / 80°C
2. Whisk all ingredients in a mixing bowl until smooth (ensure matcha powder is fully dissolved)
3. Divide the mixture into jars and seal or cover ramekins (leave space for expansion)
4. Cook jars in a water bath for 60 minutes (fully submerge jars in the bath)
5. Cool, then refrigerate for 2 hours before serving (chill thoroughly for best texture)

Cooking Temperature Range:
Optimal 176°F / 80°C (permissible range 176°F / 80°C to 180°F / 82°C).

Panna Cotta

Yield: 2 servings | Prep time: 15 minutes | Cook time: 1 hour

Indulge in the silky elegance of our Sous Vide Panna Cotta. This classic Italian dessert, with its velvety smooth texture and rich vanilla flavor, is elevated by the precision of sous vide cooking. Perfectly creamy and delicately sweet, it's a luxurious treat that melts in your mouth.

Ingredients:
- Heavy cream - 1 cup
- Sugar - 2 tbsp
- Vanilla extract - 0.5 tsp
- Gelatin (unflavored) - 0.5 tsp
- Water (room temperature) - 1 tbsp

Nutritional Information (for 2 servings):
calories 300 kcal, protein 3g, carbohydrates 15g, fat 28g, fiber 0g, cholesterol 90mg, sodium 25mg, potassium 100mg

Directions:
1. Bloom gelatin with cold water (ensure gelatin is fully hydrated before adding it to the mixture)
2. Heat cream and sugar; stir until sugar dissolves (do not let the cream boil)
3. Stir in vanilla and gelatin, then pour into jars (stir until gelatin is dissolved)
4. Cook jars in a water bath at 176°F / 80°C for 60 minutes (ensure jars are submerged)
5. Chill jars for at least 2 hours before serving (refrigerate immediately)

Cooking Temperature Range:
Optimal 176°F / 80°C (permissible range 176°F / 80°C to 180°F / 82°C).

Peanut Butter Custard

Yield: 2 servings | Prep time: 10 minutes | Cook time: 1 hour

Indulge in the rich, nutty decadence of our Sous Vide Peanut Butter Custard! This creamy, velvety dessert combines the bold flavor of peanut butter with a hint of sweetness, creating a perfectly balanced treat. Sous vide precision ensures an ultra-smooth texture, delighting every spoonful.

Ingredients:
- Heavy cream - 0.5 cup
- White sugar - 3 tbsp
- Egg yolk (large) - 2 pieces
- Peanut butter (smooth, creamy) - 2 tbsp
- Vanilla extract (pure) - 0.5 tsp

Nutritional Information (for 2 servings):
calories 360 kcal, protein 8g, carbohydrates 18g, fat 30g, fiber 1g, cholesterol 110mg, sodium 40mg, potassium 150mg

Directions:
1. Preheat sous vide water bath to 176°F / 80°C
2. Whisk all ingredients in a mixing bowl until smooth (ensure sugar is fully dissolved)
3. Divide the mixture into jars and seal or cover ramekins (leave some space for expansion)
4. Cook jars in a water bath for 60 minutes (fully submerge jars in the bath)
5. Cool, then refrigerate for 2 hours before serving (chill thoroughly for proper texture)

Cooking Temperature Range:
Optimal 176°F / 80°C (permissible range 176°F / 80°C to 180°F / 82°C).

Pumpkin Custard

Yield: 2 servings | Prep time: 10 minutes | Cook time: 45 minutes

Cozy up with the creamy warmth of our Sous Vide Pumpkin Custard! This rich and velvety dessert is infused with the earthy sweetness of pumpkin and the comforting spices of fall. Sous vide precision ensures a perfectly smooth texture and balanced flavor, making every spoonful a delightful seasonal treat.

Ingredients:
- Pumpkin puree (canned) - 0.5 cup
- Egg (large) - 2 pieces
- Heavy Cream - 0.5 cup
- Brown Sugar - 2 tbsp
- Cinnamon (ground) - 1 pinch

Nutritional Information (for 2 servings):
calories 250 kcal, protein 7g, carbohydrates 22g, fat 15g, fiber 2g, cholesterol 80mg, sodium 160mg, potassium 300mg

Directions:
1. Whisk pumpkin, eggs, cream, sugar, and cinnamon thoroughly (ensure mixture is smooth)
2. Divide the mixture into jars or vacuum bags and seal (use the proper sealing technique for sous vide)
3. Cook in a water bath at 185°F / 85°C for 45 minutes (maintain water level, jars fully submerged)
4. Remove from the water bath, and let cool for 5 minutes (carefully handle hot jars)

Cooking Temperature Range:
Optimal 185°F / 85°C (permissible range 180°F / 82°C to 190°F / 88°C).

Salted Caramel Custard

Yield: 2 servings | Prep time: 10 minutes | Cook time: 1 hour

Dive into decadence with our Sous Vide Salted Caramel Custard! This luxuriously creamy dessert blends the rich sweetness of caramel with a hint of sea salt, creating a perfect balance of flavors. Sous vide precision ensures a flawlessly smooth texture, making every spoonful a truly indulgent treat

Ingredients:
- Heavy cream - 1 cup
- White sugar - 2 tbsp
- Salted caramel sauce - 2 tbsp
- Egg yolk (large) - 3 pieces
- Sea salt - 1 pinch

Nutritional Information (for 2 servings):
calories 310 kcal, protein 5g, carbohydrates 24g, fat 23g, fiber 0g, cholesterol 185mg, sodium 60mg, potassium 85mg

Directions:
1. Preheat sous vide water bath to 179°F / 82°C
2. Whisk egg yolks, sugar, and caramel sauce until smooth (avoid over-mixing to prevent air bubbles)
3. Heat cream and gradually mix into yolk mixture (gradual mixing prevents curdling)
4. Strain the mixture into jars and seal them tightly (to ensure a smooth texture)
5. Submerge jars and cook for 60 minutes in a water bath (cool and refrigerate before serving)

Cooking Temperature Range:
Optimal 179°F / 82°C (permissible range 179°F / 82°C to 185°F / 85°C).

Salted Caramel Pots de Crème

Yield: 2 servings | Prep time: 15 minutes | Cook time: 1 hour 30 minutes

Indulge in the luxurious decadence of our Sous Vide Salted Caramel Pots de Crème. Rich, velvety custard infused with golden caramel and a touch of sea salt creates the perfect harmony of sweet and savory. Sous vide precision ensures an irresistibly smooth texture in every creamy, indulgent bite.

Ingredients:
- Heavy cream - 1 cup
- Whole milk - 0.5 cup
- Sugar (caramelize before use) - 0.5 cup
- Egg yolk (whisked) - 2 pieces
- Vanilla extract - 1 tsp
- Sea salt - 1 pinch

Nutritional Information (for 2 servings):
calories 420 kcal, protein 6g, carbohydrates 38g, fat 28g, fiber 0g, cholesterol 200mg, sodium 60mg, potassium 90mg

Directions:
1. Caramelize sugar and add cream and milk. Cool slightly (stir constantly to avoid burning)
2. Whisk egg yolks, vanilla, and salt; add caramel mixture (whisk gradually to temper eggs)
3. Preheat sous vide bath to 180°F / 82°C
4. Pour mixture into jars; sous vide for 90 minutes (seal jars tightly to avoid water entry)
5. Cool to room temperature and refrigerate before serving (let set for at least 2 hours)

Cooking Temperature Range:
Optimal 180°F / 82°C (permissible range 180°F / 82°C to 185°F / 85°C).

Strawberry Panna Cotta

Yield: 2 servings | Prep time: 15 minutes | Cook time: 2 hours

Indulge in the elegance of our Sous Vide Strawberry Panna Cotta. This silky, creamy dessert is infused with the sweet essence of ripe strawberries, creating a luscious and vibrant treat. Sous vide precision ensures a flawless texture and rich flavor, making every spoonful a moment of pure bliss.

Ingredients:
- Heavy cream - 1 cup
- Whole milk - 0.5 cup
- Sugar - 2 tbsp
- Strawberry puree (blend fresh strawberries) - 0.5 cup
- Gelatin (unflavored) - 1 tsp

Nutritional Information (for 2 servings):
calories 290 kcal, protein 4g, carbohydrates 21g, fat 22g, fiber 0g, cholesterol 70mg, sodium 50mg, potassium 100mg

Directions:
1. Mix cream, milk, sugar, puree, and bloom gelatin (let gelatin bloom for better setting)
2. Preheat sous vide water bath to 176°F / 80°C
3. Pour mixture into jars and cook sous vide for 120 minutes (ensure jars are sealed properly)
4. Cool jars to room temperature and refrigerate (refrigerate until fully set)
5. Serve chilled. Garnish with strawberries if desired (optional garnish enhances appearance)

Cooking Temperature Range:
Optimal 176°F / 80°C (permissible range 176°F / 80°C to 180°F / 82°C).

Strawberry Parfait

Yield: 2 servings | Prep time: 15 minutes | Cook time: 2 hours

Delight in the layers of our Sous Vide Strawberry Parfait! Creamy yogurt, sweet strawberry compote, and crunchy granola combine perfectly. Sous vide precision enhances the rich, vibrant flavors and smooth textures, creating a fresh, indulgent treat that's as beautiful as it is delicious.

Ingredients:
- Whole milk - 2 cups
- Yogurt starter (room temperature) - 2 tbsp
- Strawberry puree (blend fresh or frozen) - 0.5 cup
- Sugar - 2 tbsp
- Granola - 0.25 cup

Nutritional Information (for 2 servings):
calories 190 kcal, protein 8g, carbohydrates 28g, fat 5g, fiber 1g, cholesterol 20mg, sodium 80mg, potassium 150mg

Directions:
1. Warm milk to 110°F / 43°C, stirring occasionally to prevent scalding (for fresh/raw/farm milk, heat milk to 180°F / 82°C, then cool to 110°F / 43°C)
2. Mix milk with yogurt starter and sugar (ensure thorough mixing)
3. Seal jars and cook in sous vide bath at 110°F / 43°C for 120 minutes (do not overheat; keep below 115°F / 46°C to preserve cultures)
4. Cool and refrigerate yogurt for 2 hours (chill for best flavor)
5. Layer yogurt, puree, and granola in glasses (adjust layers to personal preference)

Cooking Temperature Range:
Optimal 110°F / 43°C (permissible range 110°F / 43°C to 115°F / 46°C).

Tiramisu

Yield: 2 servings | Prep time: 20 minutes | Cook time: 1 hour

Experience pure indulgence with our Sous Vide Tiramisu. Layers of velvety mascarpone cream, coffee-soaked ladyfingers, and a hint of cocoa come together in this decadent dessert. Sous vide precision ensures a luxuriously smooth texture and perfectly balanced flavors, elevating the classic Italian treat to perfection.

Ingredients:
- Mascarpone - 4 oz
- Heavy cream - 0.5 cup
- Sugar - 0.33 cup
- Egg yolk (whisked) - 2 pieces
- Espresso (brewed and cooled) - 0.25 cup
- Ladyfingers - 6 pieces

Nutritional Information (for 2 servings):
calories 450 kcal, protein 8g, carbohydrates 42g, fat 28g, fiber 0g, cholesterol 240mg, sodium 80mg, potassium 150mg

Directions:
1. Whisk the mascarpone, cream, sugar, and yolks (mix until fully combined)
2. Seal the mixture in vacuum or ziplock bags (ensure airtight sealing)
3. Cook in a water bath at 185°F / 85°C for 60 minutes (make sure jars/bags are fully submerged)
4. Cool custard and refrigerate (allow proper chilling before assembly)
5. Layer coffee-soaked ladyfingers and custard (chill before serving for best flavor)

Cooking Temperature Range:
Optimal 185°F / 85°C (permissible range 185°F / 85°C to 190°F / 88°C).

Vanilla Bean Panna Cotta

Yield: 2 servings | Prep time: 10 minutes | Cook time: 1 hour

Indulge in the timeless elegance of our Sous Vide Vanilla Bean Panna Cotta! This silky, creamy dessert infuses real vanilla beans' rich, aromatic essence. Sous vide precision ensures a flawless, velvety texture, making every spoonful a luxurious and sophisticated treat.

Ingredients:
- Heavy cream - 1 cup
- White sugar - 2 tbsp
- Vanilla bean (seeds scraped) - 1 piece
- Gelatin (unflavored) - 1 tsp
- Water - 2 tbsp

Nutritional Information (for 2 servings):
calories 250 kcal, protein 4g, carbohydrates 12g, fat 22g, fiber 0g, cholesterol 75mg, sodium 25mg, potassium 50mg

Directions:
1. Preheat sous vide water bath to 180°F / 82°C
2. Bloom gelatin in cold water (stir gently to avoid clumping)
3. Heat cream, sugar, and vanilla bean until sugar dissolves (stir occasionally to prevent scorching)
4. Strain mixture into jars and seal tightly (ensures smooth texture)
5. Submerge jars and cook for 60 minutes in the water bath (cool before refrigerating)

Cooking Temperature Range:
Optimal 180°F / 82°C (permissible range 180°F / 82°C to 185°F / 85°C).

Vanilla Custard

Yield: 2 servings | Prep time: 10 minutes | Cook time: 1 hour

Dive into the lusciousness of our Sous Vide Vanilla Custard. Smooth, creamy, and infused with the delicate warmth of vanilla, this dessert is a classic comfort reimagined. Sous vide precision ensures a perfectly silky texture and balanced flavor in every spoonful, elevating simplicity to sophistication.

Ingredients:
- Whole milk - 1 cup
- Heavy cream - 0.5 cup
- Sugar - 0.33 cup
- Egg yolk (whisked) - 4 pieces
- Vanilla extract - 1 tsp

Nutritional Information (for 2 servings):
calories 280 kcal, protein 6g, carbohydrates 30g, fat 15g, fiber 0g, cholesterol 200mg, sodium 50mg, potassium 160mg

Directions:
1. Whisk together milk, cream, sugar, yolks, and vanilla (ensure ingredients are well mixed)
2. Pour mixture into jars, leaving space at the top (use jars that seal tightly)
3. Cook in a water bath at 176°F / 80°C for 60 minutes (make sure jars are fully submerged)
4. Cool jars to room temperature, then refrigerate (refrigerate for at least 2 hours)
5. Serve chilled with optional garnishes (pair with fruit or spices for extra flavor)

Cooking Temperature Range:
Optimal 176°F / 80°C (permissible range 176°F / 80°C to 180°F / 82°C).

Vanilla Flan

Yield: 2 servings | Prep time: 15 minutes | Cook time: 1 hour

Indulge in the silky elegance of our Sous Vide Vanilla Flan. This creamy custard dessert, infused with the warm essence of vanilla, is topped with a golden layer of caramelized sugar. Sous vide precision ensures a flawlessly smooth texture and rich flavor, making every spoonful a luxurious treat.

Ingredients:
- Whole milk - 1 cup
- Heavy cream - 1 cup
- Sugar - 0.25 cup
- Egg (whisked) - 2 pieces
- Vanilla extract - 1 tsp

Nutritional Information (for 2 servings):
calories 290 kcal, protein 7g, carbohydrates 28g, fat 16g, fiber 0g, cholesterol 120mg, sodium 45mg, potassium 150mg

Directions:
1. Whisk together milk, cream, sugar, eggs, and vanilla (ensure the mixture is well combined)
2. Pour mixture into jars, leaving space at the top (use jars that seal tightly)
3. Cook in a water bath at 180°F / 82°C for 60 minutes
4. Cool to room temperature, then refrigerate (refrigerate for at least 2 hours)
5. Serve chilled with optional toppings (pair with caramel or fresh fruit)

Cooking Temperature Range:
Optimal 180°F / 82°C (permissible range 180°F / 82°C to 185°F / 85°C).

INTRODUCTION TO PREPARING YOGURT DESSERTS USING SOUS VIDE TECHNOLOGY

Yogurt desserts are beloved for their creamy texture, tangy flavor, and versatility. With sous vide technology, making homemade yogurt becomes easier and more precise, ensuring consistent results every time. From classic plain yogurt to flavored variations and indulgent parfaits, sous vide allows for exact temperature control, which is crucial for fermentation.

GENERAL PRINCIPLES AND FEATURES OF SOUS VIDE YOGURT DESSERTS

Sous vide yogurt preparation involves gently heating milk to a precise temperature, inoculating it with live cultures, and allowing it to ferment in a controlled environment. This method is particularly advantageous because it is consistent and allows for the customization of flavors and textures.

Key features and benefits of sous vide yogurt include:

Temperature Precision: Sous vide ensures the milk is heated to the ideal temperature (around 110°F/43°C) for fermentation, avoiding overheating or underheating.

Consistent Fermentation: Maintaining a stable temperature allows the cultures to develop evenly, resulting in creamy and tangy yogurt.

Hands-Free Cooking: Once the mixture is prepared and packed, sous vide takes care of the rest, freeing you to focus on other tasks.

Customization: Sous vide makes creating different textures (Greek-style, drinkable yogurt) and flavors easy by adjusting ingredients and fermentation time.

HOW TO PACK YOGURT MIXTURES CORRECTLY

Proper packing is essential for achieving the desired texture and consistency in yogurt desserts. Here's how to do it:

Choose the Right Containers:
- Use heat-resistant jars with lids for individual servings.
- For larger batches, use resealable silicone pouches or vacuum-sealed bags.

Prepare the Mixture:
- Heat milk to 180°F (82°C) to pasteurize and cool it to 110°F (43°C).
- Mix in a starter culture (store-bought yogurt with live cultures or powdered yogurt starter).

Fill Containers Evenly:
- Pour the mixture into jars or bags, leaving about ½ inch of space at the top to allow for slight expansion.
- Wipe the edges of jars to ensure a clean seal.

Seal Properly:
- Screw jar lids on loosely to allow air to escape during fermentation. Tighten them after the process is complete.
- For bags, remove as much air as possible before sealing.

SHAPING YOGURT DESSERTS FOR PRESENTATION

Sous vide yogurt can be transformed into stunning desserts with creative shaping and plating techniques:

Layered Parfaits:
- Alternate yogurt, granola, and fresh fruit layers in clear jars or glasses.

Molded Yogurt:
- Use silicone molds to set thickened yogurt for unique shapes. Add gelatin for extra stability if needed.

Swirled Creations:
- Blend fruit purees or syrups into the yogurt before serving for a marbled effect.

Topped Servings:
- Serve yogurt in individual jars and top with honey, nuts, or chocolate shavings for a simple yet elegant presentation.

STORING YOGURT BEFORE AND AFTER COOKING

Before Cooking:

Refrigeration: If not fermenting immediately, store the prepared milk and culture mixture in the refrigerator for up to 24 hours.

Freezing: Avoid freezing the mixture before fermentation as freezing can damage the live cultures.

After Cooking:

Cooling: Once fermentation is complete, transfer the yogurt to an ice bath to cool quickly and halt the process.

Refrigeration: Store yogurt in sealed containers in the refrigerator for up to 7 days.

Freezing: To make frozen yogurt desserts, mix the yogurt with sweeteners or flavors and freeze them in an airtight container for up to one month.

PREPARING THE FINISHED DISH FOR SERVING

Chill Before Serving:
- Refrigerate yogurt for at least 2 hours after fermentation for the best flavor and texture.

Customize Flavors:
- Stir in honey, fruit compote, vanilla extract, or cocoa powder to enhance the yogurt.

Serve with Toppings:
- Add granola, nuts, dried fruits, or fresh berries for texture and flavor.

Use as a Base:
- Incorporate sous vide yogurt into smoothies, salad dressings, or baked goods for added tang and creaminess.

Plating Techniques:
- Use small dessert plates or bowls to showcase yogurt as the centerpiece, garnished with edible flowers or fruit slices.

COMMON MISTAKES AND HOW TO AVOID THEM

Overheating the Milk:
  Mistake: Heating milk beyond 180°F (82°C) can alter its proteins and affect texture.
  Solution: Use a thermometer to monitor temperature carefully.

Incorrect Fermentation Temperature:
  Mistake: Too low a temperature can inhibit fermentation, while too high can kill the cultures.
  Solution: Keep the sous vide water bath at 110°F (43°C) for optimal results.

Skipping the Ice Bath:
  Mistake: Failing to cool yogurt quickly can result in over-fermentation and an overly tangy taste.
  Solution: Always use an ice bath to stop the fermentation process promptly.

Using Poor-Quality Starter:
  Mistake: A weak or expired starter culture can lead to inconsistent results.
  Solution: Use fresh yogurt with active cultures or a reliable powdered starter.

Not Cleaning Containers Properly:
  Mistake: Residual bacteria in jars can interfere with fermentation.
  Solution: Sterilize all containers and utensils before use.

CONCLUSION

Sous vide technology simplifies making homemade yogurt, delivering consistent and delicious results every time. By mastering the basics of packing, fermenting, and storing, you can create a variety of yogurt-based desserts tailored to your tastes. With sous vide, your yogurt desserts can range from simple, healthy snacks to show-stopping creations that impress every time.

Can fruit compote be added?

Yes, fruit compote can be added to sous vide yogurt desserts! It enhances the flavor, texture, and presentation of your yogurt. Here's how you can incorporate fruit compote into your sous vide yogurt desserts:

HOW TO ADD FRUIT COMPOTE TO SOUS VIDE YOGURT DESSERTS

1. As a Layer
  What to Do: Add a spoonful of fruit compote to the bottom or middle of jars before pouring in the yogurt mixture.

Why: It creates beautiful layers and a burst of fruity flavor when the yogurt is served.

2. As a Swirl

What to Do: After the yogurt is fermented and cooled, swirl the compote into the yogurt using a spoon or skewer.

Why: It adds a marbled look and distributes the fruity flavor throughout the yogurt.

3. As a Topping

What to Do: Spoon fruit compote on top of the yogurt before serving.

Why: It enhances visual appeal and lets guests mix it as they eat.

4. Mixed In

What to Do: Stir the fruit compote into the yogurt completely after fermentation and cooling.

Why: This infuses the entire yogurt with the fruit flavor, creating a consistent taste.

5. As a Sauce

What to Do: Warm the compote slightly and drizzle it over the yogurt.

Why: It creates a dessert-like presentation and contrasts warm compote with cool yogurt.

Best Fruits for Compotes with Yogurt
- **Berries**: Strawberries, blueberries, raspberries, or blackberries are classics.
- **Stone Fruits:** Peaches, cherries, plums, or apricots.
- **Tropical Fruits:** Mango, pineapple, or passionfruit for an exotic twist.
- **Apples and Pears:** Great for fall-inspired yogurt with cinnamon or nutmeg.
- **Citrus:** Orange or lemon compotes can add a tangy freshness.

Tips for Adding Fruit Compote

- **Cool the Compote:** Before adding the compote to the yogurt, ensure it is at room temperature or chilled to avoid affecting the fermentation or texture.
- **Use Small Jars:** Individual portions make it easier to add compote without mixing it into other jars.
- **Balance Sweetness:** Adjust the sugar in the compote to balance the tanginess of the yogurt.
- **Experiment with Herbs and Spices**: For added depth, add a sprig of mint, a dash of cinnamon, or even vanilla to the compote.

Few Fruit Compote Recipes for Yogurt

- **Berry Medley:** Simmer mixed berries with a touch of sugar and lemon juice.
- **Peach and Cardamom:** Cook diced peaches with honey and a pinch of cardamom.
- **Citrus Bliss:** Combine orange segments, a splash of honey, and grated zest for a bright compote.
- **Apple-Cinnamon:** Sauté apples with brown sugar, cinnamon, and a hint of nutmeg.
- **Mango Passionfruit:** Blend mango chunks and passionfruit pulp with a little sugar for a tropical burst.

Banana Cream Yogurt

Yield: 2 servings | Prep time: 15 minutes | Cook time: 6 hours

Treat yourself to the creamy decadence of our Sous Vide Banana Cream Yogurt! Sweet, ripe bananas blend seamlessly with velvety yogurt to create a luscious, dessert-like treat. Sous vide precision ensures a perfectly smooth texture and rich flavor, making every spoonful a delightful indulgence.

Ingredients:
- Whole Milk - 2 cups
- Plain yogurt (live cultures) - 2 tbsp
- Banana (medium. ripe. mashed) - 1 piece
- Honey - 1 tbsp
- Vanilla Extract - 0.5 tsp

Nutritional Information (for 2 servings):
calories 180 kcal, protein 6g, carbohydrates 24g, fat 6g, fiber 1g, cholesterol 5mg, sodium 50mg, potassium 300mg

Directions:
1. Warm milk to 110°F / 43°C, stirring occasionally to prevent scalding (for fresh/raw/farm milk, heat milk to 180°F / 82°C, then cool to 110°F / 43°C)
2. Mash the banana, stir it into warm milk, and whisk in the honey, vanilla extract, and plain yogurt (ensure smooth blending)
3. Pour mixture into jars, leaving headspace, and seal loosely (do not overtighten jars)
4. Place in sous vide bath, Incubate at 110°F / 43°C for 360 minutes (do not overheat; keep below 115°F / 46°C to preserve cultures)
5. Refrigerate for 4 hours (yogurt thickens further during refrigeration)

Cooking Temperature Range:
Optimal 110°F / 43°C (permissible range 100°F / 38°C to 115°F / 46°C).

Blackberry Honey Yogurt

Yield: 2 servings | Prep time: 20 minutes | Cook time: 6 hours

Indulge in the luscious harmony of our Sous Vide Blackberry Honey Yogurt! Sweet, juicy blackberries are blended with golden honey and creamy yogurt for a rich and refreshing treat. Sous vide precision ensures a silky texture and vibrant flavor, making this a nourishing delight in every spoonful.

Ingredients:
- Whole Milk - 2 cups
- Plain yogurt (live cultures) - 2 tbsp
- Blackberries - 0.5 cup
- Honey - 2 tbsp
- Vanilla Extract - 0.5 tsp

Nutritional Information (for 2 servings):
calories 190 kcal, protein 7g, carbohydrates 24g, fat 7g, fiber 2g, cholesterol 5mg, sodium 60mg, potassium 310mg

Directions:
1. Warm milk to 110°F / 43°C, stirring occasionally to prevent scalding (for fresh/raw/farm milk, heat milk to 180°F / 82°C, then cool to 110°F / 43°C)
2. Stir in honey and vanilla extract until dissolved. Whisk in plain yogurt (ensure the mixture is smooth)
3. Divide blackberries between jars, pour milk mixture, and seal loosely (leave some headspace in jars)
4. Place in sous vide bath, Incubate at 110°F / 43°C for 360 minutes (do not overheat; keep below 115°F / 46°C to preserve cultures)
5. Chill for at least 4 hours (yogurt thickens further as it chills)

Cooking Temperature Range:
Optimal 110°F / 43°C (permissible range 100°F / 38°C to 115°F / 46°C).

Blueberry Lemon Yogurt

Yield: 2 servings | Prep time: 20 minutes | Cook time: 6 hours

Brighten your day with our Blueberry Lemon Sous Vide Yogurt! Bursting with the sweet tang of blueberries and zesty lemon, this creamy treat perfectly balances refreshment and indulgence. Sous vide precision ensures a velvety texture and vibrant flavor, making it a delightful start to any morning.

Ingredients:
- Whole Milk - 2 cups
- Plain yogurt (live cultures) - 2 tbsp
- Blueberries - 0.5 cup
- Lemon zest (grated) - 1 tsp
- Honey or Maple Syrup - 2 tbsp

Nutritional Information (for 2 servings):
calories 180 kcal, protein 6g, carbohydrates 24g, fat 6g, fiber 1g, cholesterol 5mg, sodium 60mg, potassium 300mg

Directions:
1. Warm milk to 110°F / 43°C, and stir in lemon zest and honey until dissolved (for fresh/raw/farm milk, heat milk to 180°F / 82°C, then cool to 110°F / 43°C)
2. Whisk in plain yogurt until smooth (ensure no lumps remain)
3. Divide blueberries between jars, pour milk mixture, and seal loosely (leave some headspace in the jars)
4. Place in sous vide bath, Incubate at 110°F / 43°C for 360 minutes (do not overheat; keep below 115°F / 46°C to preserve cultures)
5. Chill for at least 4 hours (yogurt thickens further as it chills)

Cooking Temperature Range:
Optimal 110°F / 43°C (permissible range 100°F / 38°C to 115°F / 46°C).

Blueberry Yogurt

Yield: 2 servings | Prep time: 10 minutes | Cook time: 1 hour 30 minutes

Enjoy the perfect balance of sweet and tangy with our Sous Vide Blueberry Yogurt! Packed with the natural sweetness of ripe blueberries and the creamy richness of yogurt, this treat is a refreshing delight. Sous vide precision ensures a silky texture and vibrant flavor in every spoonful.

Ingredients:
- Blueberries (fresh) - 1 cup
- Whole milk yogurt (plain) - 2 cups
- White sugar - 0.25 cup
- Vanilla extract - 0.5 tsp

Nutritional Information (for 2 servings):
calories 220 kcal, protein 7g, carbohydrates 35g, fat 5g, fiber 1g, cholesterol 15mg, sodium 50mg, potassium 120mg

Directions:
1. Preheat sous vide water bath to 110°F / 43°C
2. Blend blueberries, sugar, and vanilla until smooth (use a blender for best consistency)
3. Mix with yogurt and pour into jars; seal tightly (ensure jars are airtight)
4. Sous vide for 90 minutes (keep jars submerged in the water bath)
5. Chill jars in the refrigerator before serving (allow at least 2 hours for chilling)

Cooking Temperature Range:
Optimal 110°F / 43°C (permissible range 100°F / 38°C to 115°F / 46°C).

Chai-Spiced Yogurt

Yield: 2 servings | Prep time: 20 minutes | Cook time: 6 hours

Warm your senses with our Chai-Spiced Sous Vide Yogurt! This creamy, velvety treat is infused with an aromatic blend of cinnamon, cardamom, ginger, and cloves, capturing the essence of chai tea in every bite. Sous vide precision ensures a perfectly smooth texture, making this yogurt a cozy and flavorful delight.

Ingredients:
- Whole Milk - 2 cups
- Plain yogurt (live cultures) - 2 tbsp
- Honey or Maple Syrup - 2 tbsp
- Chai Spice Mix - 1 tsp
- Vanilla Extract (optional) - 0.5 tsp

Nutritional Information (for 2 servings):
calories 200 kcal, protein 6g, carbohydrates 26g, fat 8g, fiber 0g, cholesterol 5mg, sodium 60mg, potassium 350mg

Directions:
1. Warm milk to 110°F / 43°C. Stir in chai spice mix, honey, and vanilla extract (for fresh/raw/farm milk, heat milk to 180°F / 82°C, then cool to 110°F / 43°C)
2. Whisk in plain yogurt until smooth (ensure no lumps remain)
3. Pour into jars and cover loosely (leave some headspace in the jars)
4. Place in sous vide bath, Incubate at 110°F / 43°C for 360 minutes (do not overheat; keep below 115°F / 46°C to preserve cultures)
5. Chill for at least 4 hours (yogurt thickens further as it chills)

Cooking Temperature Range:
Optimal 110°F / 43°C (permissible range 100°F / 38°C to 115°F / 46°C).

Chocolate Almond Yogurt

Yield: 2 servings | Prep time: 20 minutes | Cook time: 6 hours

Indulge in the decadent harmony of our Chocolate Almond Sous Vide Yogurt! Creamy and rich, this yogurt blends the deep flavor of chocolate with the nutty sweetness of almonds. Sous vide precision ensures a velvety texture, making every spoonful a luxurious and nourishing treat.

Ingredients:
- Almond milk (unsweetened) - 2 cups
- Plain yogurt (live cultures) - 2 tbsp
- Cocoa powder (unsweetened, sifted) - 1 tbsp
- Honey or Maple Syrup - 2 tbsp
- Almond extract (optional) - 0.25 tsp

Nutritional Information (for 2 servings):
calories 180 kcal, protein 4g, carbohydrates 20g, fat 8g, fiber 2g, cholesterol 5mg, sodium 50mg, potassium 300mg

Directions:
1. Heat almond milk to 110°F / 43°C. Stir in cocoa powder and honey until dissolved (do not overheat; keep below 115°F / 46°C to preserve cultures)
2. Whisk in plain yogurt and almond extract until smooth (ensure no lumps remain)
3. Pour into jars and cover loosely (leave some headspace in the jars)
4. Place in sous vide bath. Incubate at 110°F / 43°C for 360 minutes (make sure jars are fully submerged but lids are not airtight)
5. Chill for at least 4 hours (yogurt thickens further as it chills)

Cooking Temperature Range:
Optimal 110°F / 43°C (permissible range 100°F / 38°C to 115°F / 46°C).

Chocolate Yogurt

Yield: 2 servings | Prep time: 10 minutes | Cook time: 2 hours

Treat yourself to the velvety richness of Sous Vide Chocolate Yogurt! This creamy, indulgent delight combines the smooth tang of yogurt with chocolate's deep, luscious flavor. Sous vide precision ensures a perfectly silky texture, making every spoonful a luxurious and nourishing treat.

Ingredients:
- Greek yogurt (full-fat) - 1 cup
- Cocoa powder (unsweetened, sifted) - 2 tbsp
- Dark chocolate (melt before mixing) - 2 oz
- Honey - 2 tbsp
- Vanilla extract (pure) - 1 tsp

Nutritional Information (for 2 servings):
calories 240 kcal, protein 9g, carbohydrates 25g, fat 12g, fiber 1g, cholesterol 10mg, sodium 25mg, potassium 190mg

Directions:
1. Preheat sous vide water bath to 110°F / 43°C
2. Mix yogurt, cocoa, chocolate, honey, and vanilla (ensure smooth consistency)
3. Divide the mixture into jars and seal them tightly (leave some space for expansion)
4. Cook jars in the water bath for 120 minutes (ensure jars are fully submerged)
5. Cool and refrigerate for 2 hours before serving (enhances flavor and texture)

Cooking Temperature Range:
Optimal 110°F / 43°C (permissible range 100°F / 38°C to 115°F / 46°C).

Coconut Milk Yogurt

Yield: 2 servings | Prep time: 15 minutes | Cook time: 6 hours

Dive into tropical bliss with our Coconut Milk Sous Vide Yogurt! This creamy, dairy-free delight combines the smooth richness of coconut milk with a subtle tang, creating a velvety, indulgent, refreshing treat. Sous vide precision ensures perfect texture and bold, exotic flavor in every spoonful.

Ingredients:
- Coconut Milk (full-fat) - 2 cups
- Plain yogurt (dairy-free) - 2 tbsp
- Maple Syrup or Honey - 1 tbsp
- Vanilla extract (optional) - 0.5 tsp

Nutritional Information (for 2 servings):
calories 190 kcal, protein 3g, carbohydrates 14g, fat 16g, fiber 1g, cholesterol 0mg, sodium 25mg, potassium 250mg

Directions:
1. Heat coconut milk to 110°F / 43°C, stir in maple syrup or honey (do not overheat; keep below 115°F / 46°C to preserve cultures)
2. Whisk in yogurt and vanilla extract until smooth (ensure the mixture is fully blended)
3. Pour into jars and cover loosely (leave some headspace in the jars)
4. Place in sous vide bath. Incubate at 110°F / 43°C for 360 minutes (make sure jars are fully submerged but lids are not airtight)
5. Chill for at least 4 hours (yogurt thickens further as it chills)

Cooking Temperature Range:
Optimal 110°F / 43°C (permissible range 100°F / 38°C to 115°F / 46°C).

Greek Yogurt

Yield: 2 servings | Prep time: 15 minutes | Cook time: 6 hours

Discover the creamy richness of our Sous Vide Greek Yogurt! Thick, tangy, and protein-packed, this homemade yogurt balances indulgence and nutrition. Sous vide precision ensures a silky-smooth texture and bold flavor, making it ideal for breakfasts, snacks, or desserts.

Ingredients:
- Whole Milk - 2 cups
- Plain yogurt (live cultures) - 2 tbsp
- Heavy Cream - 0.25 cup
- Honey (optional) - 1 tbsp

Nutritional Information (for 2 servings):
calories 190 kcal, protein 8g, carbohydrates 14g, fat 11g, fiber 0g, cholesterol 30mg, sodium 60mg, potassium 300mg

Directions:
1. Heat warm milk and cream to 110°F / 43°C, stirring occasionally to avoid scalding (for fresh/raw/farm milk, heat milk to 180°F / 82°C, then cool to 110°F / 43°C)
2. Whisk in plain yogurt and honey (if using) until fully blended (ensure smooth consistency)
3. Pour mixture into jars, leaving headspace, and seal loosely (do not overtighten lids)
4. Incubate jars in a sous vide bath at 110°F / 43°C for 360 minutes (do not overheat; keep below 115°F / 46°C to preserve cultures)
5. Refrigerate for 4 hours (allow yogurt to chill for at least 4 hours)

Cooking Temperature Range:
Optimal 110°F / 43°C (permissible range 100°F / 38°C to 115°F / 46°C).

Honey-Sweetened Yogurt

Yield: 2 servings | Prep time: 15 minutes | Cook time: 6 hours

Savor the natural goodness of our Honey-Sweetened Yogurt! Creamy and velvety smooth, this delightful treat is lightly sweetened with golden honey, adding a touch of floral richness. Perfectly balanced and nourishing, every spoonful offers a comforting blend of sweetness and wholesome flavor.

Ingredients:
- Whole Milk - 2 cups
- Plain yogurt (live cultures) - 2 tbsp
- Honey - 1 tbsp
- Vanilla extract (optional) - 0.5 tsp

Nutritional Information (for 2 servings):
calories 180 kcal, protein 8g, carbohydrates 20g, fat 6g, fiber 0g, cholesterol 25mg, sodium 80mg, potassium 210mg

Directions:
1. Warm milk to 110°F / 43°C, and stir in honey until dissolved (for fresh/raw/farm milk, heat milk to 180°F / 82°C, and cool to 110°F / 43°C)
2. Whisk in yogurt and vanilla extract until smooth (ensure the mixture is fully blended)
3. Pour into jars and cover loosely (leave some headspace in the jars)
4. Place in sous vide bath, Incubate at 110°F / 43°C for 360 minutes (do not overheat; keep below 115°F / 46°C to preserve cultures)
5. Chill for at least 4 hours (yogurt thickens further as it chills)

Cooking Temperature Range:
Optimal 110°F / 43°C (permissible range 100°F / 38°C to 115°F / 46°C).

Key Lime Yogurt

Yield: 2 servings | Prep time: 15 minutes | Cook time: 6 hours

Brighten your day with our Key Lime Sous Vide Yogurt! Creamy and tangy, this luscious yogurt is infused with the zesty freshness of key limes, delivering a perfect balance of tart and sweet. Sous vide precision ensures a velvety texture and vibrant flavor, making every spoonful a tropical delight.

Ingredients:
- Whole Milk - 2 cups
- Plain yogurt (live cultures) - 2 tbsp
- Key lime juice (fresh) - 1 tbsp
- Key Lime Zest (grated) - 1 tsp
- Honey (optional) - 1 tbsp

Nutritional Information (for 2 servings):
calories 170 kcal, protein 8g, carbohydrates 19g, fat 6g, fiber 0g, cholesterol 25mg, sodium 80mg, potassium 200mg

Directions:
1. Warm milk to 110°F / 43°C; stir in honey if using (for fresh/raw/farm milk, heat milk to 180°F / 82°C, then cool to 110°F / 43°C)
2. Whisk in yogurt, lime juice, and zest (mix thoroughly for even flavor distribution)
3. Pour into jars, cover loosely (leave some space in jars)
4. Place in sous vide bath, Incubate at 110°F / 43°C for 360 minutes (do not overheat; keep below 115°F / 46°C to preserve cultures)
5. Chill for at least 4 hours (yogurt thickens further in the refrigerator)

Cooking Temperature Range:
Optimal 110°F / 43°C (permissible range 100°F / 38°C to 115°F / 46°C).

Mango Lassi Yogurt

Yield: 2 servings | Prep time: 15 minutes | Cook time: 6 hours

Transport your taste buds to the tropics with our Mango Lassi Sous Vide Yogurt! Creamy, tangy yogurt is blended with sweet, juicy mangoes and a hint of cardamom for a refreshing treat. Sous vide precision ensures a silky-smooth texture and vibrant flavor, making this a luscious and nourishing delight.

Ingredients:
- Whole Milk - 2 cups
- Plain yogurt (live cultures) - 2 tbsp
- Mango puree (canned or fresh, remove excess liquid if too thin) - 2 tbsp
- Sugar (optional) - 1 tbsp
- Cardamom (ground) - 1 pinch

Nutritional Information (for 2 servings):
calories 190 kcal, protein 8g, carbohydrates 22g, fat 6g, fiber 1g, cholesterol 25mg, sodium 80mg, potassium 210mg

Directions:
1. Warm milk to 110°F / 43°C, and stir in sugar if using (for fresh/raw/farm milk, heat milk to 180°F / 82°C, and cool to 110°F / 43°C)
2. Whisk in yogurt, mango purée, and cardamom (blend well for an even flavor)
3. Pour into jars, cover loosely (leave space at the top of jars)
4. Place in sous vide bath, Incubate at 110°F / 43°C for 360 minutes (do not overheat; keep below 115°F / 46°C to preserve cultures)
5. Chill for at least 4 hours (yogurt thickens more in the refrigerator)

Cooking Temperature Range:
Optimal 110°F / 43°C (permissible range 100°F / 38°C to 115°F / 46°C).

Maple Cinnamon Yogurt

Yield: 2 servings | Prep time: 15 minutes | Cook time: 6 hours

Cozy up with the warm, inviting flavors of Maple Cinnamon Sous Vide Yogurt! This creamy, silky treat is infused with the rich sweetness of maple syrup and a hint of cinnamon spice. Sous vide precision ensures a perfectly smooth texture, making every spoonful a comforting, indulgent delight.

Ingredients:
- Whole Milk - 2 cups
- Plain yogurt (live cultures) - 2 tbsp
- Maple Syrup - 1 tbsp
- Cinnamon (ground) - 0.5 tsp

Nutritional Information (for 2 servings):
calories 180 kcal, protein 8g, carbohydrates 20g, fat 6g, fiber 0g, cholesterol 30mg, sodium 80mg, potassium 250mg

Directions:
1. Warm milk to 110°F / 43°C, and stir in maple syrup (for fresh/raw/farm milk, heat milk to 180°F / 82°C, then cool to 110°F / 43°C)
2. Remove from heat, whisk in yogurt and cinnamon (ensure ingredients are well combined)
3. Pour into jars, cover loosely (leave some space in jars)
4. Place in sous vide bath, Incubate at 110°F / 43°C for 360 minutes (do not overheat; keep below 115°F / 46°C to preserve cultures)
5. Chill for at least 4 hours (yogurt thickens further in the fridge)

Cooking Temperature Range:
Optimal 110°F / 43°C (permissible range 100°F / 38°C to 115°F / 46°C).

Matcha Green Tea Yogurt

Yield: 2 servings | Prep time: 15 minutes | Cook time: 6 hours

Awaken your senses with the earthy elegance of Matcha Green Tea Yogurt! This creamy, vibrant treat combines the smooth richness of yogurt with matcha's bold, antioxidant-packed flavor. Perfectly balanced and refreshing, it's a nourishing delight that brings a taste of Zen to every spoonful.

Ingredients:
- Whole Milk - 2 cups
- Plain yogurt (live cultures) - 2 tbsp
- Matcha green tea powder - 1 tsp
- Honey (optional) - 1 tbsp

Nutritional Information (for 2 servings):
calories 160 kcal, protein 8g, carbohydrates 15g, fat 7g, fiber 0g, cholesterol 25mg, sodium 80mg, potassium 200mg

Directions:
1. Warm whole milk to 110°F / 43°C; stir in honey if using (for fresh/raw/farm milk, heat milk to 180°F / 82°C, then cool to 110°F / 43°C)
2. Remove from heat. Whisk in yogurt and matcha powder (ensure matcha is fully dispersed to avoid clumps)
3. Pour into jars, cover loosely (leave some headspace in jars)
4. Place in sous vide bath, Incubate at 110°F / 43°C for 360 minutes (do not overheat; keep below 115°F / 46°C to preserve cultures)
5. Chill for at least 4 hours (yogurt thickens further upon refrigeration)

Cooking Temperature Range:
Optimal 110°F / 43°C (permissible range 100°F / 38°C to 115°F / 46°C).

Orange Blossom Yogurt

Yield: 2 servings | Prep time: 15 minutes | Cook time: 6 hours

Delight in the floral elegance of Orange Blossom Sous Vide Yogurt! Creamy and velvety, this yogurt is delicately infused with the fragrant sweetness of orange blossom, creating a refreshing and sophisticated treat. Sous vide precision ensures a silky texture and balanced flavor in every luscious spoonful.

Ingredients:
- Whole Milk - 2 cups
- Plain yogurt (live cultures) - 2 tbsp
- Orange zest (grated) - 1 pinch
- Orange Blossom Water (add for subtle floral aroma) - 1 tsp
- Honey (optional) - 1 tbsp

Nutritional Information (for 2 servings):
calories 170 kcal, protein 8g, carbohydrates 18g, fat 7g, fiber 0g, cholesterol 25mg, sodium 80mg, potassium 220mg

Directions:
1. Warm milk to 110°F / 43°C; stir in honey if using (for fresh/raw/farm milk, heat milk to 180°F / 82°C, then cool to 110°F / 43°C)
2. Remove from heat and whisk in yogurt, orange blossom water, and orange zest (blend thoroughly for even flavor distribution)
3. Pour into jars and cover loosely (leave headspace for expansion)
4. Place in sous vide bath, Incubate at 110°F / 43°C for 360 minutes (do not overheat; keep below 115°F / 46°C to preserve cultures)
5. Chill for at least 4 hours (yogurt thickens further in the refrigerator)

Cooking Temperature Range:
Optimal 110°F / 43°C (permissible range 100°F / 38°C to 115°F / 46°C).

Peach Ginger Yogurt

Yield: 2 servings | Prep time: 15 minutes | Cook time: 6 hours

Savor the harmonious blend of sweet and spicy with our Peach Ginger Sous Vide Yogurt! Juicy, ripe peaches pair perfectly with the warm zing of ginger in this creamy, velvety treat. Sous vide precision enhances the flavors, creating a refreshing and indulgent yogurt as vibrant as it is delicious.

Ingredients:
- Whole Milk - 2 cups
- Plain yogurt (live cultures) - 2 tbsp
- Ginger (fresh, grated) - 1 tsp
- Peaches (fresh or canned, remove pits, dice, or purée) - 2 tbsp
- Honey (optional) - 1 tbsp

Nutritional Information (for 2 servings):
calories 190 kcal, protein 8g, carbohydrates 22g, fat 7g, fiber 1g, cholesterol 25mg, sodium 80mg, potassium 200mg

Directions:
1. Warm whole milk to 110°F / 43°C; stir in honey if using (for fresh/raw/farm milk, heat milk to 180°F / 82°C, then cool to 110°F / 43°C)
2. Remove from heat and whisk in yogurt, peaches, and ginger (evenly combine all ingredients)
3. Pour into jars and cover loosely (leave space at the top of jars for expansion)
4. Place in sous vide bath, Incubate at 110°F / 43°C for 360 minutes (do not overheat; keep below 115°F / 46°C to preserve cultures)
5. Refrigerate for at least 4 hours (yogurt thickens upon chilling)

Cooking Temperature Range:
Optimal 110°F / 43°C (permissible range 100°F / 38°C to 115°F / 46°C).

Pineapple Coconut Yogurt

Yield: 2 servings | Prep time: 15 minutes | Cook time: 6 hours

Transport yourself to a tropical paradise with Pineapple Coconut Sous Vide Yogurt! Creamy, silky yogurt is infused with the sweet tang of pineapple and the luscious richness of coconut, creating a refreshing and indulgent treat. Sous vide precision ensures perfect texture and vibrant island-inspired flavor in every bite.

Ingredients:
- Whole Milk - 2 cups
- Plain yogurt (live cultures) - 2 tbsp
- Crushed Pineapple (canned. drain excess juice if needed) - 2 tbsp
- Shredded coconut (unsweetened) - 1 tbsp
- Honey (optional) - 1 tbsp

Nutritional Information (for 2 servings):
calories 200 kcal, protein 8g, carbohydrates 25g, fat 6g, fiber 1g, cholesterol 25mg, sodium 90mg, potassium 200mg

Directions:
1. Warm milk to about 110°F / 43°C; stir in honey if using (for fresh/raw/farm milk, heat milk to 180°F / 82°C, then cool to 110°F / 43°C)
2. Whisk in yogurt, crushed pineapple, and shredded coconut (combine thoroughly for even flavor distribution)
3. Pour into jars, cover loosely (leave some headspace in jars)
4. Place in sous vide bath, Incubate at 110°F / 43°C for 360 minutes (do not overheat; keep below 115°F / 46°C to preserve cultures)
5. Chill for at least 4 hours (yogurt thickens more after refrigeration)

Cooking Temperature Range:
Optimal 110°F / 43°C (permissible range 100°F / 38°C to 115°F / 46°C).

Pumpkin Spice Yogurt

Yield: 2 servings | Prep time: 15 minutes | Cook time: 6 hours

Embrace the cozy flavors of fall with Pumpkin Spice Yogurt! This creamy, velvety treat is infused with the warm spices of cinnamon, nutmeg, and cloves, perfectly complemented by the natural sweetness of pumpkin. It's a festive, nourishing delight that captures the essence of autumn in every spoonful.

Ingredients:
- Whole Milk - 2 cups
- Plain yogurt (live cultures) - 2 tbsp
- Pumpkin puree (canned) - 2 tbsp
- Pumpkin Spice Blend - 1 tsp
- Honey (optional) - 1 tbsp

Nutritional Information (for 2 servings):
calories 180 kcal, protein 9g, carbohydrates 20g, fat 7g, fiber 1g, cholesterol 25mg, sodium 80mg, potassium 260mg

Directions:
1. Warm whole milk to 110°F / 43°C; stir in honey if using (for fresh/raw/farm milk, heat milk to 180°F / 82°C, then cool to 110°F / 43°C)
2. Remove from heat and whisk in yogurt, pumpkin puree, and pumpkin spice until combined (proper whisking ensures even distribution of cultures and flavors)
3. Pour mixture into jars, cover loosely, and leave space at the top (allows for expansion and airflow if using breathable lids)
4. Place in sous vide bath, Incubate at 110°F / 43°C for 360 minutes (do not overheat; keep below 115°F / 46°C to preserve cultures)
5. Remove jars, seal if needed, then refrigerate for at least 4 hours (yogurt will thicken further in the fridge)

Cooking Temperature Range:
Optimal 110°F / 43°C (permissible range 100°F / 38°C to 115°F / 46°C).

Raspberry Swirl Yogurt

Yield: 2 servings | Prep time: 15 minutes | Cook time: 6 hours

Treat yourself to the vibrant delight of Raspberry Swirl Yogurt! Creamy, velvety yogurt is beautifully swirled with a sweet and tangy raspberry compote, creating a visually stunning and flavorful treat. This refreshing blend balances richness and fruity brightness in every spoonful, perfect for breakfast or a snack.

Ingredients:
- Whole Milk - 2 cups
- Plain yogurt (live cultures) - 2 tbsp
- Raspberry Jam or Purée - 2 tbsp
- Honey (optional) - 1 tbsp

Nutritional Information (for 2 servings):
calories 180 kcal, protein 9g, carbohydrates 18g, fat 8g, fiber 0g, cholesterol 25mg, sodium 80mg, potassium 250mg

Directions:
1. Warm whole milk to 110°F / 43°C; stir in honey if using (for fresh/raw/farm milk, heat milk to 180°F / 82°C, then cool to 110°F / 43°C)
2. Whisk in plain yogurt (live cultures; ensure it blends evenly)
3. Pour mixture into jars, cover loosely, or use breathable lids (leave a little headspace in jars)
4. Place in sous vide bath, Incubate at 110°F / 43°C for 360 minutes (do not overheat; keep below 115°F / 46°C to preserve cultures)
5. Remove jars, gently swirl in raspberry jam or purée, then chill for at least 4 hours (yogurt thickens more in the fridge)

Cooking Temperature Range:
Optimal 110°F / 43°C (permissible range 100°F / 38°C to 115°F / 46°C).

Strawberry Yogurt

Yield: 2 servings | Prep time: 10 minutes | Cook time: 5 hours

Savor the creamy delight of our Sous Vide Strawberry Yogurt. Bursting with the natural sweetness of ripe strawberries, this velvety yogurt is perfectly balanced and irresistibly fresh. Sous vide precision ensures a silky-smooth texture and vibrant flavor in every spoonful, making it a refreshing treat anytime!

Ingredients:
- Whole milk - 2 cups
- Yogurt starter (room temperature) - 2 tbsp
- Strawberry puree (blend fresh or frozen) - 0.25 cup
- Sugar - 2 tbsp

Nutritional Information (for 2 servings):
calories 150 kcal, protein 8g, carbohydrates 20g, fat 4g, fiber 0g, cholesterol 20mg, sodium 80mg, potassium 150mg

Directions:
1. Warm milk to 110°F / 43°C, stirring occasionally to prevent scalding (for fresh/raw/farm milk, heat milk to 180°F / 82°C, then cool to 110°F / 43°C)
2. Combine milk, yogurt starter, and sugar (mix well to avoid lumps)
3. Pour into jars and place in sous vide bath at 110°F / 43°C for 300 minutes (do not overheat; keep below 115°F / 46°C to preserve cultures)
4. Chill jars after cooking for 2 hours (refrigerate for best flavor)
5. Stir in strawberry puree before serving (adjust sweetness as needed)

Cooking Temperature Range:
Optimal 110°F / 43°C (permissible range 100°F / 38°C to 115°F / 46°C).

Vanilla Bean and Lavender Yogurt

Yield: 2 servings | Prep time: 15 minutes | Cook time: 6 hours

This Vanilla Bean and Lavender Sous Vide Yogurt combines the creamy richness of homemade yogurt with the subtle floral scent of lavender and the sweet aroma of fresh vanilla beans. The gentle, precise heat of the sous vide method helps ensure a thick, luscious texture every time.

Ingredients:
- Whole Milk - 2 cups
- Plain yogurt (live cultures) - 2 tbsp
- Vanilla bean (split and scrape seeds) - 1 piece
- Culinary Lavender (dried) - 1 pinch
- Honey - 1 tbsp

Nutritional Information (for 2 servings):
calories 160 kcal, protein 8g, carbohydrates 15g, fat 8g, fiber 0g, cholesterol 25mg, sodium 90mg, potassium 280mg

Directions:
1. Warm milk and honey to 110°F / 43°C. Add scraped vanilla bean seeds and lavender (for fresh/raw/farm milk, heat milk to 180°F / 82°C, then cool to 110°F / 43°C)
2. Cool slightly and whisk in plain yogurt (live cultures;)
3. Pour mixture into jars, cover loosely, or use breathable lids (leave a little headspace in jars)
4. Incubate in a 110°F / 43°C water bath for 360 minutes (do not overheat; keep below 115°F / 46°C to preserve cultures)
5. Remove from the bath, tighten the lids if needed, and chill at least 4 hours (yogurt will thicken further in the refrigerator)

Cooking Temperature Range:
Optimal 110°F / 43°C (permissible range 100°F / 38°C to 115°F / 46°C).

Vanilla Yogurt

Yield: 2 servings | Prep time: 10 minutes | Cook time: 6 hours

Indulge in the creamy simplicity of our Sous Vide Vanilla Yogurt. Smooth, velvety, and infused with the rich warmth of vanilla, this homemade treat is both nourishing and delightful. Sous vide precision ensures perfect consistency and flavor in every spoonful, elevating yogurt to a new level of deliciousness.

Ingredients:
- Whole milk - 2 cups
- Plain yogurt (live cultures) - 2 tbsp
- Sugar - 1 tbsp
- Vanilla extract - 1 tsp

Nutritional Information (for 2 servings):
calories 140 kcal, protein 6g, carbohydrates 18g, fat 5g, fiber 0g, cholesterol 10mg, sodium 90mg, potassium 200mg

Directions:
1. Whisk together all ingredients (ensure no lumps in the mixture)
2. Pour into jars and seal tightly (use heat-safe jars for sous vide cooking)
3. Cook in water bath at 110°F / 43°C for for 360 minutes
4. Cool and refrigerate before serving (improves texture and flavor)
5. Serve with toppings or plain (customize with fruits, granola, or nuts)

Cooking Temperature Range:
Optimal 110°F / 43°C (permissible range 100°F / 38°C to 115°F / 46°C).

INTRODUCTION TO PREPARING CAKES AND PUDDINGS USING SOUS VIDE TECHNOLOGY

Sous vide technology is renowned for delivering precise and consistent results, making it an excellent method for crafting cakes and puddings. These desserts, which are known for their soft textures and rich flavors, benefit immensely from the controlled environment sous vide provides.

GENERAL PRINCIPLES AND FEATURES OF SOUS VIDE CAKES AND PUDDINGS

Sous vide cooking ensures even heating for cakes and puddings, preventing common issues like overbaking or uneven textures. These desserts typically involve a batter or custard-like mixture that is cooked gently to achieve a moist and uniform consistency.

Key features of sous vide cakes and puddings include:

Temperature Control: Sous vide allows you to set a precise temperature, usually between 175°F–185°F (79°C–85°C), ensuring the dessert is cooked just right.

Moisture Retention: The sealed environment prevents evaporation, keeping cakes and puddings moist and tender.

Even Cooking: The water bath surrounds the dessert with consistent heat, eliminating hot spots and uneven cooking.

Hands-Free Cooking: Once the desserts are packed and placed in the water bath, you can step away without worrying about overcooking.

HOW TO PACK CAKES AND PUDDINGS CORRECTLY

Proper packing is crucial for achieving the best results with sous vide cakes and puddings. Here's how to do it:

Choose the Right Containers:
- Use small, heat-resistant jars (like mason jars) for individual servings.
- For larger cakes or puddings, use vacuum-sealed bags or silicone molds that can withstand sous vide temperatures.

Prepare the Containers:
- Lightly grease the inside of the jars or molds to prevent sticking.
- If using vacuum-sealed bags, ensure the batter or mixture is thick enough to hold its shape.

Fill Evenly:
- Pour the batter or pudding mixture into the jars or molds, leaving about ½ inch of space at the top to allow for expansion.
- Tap the containers gently on the counter to release any trapped air bubbles.

Seal Properly:
- If using jars, screw the lids on loosely to allow air to escape during cooking. Tighten them after cooling.
- Use a gentle setting for vacuum bags to avoid compressing the batter excessively.

SHAPING CAKES AND PUDDINGS FOR PRESENTATION

Sous vide makes it easy to create desserts with beautiful shapes and textures:

Individual Servings:
- Small jars or molds create perfectly portioned servings that can be served directly from the container or unmolded for plating.

Layered Desserts:
- Create layered cakes or puddings by cooking different components separately and assembling them after cooling.

Decorative Molds:
- Use silicone molds with intricate designs for a visually striking presentation. Sous vide ensures even cooking, even with complex shapes.

Garnishes:
- Add garnishes like powdered sugar, fruit compote, or whipped cream to enhance the appearance and flavor of the dessert.

STORING CAKES AND PUDDINGS BEFORE AND AFTER COOKING

Before Cooking:

Refrigeration: Batter or pudding mixture can be stored in jars or molds in the refrigerator for up to 24 hours before cooking.

Freezing: If you prepare the mixture in advance, freeze it in jars or molds. Thaw it in the refrigerator before cooking.

After Cooking:

Cooling: Once cooked, cool the desserts in an ice bath to halt the cooking process and set the texture.

Refrigeration: Cool cakes and puddings and store them in the refrigerator, covered, for up to 5 days to prevent drying out.

Freezing: Some puddings and dense cakes can be frozen for up to 2 months. Wrap tightly in plastic wrap or use airtight containers.

PREPARING THE FINISHED DISH FOR SERVING

Serve Warm or Chilled:
- Many puddings, like sticky toffee or bread pudding, are best served warm. To prepare them, gently heat them in a sous vide water bath.
- Cakes like chocolate fondant can also be warmed to enhance their flavor.

Unmold Carefully:
- Run a knife around the edge of the jar or mold to loosen the dessert before inverting it onto a plate.

Add Toppings:
- Drizzle sauces like caramel, chocolate, or fruit compote over the dessert.
- Garnish with fresh fruit, whipped cream, or a dusting of powdered sugar.

Plating for Presentation:
- For an eye-catching presentation, use contrasting colors and textures. For example, pair dark chocolate pudding with bright red berries.

COMMON MISTAKES AND HOW TO AVOID THEM

Overfilling Containers:
　Mistake: Overfilled jars or molds can cause the batter to spill or cook unevenly.
　Solution: Leave ½ inch of space at the top for expansion.

Tightening Lids Too Much:
　Mistake: Tight lids can trap air and cause jars to float.
　Solution: Screw lids on finger-tight to allow air to escape.

Inconsistent Filling:
　Mistake: Unevenly filled containers result in uneven cooking times.
　Solution: Measure the batter carefully and ensure even distribution.

Skipping the Ice Bath:
　Mistake: Failing to cool desserts quickly can result in overcooking and texture issues.
　Solution: Always cool food in an ice bath immediately after cooking.

Cooking at the Wrong Temperature:
　Mistake: Too high a temperature can cause puddings to curdle or cakes to dry out.
　Solution: Double-check temperature settings and use reliable recipes.

CONCLUSION

Sous vide technology offers an innovative and foolproof way to prepare cakes and puddings. You can create moist, flavorful, and visually stunning desserts by mastering the basics of packing, temperature control, and storage. With sous vide, your homemade cakes and puddings will rival those from the finest bakeries.

Which sauce pairs with pudding?

A good sauce can elevate the flavor and presentation of pudding, contrasting or complementing its creamy texture. Here are some of the best sauces to pair with pudding:

SOME OF THE SAUCES TO PAIR WITH PUDDING

1. Caramel Sauce
　Why: Caramel's rich, buttery sweetness complements the creamy, mild flavors of puddings like vanilla, chocolate, or bread pudding.
　Best Variations:

- Salted caramel for a sweet-salty contrast.
- Rum or bourbon-infused caramel for a boozy kick.

2. Chocolate Sauce
Why: It adds richness and decadence, perfect for vanilla, banana, or coconut pudding.
Best Variations:
- Dark chocolate sauce for bittersweet depth.
- White chocolate sauce for a creamy, sweet touch.

3. Fruit Coulis
Why: The bright, tangy fruit flavors can balance the pudding's richness.
Best Variations:
- Raspberry or strawberry coulis for vanilla or chocolate pudding.
- Mango or passionfruit coulis is great for tropical puddings like coconut or banana.

4. Butterscotch Sauce
Why: The warm, buttery sweetness pairs beautifully with bread pudding, rice pudding, or custard-based puddings.
Best Variations: Add a touch of sea salt or vanilla for depth.

5. Vanilla Bean Crème Anglaise
Why: This classic custard sauce adds a luxurious creaminess that enhances simple puddings.
Best Variations: Infuse with cinnamon or cardamom for an aromatic twist.

6. Maple Syrup
Why: Its earthy sweetness pairs perfectly with bread, rice, or spiced puddings.
Best Variations: Combine with pecans or walnuts for added texture.

7. Berry Compote
Why: Cooked berries add a sweet-tart contrast to creamy puddings.
Best Variations: Blueberry, cherry, or mixed berry compote.

8. Coffee Sauce
Why: It adds a bittersweet depth that complements chocolate or vanilla puddings.
Best Variations: Espresso or mocha sauce for added richness.

9. Spiced Syrup
Why: Warm spices, such as cinnamon, nutmeg, and cloves, enhance the flavor of puddings like pumpkin or bread pudding.
Best Variations: Try a chai-spiced syrup or maple-cinnamon glaze.

10. Citrus Sauce
Why: Bright and tangy citrus sauces cut through the richness of creamy puddings.
Best Variations: Orange, lemon, or lime curd for a zesty pairing.

11. Rum or Whiskey Sauce
Why: A boozy sauce adds warmth and depth, which is ideal for bread pudding or sticky toffee pudding.
Best Variations: Add vanilla or spices for complexity.

12. Nutty Sauces
Why: Adds crunch and nutty richness to puddings like chocolate or vanilla.
Best Variations: Peanut butter, almond, or hazelnut sauces.

13. Honey Sauce
Why: The floral sweetness of honey enhances mild puddings like rice pudding or panna cotta.
Best Variations: Infuse lavender, rosemary, or lemon for unique flavors.

Pro Tips for Pairing Sauces with Pudding:
- **Balance Flavors:** Choose a sauce that enhances the pudding without overpowering it.
- **Add Texture:** Pair smooth sauces with crunchy garnishes like nuts, brittle, or toffee.
- **Warm or Chill:** Serve warm sauces with warm puddings and chilled sauces with cold puddings for harmony.

What is the best sauce for bread pudding?

The perfect sauce for bread pudding depends on the flavors you want to highlight, but some classics and creative options stand out as favorites:

THE PERFECT SAUCE FOR BREAD PUDDING

1. Classic Vanilla Sauce
Why: This rich and creamy custard-based sauce enhances the bread pudding's warm, comforting flavors.
How: Combine milk, cream, sugar, egg yolks, and a splash of vanilla extract. Cook gently until thickened.

2. Bourbon Sauce
Why: It adds a warm, boozy kick that pairs beautifully with the sweetness of bread pudding.
How: Cook butter, sugar, and heavy cream until smooth, then stir in a splash of bourbon.

3. Caramel Sauce
Why: Its buttery sweetness complements the rich, custardy bread pudding.
How: Melt sugar until golden brown, then stir in butter, heavy cream, and a pinch of salt for depth.

4. Salted Caramel Sauce
Why: It adds a modern twist with a balance of sweet and salty flavors.
How: Follow the caramel sauce recipe and finish with flaky sea salt.

5. Rum Sauce
Why: It infuses tropical warmth into the dessert, especially if the pudding includes raisins or cinnamon.
How: Combine butter, sugar, heavy cream, and a splash of dark rum. Cook until smooth and slightly thickened.

6. Chocolate Sauce

Why: Its decadent, bittersweet richness pairs beautifully with vanilla or banana bread puddings.

How: Melt chocolate with cream, sugar, and a touch of butter for a glossy finish.

7. Maple Syrup or Maple Sauce

Why: It enhances bread pudding's cozy, autumnal vibe, especially if it is spiced with cinnamon or nutmeg.

How: Warm pure maple syrup with a little butter for added richness.

8. Spiced Anglaise

Why: A spiced custard sauce with hints of cinnamon, nutmeg, or cardamom complements warm bread pudding perfectly.

How: Prepare a classic crème anglaise and infuse it with your favorite spices.

9. Butterscotch Sauce

Why: It adds a deeper, caramel-like sweetness with buttery undertones.

How: Cook butter, brown sugar, and cream together until smooth and luscious.

10. Berry Compote

Why: It provides a tart, fruity contrast to the richness of bread pudding.

How: Simmer mixed berries with sugar and a splash of lemon juice until thickened.

Pro Tips for Serving Sauce with Bread Pudding:

- **Warm the Sauce:** A warm sauce complements bread pudding's cozy, custardy nature.
- **Serve on the Side:** Let guests drizzle their desired amount for the perfect balance.
- **Garnish for Flair:** Add a dollop of whipped cream, a sprinkle of nuts, or a dusting of powdered sugar to finish the dish.

Key Lime Pie

Yield: 2 servings | Prep time: 15 minutes | Cook time: 1 hour

Transport your taste buds to the tropics with our Sous Vide Key Lime Pie! This creamy, tangy dessert combines the zesty brightness of key limes with a rich, velvety filling atop a buttery graham cracker crust. Sous vide precision ensures a perfectly smooth texture and vibrant flavor in every bite.

Ingredients:
- Sweetened condensed milk - 7 oz
- Egg yolk (large) - 2 pieces
- Key lime juice (fresh or bottled) - 3 tbsp
- Graham cracker crumbs (crushed) - 0.25 cup
- Butter (unsalted, melted) - 1 tbsp

Nutritional Information (for 2 servings):
calories 320 kcal, protein 7g, carbohydrates 45g, fat 12g, fiber 1g, cholesterol 70mg, sodium 140mg, potassium 90mg

Directions:
1. Combine graham cracker crumbs and butter press into ramekins (ensure even crust thickness)
2. Whisk filling ingredients and pour over crusts (avoid overmixing to prevent air bubbles)
3. Seal ramekins and cook in sous vide bath at 185°F / 85°C for 60 minutes
4. Cool, refrigerate, and garnish before serving (chill for at least 2 hours for best texture)

Cooking Temperature Range:
Optimal 185°F / 85°C (permissible range 185°F / 85°C to 190°F / 88°C).

Lemon Bars

Yield: 2 servings | Prep time: 15 minutes | Cook time: 1 hour

Brighten your dessert table with our Sous Vide Lemon Bars! A buttery shortbread crust holds a luscious, tangy lemon filling that's bursting with zesty flavor. Sous vide precision ensures a velvety smooth texture and vibrant citrus taste, making these bars a sweet and refreshing delight in every bite.

Ingredients:
- Lemon juice (freshly squeezed) - 2 tbsp
- White sugar - 3 tbsp
- Egg (large. whisk thoroughly) - 1 piece
- All-purpose flour (sifted) - 1 tbsp
- Butter (unsalted, melted) - 2 tbsp
- Lemon zest (grated) - 1 tsp

Nutritional Information (for 2 servings):
calories 260 kcal, protein 5g, carbohydrates 30g, fat 13g, fiber 1g, cholesterol 140mg, sodium 50mg, potassium 90mg

Directions:
1. Whisk all ingredients and strain the mixture (straining removes lumps for a smooth texture)
2. Pour into jars or vacuum-sealed bags and seal tightly (use airtight jars or bags to avoid leaks)
3. Cook in a sous vide water bath at 180°F / 82°C for 60 minutes
4. Cool to room temperature and refrigerate for 2 hours (chilling sets the custard for clean slicing)
5. Serve chilled with garnish, if desired (powdered sugar adds an elegant touch)

Cooking Temperature Range:
Optimal 180°F / 82°C (permissible range 176°F / 80°C to 183°F / 84°C).

Lemon Cheesecake

Yield: 2 servings | Prep time: 20 minutes | Cook time: 1 hour 30 minutes

Delight in the creamy indulgence of our Sous Vide Lemon Cheesecake! This luscious dessert pairs the tangy brightness of lemon with the rich, velvety smoothness of cheesecake, all atop a buttery crust. Sous vide precision ensures a perfect texture and vibrant citrus flavor in every bite.

Ingredients:
- Cream cheese (softened) - 8 oz
- White sugar - 0.25 cup
- Egg (large, whisk before adding) - 1 piece
- Lemon juice (freshly squeezed) - 2 tbsp
- Lemon zest (grated) - 1 tsp
- Graham cracker crumbs (crushed) - 0.25 cup

Nutritional Information (for 2 servings):
calories 460 kcal, protein 8g, carbohydrates 30g, fat 34g, fiber 1g, cholesterol 190mg, sodium 150mg, potassium 90mg

Directions:
1. Mix cream cheese, sugar, eggs, lemon juice, and zest (ensure mixture is smooth for a creamy texture)
2. Pour into mason jars, leaving space at the top (do not overfill to avoid spills)
3. Cook in a sous vide water bath at 176°F / 80°C for 90 minutes
4. Cool at room temperature, then refrigerate for 2 hours (chilling sets the cheesecake)
5. Garnish with graham cracker crumbs and lemon zest (adds texture and flavor)

Cooking Temperature Range:
Optimal 176°F / 80°C (permissible range 176°F / 80°C to 183°F / 84°C).

Apricot Almond Cake

Yield: 2 servings | Prep time: 15 minutes | Cook time: 1 hour 30 minutes

Experience a moist and fluffy dessert with our Sous Vide Apricot Almond Cake! This elegant treat combines the natural sweetness of apricots with the nutty richness of almonds, perfectly baked in a water bath for a soft, melt-in-your-mouth texture. A decadent delight for any occasion!

Ingredients:
- Apricots (dried and chopped finely) - 0.25 cup
- Almond flour (sifted) - 0.5 cup
- White sugar - 0.25 cup
- Egg (whisked) - 2 pieces
- Butter (unsalted, melted) - 2 tbsp
- Vanilla extract - 1 tsp

Nutritional Information (for 2 servings):
calories 300 kcal, protein 8g, carbohydrates 30g, fat 16g, fiber 2g, cholesterol 125mg, sodium 50mg, potassium 150mg

Directions:
1. Whisk eggs, sugar, butter, and vanilla (ensure the mixture is smooth)
2. Fold in almond flour and apricots (mix gently to avoid lumps)
3. Pour batter into greased mason jars (seal jars lightly)
4. Cook in a sous vide water bath at 180°F / 82°C for 90 minutes (ensure jars are fully submerged)
5. Cool and serve from jars or unmold (let cool completely)

Cooking Temperature Range:
Optimal 180°F / 82°C (permissible range 176°F / 80°C to 190°F / 88°C).

Gooseberry Cardamom Cake

Yield: 2 servings | Prep time: 20 minutes | Cook time: 1 hour 30 minutes

Delight in the unique fusion of tart gooseberries and aromatic cardamom with our Sous Vide Gooseberry Cardamom Cake. This moist, spiced cake highlights the fruit's tangy sweetness and cardamom's warm depth, creating a luscious dessert perfect for any celebration.

Ingredients:
- Gooseberries (fresh. chop finely) - 0.33 cup
- All-purpose flour (sifted) - 0.5 cup
- White sugar - 0.25 cup
- Egg (whisked) - 2 pieces
- Butter (unsalted, melted) - 2 tbsp
- Cardamom (ground) - 0.5 tsp

Nutritional Information (for 2 servings):
calories 310 kcal, protein 7g, carbohydrates 34g, fat 15g, fiber 1g, cholesterol 120mg, sodium 60mg, potassium 160mg

Directions:
1. Whisk eggs, sugar, butter, and cardamom (ensure smooth mixing)
2. Fold in flour and gooseberries (do not overmix)
3. Divide batter into greased jars (seal loosely)
4. Cook in a sous vide water bath at 185°F / 85°C for 90 minutes (ensure jars are submerged)
5. Cool and serve directly from jars or unmold (let cool completely)

Cooking Temperature Range:
Optimal 185°F / 85°C (permissible range 176°F / 80°C to 190°F / 88°C).

Fig Honey Cake

Yield: 2 servings | Prep time: 15 minutes | Cook time: 1 hour 30 minutes

Indulge in the luxurious combination of figs and honey with our Sous Vide Fig Honey Cake. This tender, golden cake bursts with the natural sweetness of figs and a drizzle of warm honey, achieving perfect texture and depth of flavor through precise sous vide cooking.

Ingredients:
- Figs (fresh, diced finely) - 0.33 cup
- All-purpose flour (sifted) - 0.5 cup
- Honey - 2 tbsp
- Egg (whisked) - 2 pieces
- Butter (unsalted, melted) - 2 tbsp
- Baking powder - 0.5 tsp

Nutritional Information (for 2 servings):
calories 320 kcal, protein 6g, carbohydrates 36g, fat 15g, fiber 2g, cholesterol 120mg, sodium 65mg, potassium 150mg

Directions:
1. Whisk eggs, melted butter, and honey (ensure smooth mixing)
2. Fold in flour, baking powder, and figs (do not overmix)
3. Divide batter into greased jars (seal loosely)
4. Cook in a sous vide water bath at 185°F / 85°C for 90 minutes (ensure jars are submerged)
5. Cool and serve directly or unmold onto a plate (let cool completely)

Cooking Temperature Range:
Optimal 185°F / 85°C (permissible range 176°F / 80°C to 190°F / 88°C).

Kiwi Lime Cake

Yield: 2 servings | Prep time: 20 minutes | Cook time: 1 hour 30 minutes

Brighten your day with the zesty fusion of kiwi and lime in our Sous Vide Kiwi Lime Cake. This vibrant dessert combines tangy citrus notes with the natural sweetness of kiwi, creating a refreshingly moist and tender cake with a tropical twist, perfected in a water bath.

Ingredients:
- Kiwi (diced finely) - 0.33 cup
- All-purpose flour (sifted) - 0.5 cup
- Lime juice (freshly squeezed) - 2 tbsp
- Egg (whisked) - 2 pieces
- Butter (unsalted, melted) - 2 tbsp
- Baking powder - 0.5 tsp

Nutritional Information (for 2 servings):
calories 310 kcal, protein 6g, carbohydrates 35g, fat 14g, fiber 1g, cholesterol 120mg, sodium 60mg, potassium 140mg

Directions:
1. Whisk eggs, melted butter, and lime juice (ensure smooth mixing)
2. Fold in flour, baking powder, and kiwi (do not overmix)
3. Divide batter into greased jars (seal loosely)
4. Cook in a sous vide water bath at 185°F / 85°C for 90 minutes (ensure jars are submerged)
5. Cool and serve directly or unmold onto a plate (let cool completely)

Cooking Temperature Range:
Optimal 185°F / 85°C (permissible range 176°F / 80°C to 190°F / 88°C).

Pear Ginger Cake

Yield: 2 servings | Prep time: 30 minutes | Cook time: 1 hour 30 minutes

Savor the warm embrace of ginger and the delicate sweetness of pears in our Sous Vide Pear Ginger Cake. This perfectly spiced dessert boasts a moist, tender crumb, with every bite infused with fruity and aromatic flavors, elevated by precise sous vide cooking.

Ingredients:
- Pears (diced fresh) - 0.5 cup
- All-purpose flour (sifted) - 0.5 cup
- Ginger (fresh, grated) - 1 tsp
- Egg (whisked) - 2 pieces
- Butter (unsalted, melted) - 2 tbsp
- Baking powder - 0.5 tsp

Nutritional Information (for 2 servings):
calories 330 kcal, protein 7g, carbohydrates 42g, fat 14g, fiber 3g, cholesterol 120mg, sodium 60mg, potassium 140mg

Directions:
1. Whisk eggs, butter, and grated ginger (ensure smooth mixing)
2. Fold in flour, baking powder, and pears (do not overmix)
3. Divide batter into greased jars (seal jars loosely)
4. Cook in sous vide water bath at 185°F / 85°C for 90 minutes (ensure jars are fully submerged)
5. Cool jars and serve or unmold onto plates (let cool completely)

Cooking Temperature Range:
Optimal 185°F / 85°C (permissible range 176°F / 80°C to 190°F / 88°C).

Blackberry Sage Cake

Yield: 2 servings | Prep time: 25 minutes | Cook time: 1 hour 30 minutes

Discover a harmonious blend of bold blackberries and earthy sage in our Sous Vide Blackberry Sage Cake. This unique dessert balances fresh berries' juicy sweetness with sage's herbal aroma, creating a moist, fragrant, and unforgettable cake through the precision of sous vide cooking.

Ingredients:
- Blackberries (fresh, whole) - 0.5 cup
- All-purpose flour (sifted) - 0.5 cup
- Sage (fresh, finely chopped) - 1 tsp
- Egg (whisked) - 2 pieces
- Butter (unsalted, melted) - 2 tbsp
- Baking powder - 0.5 tsp

Nutritional Information (for 2 servings):
calories 310 kcal, protein 6g, carbohydrates 40g, fat 12g, fiber 4g, cholesterol 110mg, sodium 70mg, potassium 160mg

Directions:
1. Whisk eggs, butter, and sage until combined (ensure sage is finely chopped)
2. Fold in flour, baking powder, and berries (do not overmix)
3. Pour batter into greased jars (seal jars loosely)
4. Cook in sous vide water bath at 185°F / 85°C for 90 minutes (ensure jars are fully submerged)
5. Cool jars and serve or unmold onto plates (let cool completely)

Cooking Temperature Range:
Optimal 185°F / 85°C (permissible range 176°F / 80°C to 190°F / 88°C).

Cranberry Orange Cake

Yield: 2 servings | Prep time: 30 minutes | Cook time: 1 hour 30 minutes

Bright and festive, our Sous Vide Cranberry Orange Cake marries the tangy zing of cranberries with the sunny sweetness of orange. This moist, citrus-infused dessert is perfectly balanced and elevated with sous vide precision for a tender, flavor-packed treat that shines on any occasion.

Ingredients:
- Cranberries (fresh, whole) - 0.5 cup
- All-purpose flour (sifted) - 0.5 cup
- Orange zest (grated) - 1 tsp
- Egg (whisked) - 2 pieces
- Butter (unsalted, melted) - 2 tbsp
- Baking powder - 0.5 tsp

Nutritional Information (for 2 servings):
calories 320 kcal, protein 7g, carbohydrates 42g, fat 13g, fiber 4g, cholesterol 110mg, sodium 75mg, potassium 170mg

Directions:
1. Whisk eggs, butter, and orange zest until smooth (ensure orange zest is fresh)
2. Fold in flour, baking powder, and cranberries (do not overmix)
3. Pour batter into greased jars (seal jars loosely)
4. Cook in sous vide water bath at 185°F / 85°C for 90 minutes (ensure jars are fully submerged)
5. Cool jars and serve or unmold onto plates (let cool completely)

Cooking Temperature Range:
Optimal 185°F / 85°C (permissible range 176°F / 80°C to 190°F / 88°C).

Pineapple Upside-Down Cake

Yield: 2 servings | Prep time: 25 minutes | Cook time: 1 hour 30 minutes

Indulge in the classic charm of our Sous Vide Pineapple Upside-Down Cake. This tropical delight features caramelized pineapple slices atop a buttery, moist cake. Perfectly cooked in a sous vide water bath, every bite is tender, fruity, and irresistibly rich with caramelized sweetness.

Ingredients:
- Pineapple slices (fresh, 0.5-inch thick) - 2 pieces
- Brown sugar - 2 tbsp
- Butter (unsalted, melted) - 3 tbsp
- All-purpose flour (sifted) - 0.5 cup
- Baking powder - 0.5 tsp
- Egg (whisked) - 2 pieces

Nutritional Information (for 2 servings):
calories 340 kcal, protein 6g, carbohydrates 42g, fat 15g, fiber 2g, cholesterol 110mg, sodium 80mg, potassium 160mg

Directions:
1. Caramelize pineapple slices with sugar and butter (let cool before assembling)
2. Mix eggs, butter, flour, and baking powder (avoid overmixing the batter)
3. Layer caramelized pineapple in jars, add batter (fill jars only 2/3 full)
4. Cook jars in a sous vide bath at 185°F / 85°C for 90 minutes (ensure jars are fully submerged)
5. Cool jars and serve or unmold (let cakes cool completely)

Cooking Temperature Range:
Optimal 185°F / 85°C (permissible range 176°F / 80°C to 190°F / 88°C).

Banana Walnut Cake

Yield: 2 servings | Prep time: 20 minutes | Cook time: 1 hour 30 minutes

Elevate your dessert game with our Sous Vide Banana Walnut Cake. This moist, nutty delight combines the natural sweetness of ripe bananas with the crunch of toasted walnuts, perfectly balanced and cooked to tender perfection using sous vide for a rich and comforting treat.

Ingredients:
- Banana (medium. ripe. mashed) - 2 pieces
- All-purpose flour (sifted) - 0.5 cup
- Baking powder - 0.5 tsp
- Brown sugar - 2 tbsp
- Butter (unsalted, melted) - 3 tbsp
- Chopped walnuts (roughly chopped) - 2 tbsp

Nutritional Information (for 2 servings):
calories 320 kcal, protein 5g, carbohydrates 40g, fat 14g, fiber 2g, cholesterol 100mg, sodium 80mg, potassium 150mg

Directions:
1. Mash the banana, then mix it with sugar, butter, and walnuts (ensure the banana is well-mashed)
2. Combine flour and baking powder mix with banana mixture (mix until just combined to avoid overmixing)
3. Pour batter into jars, filling 2/3 full (grease jars for easy removal)
4. Cook jars in a sous vide bath at 185°F / 85°C for 90 minutes (ensure jars are fully submerged)
5. Cool jars before serving or unmolding (let cakes cool completely)

Cooking Temperature Range:
Optimal 185°F / 85°C (permissible range 176°F / 80°C to 190°F / 88°C).

Mango Coconut Cake

Yield: 2 servings | Prep time: 25 minutes | Cook time: 1 hour 30 minutes

Transport your taste buds to paradise with our Sous Vide Mango Coconut Cake. This tropical dessert features sweet, juicy mangoes and creamy coconut, creating a moist and flavorful cake. Sous vide precision ensures every bite is perfectly tender and packed with island-inspired bliss.

Ingredients:

- Mango (ripe, medium, pureed) - 2 pieces
- Coconut milk (unsweetened) - 0.25 cup
- All-purpose flour (sifted) - 0.5 cup
- Baking powder - 0.5 tsp
- Sugar - 2 tbsp
- Shredded coconut (unsweetened, finely shredded) - 2 tbsp

Nutritional Information (for 2 servings):

calories 280 kcal, protein 4g, carbohydrates 40g, fat 10g, fiber 3g, cholesterol 0mg, sodium 40mg, potassium 180mg

Directions:

1. Blend mango and mix with coconut milk, sugar, and shredded coconut (blend until smooth)
2. Combine flour and baking powder and mix with mango mixture (mix until just combined)
3. Pour batter into jars, filling 2/3 full (grease jars for easy removal)
4. Cook jars in the sous vide bath at 185°F / 85°C for 90 minutes (ensure jars are fully submerged)
5. Cool jars before serving or unmolding (let cakes cool completely)

Cooking Temperature Range:

Optimal 185°F / 85°C (permissible range 176°F / 80°C to 190°F / 88°C).

Lemon Blueberry Bundt Cake

Yield: 2 servings | Prep time: 15 minutes | Cook time: 1 hour 30 minutes

Brighten your dessert table with our Sous Vide Lemon Blueberry Bundt Cake. Bursting with zesty lemon and juicy blueberries, this perfectly moist cake balances tart and sweet flavors. Sous vide precision ensures even cooking for a tender, show-stopping treat.

Ingredients:

- All-purpose flour (sifted) - 1 cup
- White sugar - 0.5 cup
- Baking powder - 1 tsp
- Blueberries (fresh, washed, patted dry) - 4 oz
- Lemon zest (grated) - 1 tsp
- Butter (unsalted, melted) - 4 tbsp

Nutritional Information (for 2 servings):

calories 320 kcal, protein 4g, carbohydrates 42g, fat 14g, fiber 2g, cholesterol 40mg, sodium 30mg, potassium 90mg

Directions:

1. Mix dry ingredients and lemon zest (use freshly grated lemon zest)
2. Fold in blueberries and melted butter (ensure even distribution)
3. Transfer batter to a greased bundt mold (seal mold securely in the bag)
4. Cook in sous vide bath at 185°F / 85°C for 90 minutes (ensure the mold is submerged)
5. Cool and invert onto a plate. Serve (allow cooling for easy removal)

Cooking Temperature Range:

Optimal 185°F / 85°C (permissible range 185°F / 85°C to 190°F / 88°C).

Black Forest Cake

Yield: 2 servings | Prep time: 20 minutes | Cook time: 1 hour 30 minutes

Dive into decadence with our Sous Vide Black Forest Cake. Layers of rich chocolate cake, luscious cherries, and velvety whipped cream are brought together with sous vide precision, creating a moist, indulgent dessert that's both elegant and irresistibly flavorful.

Ingredients:
- All-purpose flour (sifted) - 0.75 cup
- White sugar - 0.5 cup
- Cocoa powder (unsweetened, sifted) - 0.25 cup
- Baking powder - 1 tsp
- Sweet cherries (pitted, fresh, or canned) - 6 oz
- Heavy cream (whipped) - 0.5 cup

Nutritional Information (for 2 servings):
calories 320 kcal, protein 5g, carbohydrates 46g, fat 12g, fiber 3g, cholesterol 40mg, sodium 35mg, potassium 100mg

Directions:
1. Mix dry ingredients in a bowl (use unsweetened cocoa powder)
2. Fold in cherries and transfer to mold (grease mold for easy release)
3. Seal the mold and submerge it in the water bath (ensure the bag is securely sealed)
4. Cook in sous vide bath at 185°F / 85°C for 90 minutes
5. Cool, top with whipped cream, and serve (add extra cherries for garnish)

Cooking Temperature Range:
Optimal 185°F / 85°C (permissible range 185°F / 85°C to 190°F / 88°C).

Cherry Vanilla Cake

Yield: 2 servings | Prep time: 25 minutes | Cook time: 1 hour 30 minutes

Celebrate elegance with our Sous Vide Cherry Vanilla Cake. This tender and flavorful dessert blends sweet cherries with fragrant vanilla, creating a perfectly moist cake with a delicate balance and irresistible charm. Sous vide precision ensures even baking for a truly delightful treat.

Ingredients:
- All-purpose flour (sifted) - 0.75 cup
- White sugar - 0.5 cup
- Baking powder - 1 tsp
- Sweet cherries (pitted, fresh, or canned) - 6 oz
- Vanilla extract (pure) - 1 tsp
- Butter (unsalted, melted) - 4 tbsp

Nutritional Information (for 2 servings):
calories 380 kcal, protein 5g, carbohydrates 48g, fat 18g, fiber 3g, cholesterol 50mg, sodium 35mg, potassium 110mg

Directions:
1. Mix dry ingredients in a bowl (ensure even mixing)
2. Add wet ingredients and cherries. Stir well (do not overmix)
3. Pour batter into mold and seal bag (grease mold for easy release)
4. Cook in sous vide bath at 185°F / 85°C for 90 minutes
5. Cool, then serve (add a dusting of powdered sugar)

Cooking Temperature Range:
Optimal 185°F / 85°C (permissible range 185°F / 85°C to 190°F / 88°C).

Raspberry Almond Cake

Yield: 2 servings | Prep time: 20 minutes | Cook time: 1 hour 30 minutes

Delight in the elegance of our Sous Vide Raspberry Almond Cake. Bursting with the tart sweetness of raspberries and the nutty richness of almonds, this cake is perfectly moist and flavorful. Sous vide precision ensures a tender crumb and even baking for a sophisticated and irresistible dessert.

Ingredients:
- All-purpose flour (sifted) - 0.75 cup
- Almond flour (sifted) - 0.25 cup
- White sugar - 0.5 cup
- Raspberries (fresh, washed) - 6 oz
- Butter (unsalted, melted) - 4 tbsp
- Almond extract - 1 tsp

Nutritional Information (for 2 servings):
calories 410 kcal, protein 6g, carbohydrates 50g, fat 20g, fiber 4g, cholesterol 45mg, sodium 40mg, potassium 120mg

Directions:
1. Mix dry ingredients in a bowl (ensure all dry ingredients are well combined)
2. Add wet ingredients and raspberries. Stir (be gentle to avoid smashing the raspberries)
3. Pour into the greased mold and seal the bag (grease mold to prevent sticking)
4. Cook in sous vide bath at 185°F / 85°C for 90 minutes
5. Cool and serve (optional: dust with powdered sugar)

Cooking Temperature Range:
Optimal 185°F / 85°C (permissible range 185°F / 85°C to 190°F / 88°C).

Peach Cobbler Cake

Yield: 2 servings | Prep time: 15 minutes | Cook time: 1 hour 30 minutes

Savor the comfort of summer with our Sous Vide Peach Cobbler Cake. Juicy peaches are nestled in a tender, buttery cake with hints of warm spices, capturing the essence of classic cobbler. Sous vide cooking ensures a perfectly moist and flavorful dessert, ready to delight your taste buds.

Ingredients:
- All-purpose flour (sifted) - 0.75 cup
- White sugar - 0.5 cup
- Butter (unsalted, melted) - 4 tbsp
- Peaches (fresh, sliced) - 6 oz
- Baking powder - 1 tsp
- Vanilla extract - 1 tsp

Nutritional Information (for 2 servings):
calories 430 kcal, protein 6g, carbohydrates 52g, fat 20g, fiber 2g, cholesterol 45mg, sodium 40mg, potassium 150mg

Directions:
1. Mix dry ingredients in a bowl (ensure even distribution of baking powder)
2. Add wet ingredients and peaches. Stir gently (avoid overmixing to keep peaches intact)
3. Pour batter into the greased mold and seal the bag (grease mold to prevent sticking)
4. Cook in sous vide bath at 185°F / 85°C for 90 minutes
5. Cool for 10 minutes and serve (serve with whipped cream for extra indulgence)

Cooking Temperature Range:
Optimal 185°F / 85°C (permissible range 185°F / 85°C to 190°F / 88°C).

Mixed Berry Cheesecake

Yield: 2 servings | Prep time: 20 minutes | Cook time: 1 hour 30 minutes

Indulge in the creamy decadence of our Sous Vide Mixed Berry Cheesecake. This velvety dessert pairs the tangy sweetness of mixed berries with the smooth richness of cheesecake, all atop a buttery crust. Sous vide precision ensures every bite's perfectly set, lusciously creamy texture.

Ingredients:
- Cream cheese (softened) - 8 oz
- White sugar - 0.25 cup
- Egg (large) - 1 piece
- Mixed berries - 6 oz
- Vanilla extract - 1 tsp
- Graham cracker crumbs (crushed) - 0.5 cup

Nutritional Information (for 2 servings):
calories 420 kcal, protein 7g, carbohydrates 32g, fat 28g, fiber 2g, cholesterol 85mg, sodium 150mg, potassium 180mg

Directions:
1. Mix cream cheese, sugar, eggs, and vanilla (ensure cream cheese is at room temperature for smooth mixing)
2. Fold in mixed berries gently (avoid crushing berries to maintain texture)
3. Prepare the crust and pour the cheesecake mixture (press crumbs firmly to create a solid base)
4. Cook in sous vide bath at 176°F / 80°C for 90 minutes
5. Chill for 1 hour before serving (garnish with extra berries for presentation)

Cooking Temperature Range:
Optimal 176°F / 80°C (permissible range 176°F / 80°C to 180°F / 82°C).

Strawberry Shortcake

Yield: 2 servings | Prep time: 15 minutes | Cook time: 1 hour 30 minutes

Relish the timeless charm of our Sous Vide Strawberry Shortcake. Fluffy, buttery cake layers meet juicy, sweet strawberries and pillows of whipped cream, creating a perfectly balanced dessert. Sous vide cooking ensures a moist, tender cake with vibrant berry flavors that shine in every bite.

Ingredients:
- All-purpose flour (sifted) - 0.5 cup
- Sugar - 0.33 cup
- Baking powder - 1 tsp
- Strawberries (sliced) - 6 oz
- Heavy cream - 0.25 cup
- Butter (unsalted, melted) - 2 tbsp

Nutritional Information (for 2 servings):
calories 380 kcal, protein 6g, carbohydrates 42g, fat 20g, fiber 2g, cholesterol 70mg, sodium 150mg, potassium 180mg

Directions:
1. Mix dry and wet ingredients to form batter (ensure the batter is smooth without lumps)
2. Pour batter into molds and seal in vacuum bags (grease molds to prevent sticking)
3. Cook in sous vide bath at 180°F / 82°C for 90 minutes
4. Cool cakes and layer with strawberries (use chilled strawberries for best flavor)
5. Garnish with whipped cream and extra berries (add mint leaves for a refreshing touch)

Cooking Temperature Range:
Optimal 180°F / 82°C (permissible range 180°F / 82°C to 185°F / 85°C).

Blueberry Lemon Cake

Yield: 2 servings | Prep time: 20 minutes | Cook time: 1 hour 30 minutes

Brighten your day with our Sous Vide Blueberry Lemon Cake! Bursting with juicy blueberries and zesty lemon, this moist and flavorful cake balances sweet and tangy notes perfectly. Sous vide precision ensures even baking and a tender crumb, making every bite a sunny delight.

Ingredients:
- All-purpose flour (sifted) - 0.5 cup
- Sugar - 0.33 cup
- Baking powder - 1 tsp
- Blueberries (fresh) - 4 oz
- Lemon zest (grated) - 1 tsp
- Butter (unsalted, melted) - 2 tbsp

Nutritional Information (for 2 servings):
calories 350 kcal, protein 6g, carbohydrates 40g, fat 18g, fiber 2g, cholesterol 60mg, sodium 140mg, potassium 160mg

Directions:
1. Combine dry ingredients and lemon zest (ensure the batter is smooth without lumps)
2. Fold in blueberries gently to avoid crushing (use fresh blueberries for best flavor)
3. Pour batter into greased molds and seal (ensure an airtight seal for proper cooking)
4. Cook in a water bath at 180°F / 82°C for 90 minutes
5. Cool cakes and remove from molds for serving (add extra blueberries or a lemon glaze)

Cooking Temperature Range:
Optimal 180°F / 82°C (permissible range 180°F / 82°C to 185°F / 85°C).

Apple Spice Cake

Yield: 2 servings | Prep time: 25 minutes | Cook time: 1 hour 30 minutes

Warm up with our Sous Vide Apple Spice Cake, a cozy blend of tender apples and aromatic spices. This moist and flavorful dessert combines the comforting essence of cinnamon, nutmeg, and cloves with the natural sweetness of apples. Sous vide precision ensures a perfectly soft and decadent cake in every slice.

Ingredients:
- All-purpose flour (sifted) - 0.5 cup
- Sugar - 0.33 cup
- Baking powder - 1 tsp
- Apple (peeled, diced) - 1 piece
- Cinnamon (ground) - 0.5 tsp
- Butter (unsalted, melted) - 2 tbsp

Nutritional Information (for 2 servings):
calories 360 kcal, protein 5g, carbohydrates 42g, fat 16g, fiber 3g, cholesterol 55mg, sodium 150mg, potassium 180mg

Directions:
1. Combine dry ingredients with melted butter (mix until batter is smooth without lumps)
2. Fold in diced apples evenly (use fresh apples for best flavor)
3. Pour batter into greased molds and seal (ensure molds are tightly sealed)
4. Cook in a water bath at 180°F / 82°C for 90 minutes
5. Cool cakes and remove from molds for serving (garnish with powdered sugar or cream)

Cooking Temperature Range:
Optimal 180°F / 82°C (permissible range 180°F / 82°C to 185°F / 85°C).

S'mores Cake

Yield: 2 servings | Prep time: 20 minutes | Cook time: 1 hour 30 minutes

Experience campfire magic with our Sous Vide S'mores Cake! Layers of moist chocolate cake, graham cracker crumbles, and gooey marshmallows come together in a decadent dessert. Sous vide precision ensures perfect texture and bold flavors, turning this nostalgic treat into a show-stopping indulgence.

Ingredients:
- Graham cracker crumbs (crushed) - 0.5 cup
- Butter (unsalted, melted) - 2 tbsp
- White sugar (divided for crust and batter) - 0.33 cup
- Egg (large. whisk into batter) - 2 pieces
- Semi-sweet chocolate chips (melted) - 0.5 cup
- Marshmallow fluff - 0.5 cup

Nutritional Information (for 2 servings):
calories 540 kcal, protein 6g, carbohydrates 58g, fat 32g, fiber 1g, cholesterol 110mg, sodium 100mg, potassium 150mg

Directions:
1. Mix crumbs, butter, and sugar; press into mason jars (ensure a firm base)
2. Prepare chocolate batter and pour over crust (whisk until smooth)
3. Preheat sous vide bath to 185°F / 85°C
4. Sous vide for 90 minutes (seal jars tightly to prevent water entry)
5. Cool slightly, top with marshmallow, and torch for effect (torch carefully to avoid burning)

Cooking Temperature Range:
Optimal 185°F / 85°C (permissible range 185°F / 85°C to 190°F / 88°C).

Raspberry Lemon Bars

Yield: 2 servings | Prep time: 25 minutes | Cook time: 1 hour 15 minutes

Brighten your day with our Sous Vide Raspberry Lemon Bars! A buttery shortbread crust supports a luscious, tangy lemon filling swirled with vibrant raspberry. Sous vide precision ensures a perfectly smooth texture and balanced flavor, making these bars a sweet, zesty delight in every bite.

Ingredients:
- All-purpose flour (sifted) - 0.5 cup
- Butter (unsalted, melted) - 3 tbsp
- White sugar (divided for crust and custard) - 0.33 cup
- Egg (large. whisk into custard) - 2 pieces
- Lemon juice (freshly squeezed) - 2 tbsp
- Raspberries (fresh, puree before using) - 0.33 cup

Nutritional Information (for 2 servings):
calories 320 kcal, protein 6g, carbohydrates 40g, fat 15g, fiber 2g, cholesterol 110mg, sodium 50mg, potassium 120mg

Directions:
1. Mix flour, butter, and sugar for the crust. Press into jars (ensure an even crust)
2. Prepare custard with eggs, sugar, and lemon juice (whisk until smooth)
3. Preheat sous vide bath to 176°F / 80°C
4. Sous vide for 75 minutes (seal jars tightly to prevent water entry)
5. Cool slightly and spread raspberry puree before serving (chill jars for easier handling)

Cooking Temperature Range:
Optimal 176°F / 80°C (permissible range 176°F / 80°C to 180°F / 82°C).

Pumpkin Pie

Yield: 2 servings | Prep time: 30 minutes | Cook time: 1 hour 15 minutes

Celebrate fall flavors with our Sous Vide Pumpkin Pie! Creamy, spiced pumpkin filling meets a buttery, flaky crust in this classic dessert reimagined. Sous vide precision ensures a perfectly smooth texture and even baking, delivering a slice of holiday magic in every bite.

Ingredients:
- Pumpkin puree (canned, unsweetened) - 0.5 cup
- Heavy cream (chilled) - 0.33 cup
- White sugar - 0.33 cup
- Egg (large, whisk before adding) - 1 piece
- Pumpkin pie spice (fresh) - 1 tsp
- Pre-made pie crust (cut to fit jars) - 1 piece

Nutritional Information (for 2 servings):
calories 320 kcal, protein 6g, carbohydrates 40g, fat 15g, fiber 2g, cholesterol 80mg, sodium 50mg, potassium 140mg

Directions:
1. Prepare and press crust into jars (use small jars for even baking)
2. Combine filling ingredients and pour into jars (ensure smooth consistency)
3. Preheat sous vide bath to 176°F / 80°C
4. Sous vide jars for 75 minutes (seal tightly to prevent water entry)
5. Cool to room temperature, then refrigerate (chill thoroughly before serving)

Cooking Temperature Range:
Optimal 176°F / 80°C (permissible range 176°F / 80°C to 180°F / 82°C).

Pumpkin Cheesecake

Yield: 2 servings | Prep time: 35 minutes | Cook time: 1 hour 30 minutes

Delight in the creamy decadence of our Sous Vide Pumpkin Cheesecake! This luxurious dessert combines pumpkin pie's warm spices with cheesecake's silky smoothness. Sous vide precision ensures a perfectly creamy texture and rich flavor, making every slice a festive and unforgettable treat.

Ingredients:
- Cream cheese (softened) - 8 oz
- Pumpkin puree (unsweetened) - 0.5 cup
- White sugar - 0.33 cup
- Egg (large, whisk before adding) - 1 piece
- Pumpkin pie spice (fresh) - 1 tsp
- Graham cracker crust (cut to fit jars) - 1 piece

Nutritional Information (for 2 servings):
calories 400 kcal, protein 8g, carbohydrates 38g, fat 26g, fiber 2g, cholesterol 95mg, sodium 130mg, potassium 150mg

Directions:
1. Prepare jars with graham cracker crust (ensure the crust is evenly pressed)
2. Mix filling ingredients until smooth (avoid lumps for a creamy texture)
3. Preheat sous vide bath to 176°F / 80°C
4. Sous vide jars for 90 minutes (seal jars tightly to prevent leaks)
5. Cool jars at room temperature, then refrigerate (chill thoroughly before serving)

Cooking Temperature Range:
Optimal 176°F / 80°C (permissible range 176°F / 80°C to 180°F / 82°C).

Lemon Pudding

Yield: 2 servings | Prep time: 10 minutes | Cook time: 2 hours

Treat yourself to the zesty delight of our Sous Vide Lemon Pudding! This creamy, velvety dessert bursts with vibrant lemon flavor and just the right touch of sweetness. Sous vide precision ensures a perfectly smooth texture, making every spoonful a luscious, refreshing indulgence.

Ingredients:
- Whole milk - 0.75 cup
- Heavy cream - 0.25 cup
- White sugar - 0.25 cup
- Lemon juice (freshly squeezed) - 2 tbsp
- Lemon zest (grated) - 1 tsp
- Egg yolk (whisked) - 2 pieces

Nutritional Information (for 2 servings):
calories 270 kcal, protein 6g, carbohydrates 30g, fat 14g, fiber 0g, cholesterol 120mg, sodium 35mg, potassium 150mg

Directions:
1. Whisk egg yolks, sugar, and lemon zest until smooth (ensure no lumps remain in the mixture)
2. Add milk, cream, and lemon juice while whisking (combine gradually to prevent curdling)
3. Pour mixture into jars and seal loosely (leave space for expansion)
4. Cook jars in the water bath at 176°F / 80°C for 120 minutes (use a rack to keep jars submerged evenly)
5. Cool and refrigerate jars for at least 2 hours (chill for best consistency)

Cooking Temperature Range:
Optimal 176°F / 80°C (permissible range 176°F / 80°C to 180°F / 82°C).

Lemon Tart

Yield: 2 servings | Prep time: 15 minutes | Cook time: 2 hours

Savor the sunshine with our Sous Vide Lemon Tart! A buttery, crisp crust cradles a silky-smooth lemon filling bursting with bright, tangy flavor. Sous vide precision ensures perfect consistency and vibrant citrus notes, making this elegant dessert a refreshing and irresistible treat.

Ingredients:
- Lemon juice (freshly squeezed) - 3 tbsp
- Lemon zest (grated) - 1 tsp
- White sugar - 0.33 cup
- Egg yolk (whisked) - 3 pieces
- Heavy cream - 0.33 cup
- Tart crust (pre-baked) - 2 pieces

Nutritional Information (for 2 servings):
calories 320 kcal, protein 5g, carbohydrates 38g, fat 16g, fiber 0g, cholesterol 160mg, sodium 50mg, potassium 110mg

Directions:
1. Whisk egg yolks, sugar, lemon juice, and zest until smooth (ensure no lumps for a creamy filling)
2. Gradually whisk in heavy cream (combine slowly to avoid curdling)
3. Pour mixture into sous vide-safe bags or jars and seal (ensure a tight seal to prevent leakage)
4. Cook in a water bath at 176°F / 80°C for 120 minutes (use a rack to keep jars stable)
5. Cool, spoon into tart crusts, and chill for 1 hour (chill for proper setting before serving)

Cooking Temperature Range:
Optimal 176°F / 80°C (permissible range 176°F / 80°C to 180°F / 82°C).

Fruit Tart

Yield: 2 servings | Prep time: 15 minutes | Cook time: 1 hour 30 minutes

Delight in the elegance of our Sous Vide Fruit Tart! A crisp, buttery crust holds a luscious, silky custard filling with vibrant, tender fruit. Sous vide precision ensures flawless textures and enhanced flavors, making this tart a stunning and delicious centerpiece for any occasion.

Ingredients:
- Heavy cream - 0.75 cup
- Egg yolk (whisked) - 3 pieces
- White sugar - 0.33 cup
- Vanilla extract - 1 tsp
- Fruits (fresh, sliced and top of the tart) - 0.5 cup
- Pre-baked tart shell (6-inch size) - 2 pieces

Nutritional Information (for 2 servings):
calories 320 kcal, protein 5g, carbohydrates 35g, fat 18g, fiber 1g, cholesterol 150mg, sodium 60mg, potassium 50mg

Directions:
1. Whisk cream, egg yolks, sugar, and vanilla until smooth (ensure the mixture is fully combined)
2. Seal custard mixture in a sous vide bag or jar (remove air to prevent water entry)
3. Preheat the water bath to 176°F / 80°C and cook for 90 minutes (keep jars stable in the bath)
4. Fill the tart shell with custard and top with fresh fruits (let the custard cool slightly before filling)
5. Chill tart for 1 hour before serving (for best results, refrigerate longer)

Cooking Temperature Range:
Optimal 176°F / 80°C (permissible range 176°F / 80°C to 180°F / 82°C).

Coconut Rice Pudding

Yield: 2 servings | Prep time: 15 minutes | Cook time: 1 hour

Savor the creamy tropical delight of our Sous Vide Coconut Rice Pudding! Tender, perfectly cooked rice is infused with coconut milk's rich, luscious flavor and a hint of sweetness. Sous vide precision ensures a silky, indulgent texture, giving every bite a comforting taste of paradise.

Ingredients:
- Coconut milk (unsweetened) - 1 cup
- Cooked white rice (pre-cooked before use) - 0.5 cup
- White sugar - 2 tbsp
- Vanilla extract - 0.5 tsp
- Cinnamon (ground) - 1 pinch

Nutritional Information (for 2 servings):
calories 310 kcal, protein 4g, carbohydrates 43g, fat 15g, fiber 1g, cholesterol 0mg, sodium 30mg, potassium 150mg

Directions:
1. Preheat sous vide water bath to 185°F / 85°C
2. Mix coconut milk, rice, sugar, vanilla, and cinnamon in a bowl (stir until fully combined)
3. Divide into jars, seal, and cook for 60 minutes (use tightly sealed jars)
4. Cool slightly and serve warm or refrigerate (can be served chilled or warm)

Cooking Temperature Range:
Optimal 185°F / 85°C (permissible range 185°F / 85°C to 190°F / 88°C).

Cinnamon Rolls

Yield: 2 servings | Prep time: 20 minutes | Cook time: 2 hours

Indulge in the gooey perfection of our Sous Vide Cinnamon Rolls! The soft, pillowy dough is swirled with a rich cinnamon-sugar filling and topped with a creamy glaze. Sous vide precision ensures perfectly tender rolls with evenly melted filling, making every bite a warm, irresistible delight.

Ingredients:
- All-purpose flour (sifted) - 1.5 cups
- Milk (whole) - 0.5 cup
- Instant yeast - 0.5 tsp
- White sugar - 2 tbsp
- Butter (unsalted, softened) - 2 tbsp
- Cinnamon (ground) - 1 tsp

Nutritional Information (for 2 servings):
calories 320 kcal, protein 6g, carbohydrates 45g, fat 12g, fiber 1g, cholesterol 20mg, sodium 120mg, potassium 100mg

Directions:
1. Preheat sous vide water bath to 180°F / 82°C
2. Combine milk, yeast, and sugar. Add flour and butter. Form dough (let the yeast bloom properly)
3. Roll the dough, spread butter, sprinkle with cinnamon, and form rolls (roll tightly for uniform shape)
4. Seal the rolls in a bag and cook in the water bath for 120 minutes (ensure the bag is fully sealed)
5. Remove from heat, cool slightly, and serve with glaze or frosting (add glaze while warm for flavor)

Cooking Temperature Range:
Optimal 180°F / 82°C (permissible range 180°F / 82°C to 185°F / 85°C).

Sticky Toffee Pudding

Yield: 2 servings | Prep time: 15 minutes | Cook time: 1 hour 30 minutes

Indulge in the ultimate comfort with our Sous Vide Sticky Toffee Pudding! Moist, tender cake infused with rich dates is smothered in a luscious toffee sauce, creating a dessert that's irresistibly decadent. Sous vide precision ensures perfect texture and flavor, making every bite a warm, caramelized delight.

Ingredients:
- Dates (pitted, chopped) - 0.5 cup
- Brown sugar - 0.25 cup
- All-purpose flour (sifted) - 0.25 cup
- Egg (large) - 1 piece
- Butter (unsalted, melted) - 2 tbsp
- Baking soda - 0.25 tsp

Nutritional Information (for 2 servings):
calories 320 kcal, protein 5g, carbohydrates 45g, fat 12g, fiber 2g, cholesterol 45mg, sodium 100mg, potassium 150mg

Directions:
1. Preheat sous vide water bath to 190°F / 88°C
2. Soak dates in hot water with baking soda (softens dates for blending)
3. Mix all ingredients and pour into jars (fill jars only halfway)
4. Seal jars and cook in the water bath for 90 minutes (check that jars are sealed properly)
5. Cool slightly and serve with toffee sauce (delicious warm or chilled)

Cooking Temperature Range:
Optimal 190°F / 88°C (permissible range 190°F / 88°C to 195°F / 90°C).

Vanilla Bean Cheesecake

Yield: 2 servings | Prep time: 20 minutes | Cook time: 1 hour 30 minutes

Experience pure indulgence with our Sous Vide Vanilla Bean Cheesecake! This creamy, velvety dessert is infused with the aromatic richness of real vanilla beans and rests atop a buttery crust. Sous vide precision ensures a perfectly smooth texture, making every bite a luxurious and flavorful treat.

Ingredients:
- Cream cheese (softened) - 8 oz
- White sugar - 0.33 cup
- Egg (large) - 1 piece
- Heavy cream - 0.33 cup
- Vanilla bean (seeds scraped) - 1 piece
- Graham cracker crumbs (crushed) - 0.25 cup

Nutritional Information (for 2 servings):
calories 450 kcal, protein 6g, carbohydrates 36g, fat 32g, fiber 0g, cholesterol 100mg, sodium 120mg, potassium 100mg

Directions:
1. Preheat sous vide water bath to 176°F / 80°C
2. Blend cream cheese, sugar, egg, cream, and vanilla seeds (mix until smooth and lump-free)
3. Pour into jars and add graham cracker crumbs on top (do not overfill jars)
4. Seal jars and cook in the water bath for 90 minutes (ensure jars are airtight)
5. Cool, then refrigerate for at least 2 hours (chill for best texture)

Cooking Temperature Range:
Optimal 176°F / 80°C (permissible range 175°F / 79°C to 180°F / 82°C).

Rice Pudding with Cinnamon

Yield: 2 servings | Prep time: 10 minutes | Cook time: 1 hour 30 minutes

Cozy up with our Sous Vide Rice Pudding with Cinnamon! Creamy, tender rice is infused with the warm cinnamon spice and a sweet touch, creating a comforting and nostalgic dessert. Sous vide precision ensures perfect consistency, making every spoonful a smooth, flavorful delight.

Ingredients:
- Arborio rice - 0.5 cup
- Whole milk - 1 cup
- Heavy cream - 0.5 cup
- White sugar - 0.25 cup
- Cinnamon (ground) - 1 tsp
- Vanilla extract - 0.5 tsp

Nutritional Information (for 2 servings):
calories 380 kcal, protein 7g, carbohydrates 45g, fat 18g, fiber 1g, cholesterol 40mg, sodium 50mg, potassium 150mg

Directions:
1. Preheat sous vide water bath to 185°F / 85°C
2. Mix all ingredients in a bowl (stir thoroughly)
3. Transfer to a sealed bag using water displacement or vacuum (seal tightly)
4. Submerge and cook for 90 minutes
5. Remove, stir, and serve warm or chilled (serve immediately or store)

Cooking Temperature Range:
Optimal 185°F / 85°C (permissible range 184°F / 84°C to 186°F / 86°C).

Carrot Cake Cheesecake

Yield: 2 servings | Prep time: 15 minutes | Cook time: 1 hour 30 minutes

Indulge in the ultimate dessert fusion with our Sous Vide Carrot Cake Cheesecake! Layers of spiced, moist carrot cake meet creamy, rich cheesecake in a perfectly balanced treat. Sous vide precision ensures flawless textures and vibrant flavors, making every bite a decadent and unforgettable delight.

Ingredients:
- Cream cheese (softened) - 8 oz
- White sugar - 0.25 cup
- Carrot puree - 0.5 cup
- Cinnamon (ground) - 1 tsp
- Vanilla extract - 1 tsp
- Graham cracker crumbs (crushed) - 0.25 cup

Nutritional Information (for 2 servings):
calories 420 kcal, protein 8g, carbohydrates 36g, fat 28g, fiber 2g, cholesterol 90mg, sodium 160mg, potassium 120mg

Directions:
1. Preheat sous vide water bath to 185°F / 85°C
2. Mix cream cheese, sugar, carrot puree, cinnamon, and vanilla (use a hand mixer for smoothness)
3. Layer the mixture and crumbs into mason jars. Seal lightly (do not over-tighten lids)
4. Submerge and cook for 90 minutes (ensure jars are fully submerged)
5. Cool, chill, and serve (chill for at least 1 hour)

Cooking Temperature Range:
Optimal 185°F / 85°C (permissible range 184°F / 84°C to 186°F / 86°C).

Gingerbread Pudding

Yield: 2 servings | Prep time: 20 minutes | Cook time: 1 hour 30 minutes

Warm your heart with our Sous Vide Gingerbread Pudding! This rich and moist dessert is infused with the cozy spices of ginger, cinnamon, and nutmeg, capturing the essence of the holidays. Sous vide precision ensures a perfectly tender texture, making every bite a comforting, flavorful treat.

Ingredients:
- All-purpose flour (sifted) - 0.5 cup
- Brown sugar - 0.25 cup
- Molasses - 2 tbsp
- Ginger (fresh. grated) - 1 tsp
- Cinnamon (ground) - 0.5 tsp
- Milk (whole) - 0.5 cup

Nutritional Information (for 2 servings):
calories 320 kcal, protein 6g, carbohydrates 52g, fat 8g, fiber 1g, cholesterol 15mg, sodium 180mg, potassium 100mg

Directions:
1. Preheat sous vide water bath to 185°F / 85°C
2. Mix dry ingredients with wet ingredients (use a whisk for smooth batter)
3. Pour into jars, leaving space at the top (do not overfill jars)
4. Submerge jars and cook for 90 minutes (ensure jars are fully submerged)
5. Cool slightly and serve (serve with toppings as desired)

Cooking Temperature Range:
Optimal 185°F / 85°C (permissible range 185°F / 85°C to 186°F / 86°C).

Butterscotch Bread Pudding

Yield: 2 servings | Prep time: 15 minutes | Cook time: 1 hour 30 minutes

Sous Vide Butterscotch Bread Pudding offers a comforting, rich dessert with a luscious texture. The butterscotch flavor is perfectly infused into the bread, delivering a sweet and creamy treat. Sous vide ensures consistent, tender results, making it ideal for a beginner-friendly dessert.

Ingredients:
- Bread (day-old, cubed) - 1 cup
- Milk (whole) - 0.5 cup
- Brown sugar - 0.25 cup
- Butter (unsalted, melted) - 2 tbsp
- Egg - 2 pieces
- Butterscotch chips - 0.25 cup

Nutritional Information (for 2 servings):
calories 420 kcal, protein 10g, carbohydrates 52g, fat 18g, fiber 1g, cholesterol 150mg, sodium 180mg, potassium 120mg

Directions:
1. Preheat sous vide water bath to 185°F / 85°C
2. Whisk wet ingredients and coat bread (use day-old bread for best texture)
3. Fill mason jars, leaving a 1-inch space (lightly seal jars for air expansion)
4. Submerge jars in the water bath for 90 minutes (ensure jars are fully submerged)
5. Remove, cool, and serve warm (top with whipped cream if desired)

Cooking Temperature Range:
Optimal 185°F / 85°C (permissible range 185°F / 85°C to 186°F / 86°C).

Tres Leches Cake

Yield: 2 servings | Prep time: 20 minutes | Cook time: 1 hour 30 minutes

Sous Vide Tres Leches Cake is a delightful dessert soaked in a mixture of three milks (tres leches). This sous vide method ensures the cake remains moist and uniformly cooked, providing a rich and creamy texture. It's perfect for anyone seeking a sweet and satisfying treat.

Ingredients:
- All-purpose flour (sifted) - 0.25 cup
- Sugar - 0.25 cup
- Baking powder - 0.5 tsp
- Egg - 2 pieces
- Sweetened condensed milk - 0.25 cup
- Evaporated milk - 0.25 cup

Nutritional Information (for 2 servings):
calories 320 kcal, protein 9g, carbohydrates 48g, fat 8g, fiber 1g, cholesterol 85mg, sodium 100mg, potassium 120mg

Directions:
1. Preheat sous vide water bath to 185°F / 85°C
2. Whisk dry ingredients with eggs until smooth (avoid lumps for a smooth batter)
3. Fill greased mason jars with batter (leave 1-inch space for expansion)
4. Cook jars in the water bath for 90 minutes (ensure jars are fully submerged)
5. Pour milk mixture over the cake, then chill (garnish before serving)

Cooking Temperature Range:
Optimal 185°F / 85°C (permissible range 185°F / 85°C to 186°F / 86°C).

Peach Cobbler Bread Pudding

Yield: 2 servings | Prep time: 20 minutes | Cook time: 1 hour 30 minutes

Sous Vide Peach Cobbler Bread Pudding combines the comforting textures of bread pudding with peach cobbler's sweet, fruity flavors. Using sous vide ensures an even, custardy consistency while preserving the freshness of the peaches. This dessert is perfect for a cozy evening or a special occasion.

Ingredients:
- Peaches (sliced) - 1 piece
- Bread (day-old, cubed) - 2 cup
- Egg (whisked) - 2 pieces
- Heavy cream - 0.5 cup
- Brown sugar - 0.25 cup
- Cinnamon (ground) - 0.5 tsp

Nutritional Information (for 2 servings):
calories 340 kcal, protein 8g, carbohydrates 50g, fat 12g, fiber 2g, cholesterol 95mg, sodium 120mg, potassium 150mg

Directions:
1. Preheat sous vide water bath to 185°F / 85°C
2. Whisk eggs, cream, sugar, and cinnamon together (blend well to avoid lumps)
3. Combine bread and peaches in jars, pour custard (leave 1-inch space in jars)
4. Submerge jars and cook in the water bath for 90 minutes (ensure jars are fully sealed)
5. Cool slightly and serve with whipped cream (chill for a firmer texture)

Cooking Temperature Range:
Optimal 185°F / 85°C (permissible range 185°F / 85°C to 186°F / 86°C).

Maple Pecan Pudding Cake

Yield: 2 servings | Prep time: 15 minutes | Cook time: 1 hour 30 minutes

Sous Vide Maple Pecan Pudding Cake is a delightful combination of rich maple syrup and crunchy pecans baked into a moist pudding-style cake. The sous vide cooking method ensures perfect consistency and deep flavors, making it an indulgent treat for dessert lovers.

Ingredients:
- Bread (day-old, cubed) - 2 cup
- Maple syrup - 0.25 cup
- Heavy cream - 0.5 cup
- Egg (whisked) - 2 pieces
- Pecans (chopped) - 0.25 cup
- Cinnamon (ground) - 0.5 tsp

Nutritional Information (for 2 servings):
calories 420 kcal, protein 9g, carbohydrates 55g, fat 20g, fiber 3g, cholesterol 120mg, sodium 140mg, potassium 180mg

Directions:
1. Preheat sous vide water bath to 185°F / 85°C
2. Whisk eggs, cream, syrup, and cinnamon together (blend well to avoid lumps)
3. Combine bread and pecans in jars, pour custard (leave 1-inch space in jars)
4. Submerge jars and cook in the water bath for 90 minutes (ensure jars are fully sealed)
5. Cool slightly and serve warm (optional topping: whipped cream)

Cooking Temperature Range:
Optimal 185°F / 85°C (permissible range 185°F / 85°C to 186°F / 86°C).

Apple Cinnamon Pudding

Yield: 2 servings | Prep time: 15 minutes | Cook time: 1 hour 30 minutes

Sous Vide Apple Cinnamon Pudding is a warm, comforting dessert that combines tender apple slices, aromatic cinnamon, and a rich custard base. The sous vide method ensures even cooking and a melt-in-your-mouth texture. Perfect for fall or any time you're craving something cozy and sweet.

Ingredients:

- Apples (diced) - 1 piece
- Bread (day-old, cubed) - 2 cup
- Egg (whisked) - 2 pieces
- Heavy cream - 0.5 cup
- Sugar - 0.25 cup
- Cinnamon (ground) - 0.5 tsp

Nutritional Information (for 2 servings):

calories 400 kcal, protein 9g, carbohydrates 52g, fat 18g, fiber 3g, cholesterol 110mg, sodium 120mg, potassium 200mg

Directions:

1. Preheat sous vide water bath to 185°F / 85°C
2. Whisk eggs, cream, sugar, and cinnamon together (blend well to avoid lumps)
3. Combine apples and bread in jars, pour custard (leave 1-inch space in jars)
4. Submerge jars and cook in the water bath for 90 minutes (ensure jars are fully sealed)
5. Cool slightly and serve warm (optional topping: whipped cream)

Cooking Temperature Range:

Optimal 185°F / 85°C (permissible range 185°F / 85°C to 186°F / 86°C).

Red Velvet Cheesecake

Yield: 2 servings | Prep time: 20 minutes | Cook time: 1 hour 30 minutes

Indulge in the elegance of our Sous Vide Red Velvet Cheesecake! This luxurious dessert combines red velvet cake's velvety richness with the cheesecake's creamy decadence. Sous vide precision ensures flawless textures and bold flavors, making every bite a stunning and unforgettable treat.

Ingredients:

- Cream cheese (softened) - 8 oz
- Sugar - 0.33 cup
- Egg (whisked) - 2 pieces
- Cocoa powder (unsweetened, sifted) - 1 tbsp
- Red food coloring - 1 tsp
- Vanilla extract - 0.5 tsp

Nutritional Information (for 2 servings):

calories 420 kcal, protein 10g, carbohydrates 30g, fat 28g, fiber 1g, cholesterol 140mg, sodium 150mg, potassium 130mg

Directions:

1. Preheat sous vide water bath to 176°F / 80°C
2. Blend all ingredients until smooth (use a hand or stand mixer)
3. Pour into mason jars and seal (leave 1 inch space)
4. Submerge in the bath and cook for 90 minutes (ensure jars are submerged fully)
5. Cool before serving (optional: add toppings)

Cooking Temperature Range:

Optimal 176°F / 80°C (permissible range 176°F / 80°C to 180°F / 82°C).

Coconut Rum Pudding Cake

Yield: 2 servings | Prep time: 15 minutes | Cook time: 1 hour 30 minutes

Escape to paradise with our Sous Vide Coconut Rum Pudding Cake! This moist, tender cake is infused with tropical coconut and a hint of rum, delivering bold, exotic flavors in every bite. Sous vide precision ensures a perfectly luscious texture, making this dessert a dreamy island-inspired indulgence.

Ingredients:
- Bread (day-old, cubed) - 4 oz
- Coconut milk (unsweetened) - 0.5 cup
- Sugar - 0.25 cup
- Egg (whisked) - 2 pieces
- Rum - 1 tbsp
- Coconut flakes (toasted) - to taste

Nutritional Information (for 2 servings):
calories 420 kcal, protein 8g, carbohydrates 50g, fat 18g, fiber 2g, cholesterol 110mg, sodium 200mg, potassium 150mg

Directions:
1. Preheat sous vide water bath to 180°F / 82°C
2. In a bowl, whisk coconut milk, sugar, eggs, and rum (beat thoroughly to incorporate)
3. Add bread cubes to soak up the mixture (let bread rest to absorb liquid fully)
4. Fill the greased mason jars, leaving 1 inch at the top. Seal jars (leave headspace for expansion)
5. Submerge jars and cook for 90 minutes. Remove, cool slightly, and top with toasted coconut flakes (serve warm for best flavor)

Cooking Temperature Range:
Optimal 180°F / 82°C (permissible range 180°F / 82°C to 185°F / 85°C).

Salted Caramel Pudding Cake

Yield: 2 servings | Prep time: 15 minutes | Cook time: 1 hour

Treat yourself to the ultimate indulgence with our Sous Vide Salted Caramel Pudding Cake! This luscious dessert features a moist, tender cake layered with rich, buttery caramel and a hint of sea salt. Sous vide precision ensures perfect textures, creating a heavenly blend of sweet and savory in every bite.

Ingredients:
- Cubed brioche or challah (cut into small cubes) - 1 cup
- Heavy cream - 0.5 cup
- Caramel sauce (store-bought or homemade) - 0.25 cup
- Egg (large) - 1 piece
- Salt - 0.12 tsp

Nutritional Information (for 2 servings):
calories 420 kcal, protein 7g, carbohydrates 46g, fat 25g, fiber 1g, cholesterol 90mg, sodium 270mg, potassium 120mg

Directions:
1. Lightly grease mason jars and divide bread (use softened butter for greasing)
2. Mix custard and pour over bread (ensure bread is fully soaked)
3. Seal jars and place them in sous vide bath (avoid over-tightening jar lids)
4. Cook at 180°F / 82°C for 60 minutes
5. Cool slightly before serving (garnish with caramel sauce)

Cooking Temperature Range:
Optimal 180°F / 82°C (permissible range 175°F / 80°C to 185°F / 85°C).

Almond Butter Brownies

Yield: 2 servings | Prep time: 15 minutes | Cook time: 1 hour

Satisfy your sweet tooth with our Sous Vide Almond Butter Brownies! These rich, fudgy delights combine intense chocolate flavor with the nutty richness of almond butter. Sous vide precision ensures a perfectly moist texture, making every bite an indulgent and wholesome treat.

Ingredients:

- Almond butter (smooth) - 0.5 cup
- White sugar - 0.33 cup
- Egg (large) - 1 piece
- Cocoa powder (unsweetened, sifted) - 1 tbsp
- Vanilla extract (pure) - 0.5 tsp
- Salt - 1 pinch

Nutritional Information (for 2 servings):

calories 320 kcal, protein 9g, carbohydrates 28g, fat 20g, fiber 4g, cholesterol 40mg, sodium 150mg, potassium 120mg

Directions:

1. Preheat sous vide water bath to 185°F / 85°C
2. Mix all ingredients until smooth batter forms (use a whisk for even blending)
3. Transfer batter to a resealable bag, remove air, and seal (use water displacement method)
4. Cook in the sous vide bath for 60 minutes (submerge bag fully)
5. Cool, cut into squares, and serve (allow cooling for easy cutting)

Cooking Temperature Range:

Optimal 185°F / 85°C (permissible range 183°F / 84°C to 190°F / 88°C).

Apple Crumble

Yield: 2 servings | Prep time: 20 minutes | Cook time: 1 hour

Warm up with our Sous Vide Apple Crumble! Tender, caramelized apples are topped with a perfectly crisp, buttery crumble, creating a comforting and delicious treat. Sous vide precision ensures the apples are tender and flavorful, making every bite a cozy, indulgent delight perfect for any occasion.

Ingredients:

- Apples (peeled, sliced) - 2 pieces
- White sugar - 0.25 cup
- Cinnamon (ground) - 1 tsp
- Butter (unsalted, softened) - 2 tbsp
- Rolled oats - 3 tbsp
- All-purpose flour (sifted) - 2 tbsp

Nutritional Information (for 2 servings):

calories 240 kcal, protein 2g, carbohydrates 40g, fat 10g, fiber 3g, cholesterol 20mg, sodium 60mg, potassium 200mg

Directions:

1. Preheat sous vide water bath to 185°F / 85°C
2. Mix apples with sugar and cinnamon in a bowl (coat apples evenly)
3. Bag the apples, seal, and cook in the sous vide bath for 45 minutes (ensure no air in the bag)
4. Mix butter, oats, and flour for crumble topping (chill topping if too soft)
5. Broil assembled dish for 5-7 min to brown topping (watch carefully to avoid burning)

Cooking Temperature Range:

Optimal 185°F / 85°C (permissible range 183°F / 84°C to 190°F / 88°C).

Banana Bread Pudding

Yield: 2 servings | Prep time: 20 minutes | Cook time: 1 hour 30 minutes

Sous Vide Banana Bread Pudding is a rich and comforting dessert, blending the flavors of ripe bananas and warm spices with a custard base. This foolproof method ensures a creamy texture while maintaining the moistness of the bread. Serve with whipped cream or caramel sauce for an indulgent finish.

Ingredients:

- Bread (day-old, cubed) - 2 cup
- Banana (ripe, mashed) - 1 piece
- Whole milk - 1 cup
- Heavy cream - 0.5 cup
- Brown sugar - 2 tbsp
- Cinnamon (ground) - 1 tsp

Nutritional Information (for 2 servings):

calories 350 kcal, protein 6g, carbohydrates 50g, fat 15g, fiber 2g, cholesterol 40mg, sodium 100mg, potassium 250mg

Directions:

1. Preheat sous vide water bath to 185°F / 85°C
2. Mix banana, milk, cream, sugar, and cinnamon in a bowl (ensure smooth blending)
3. Add bread cubes to the mixture and coat evenly (let the bread absorb liquid fully)
4. Seal the mixture in a bag or jar and cook for 90 minutes (remove air from the bag completely)
5. Serve warm with whipped cream or caramel sauce (add toppings for extra flavor)

Cooking Temperature Range:

Optimal 185°F / 85°C (permissible range 183°F / 84°C to 190°F / 88°C).

Blueberry Cheesecake

Yield: 2 servings | Prep time: 15 minutes | Cook time: 1 hour 30 minutes

Sous Vide Blueberry Cheesecake offers a creamy texture and balanced sweetness with the tartness of blueberries. This dessert is made with a simple blend of cream cheese, eggs, and sugar, cooked sous vide for a smooth consistency, and topped with a fresh blueberry sauce.

Ingredients:

- Cream cheese (softened) - 8 oz
- Sugar - 0.33 cup
- Egg (large) - 1 piece
- Vanilla extract - 0.5 tsp
- Blueberries (fresh topping) - 0.5 cup

Nutritional Information (for 2 servings):

calories 350 kcal, protein 7g, carbohydrates 30g, fat 25g, fiber 1g, cholesterol 95mg, sodium 150mg, potassium 90mg

Directions:

1. Preheat sous vide water bath to 176°F / 80°C
2. Mix cream cheese, sugar, egg, and vanilla until smooth (avoid lumps for even cooking)
3. Pour mixture into jars and seal tightly (leave space for expansion)
4. Sous vide for 90 minutes (cool jars gradually after cooking)
5. Top with fresh blueberries and serve (add toppings just before serving)

Cooking Temperature Range:

Optimal 176°F / 80°C (permissible range 175°F / 79°C to 179°F / 81°C).

Blueberry Cobbler

Yield: 2 servings | Prep time: 15 minutes | Cook time: 1 hour 30 minutes

Sous vide blueberry cobbler combines sweet blueberries and a soft, buttery crumble for a classic dessert with a modern twist. The sous vide method ensures a perfectly moist and evenly cooked texture, creating a delightful balance of tart and sweet flavors.

Ingredients:
- Blueberries (fresh) - 1 cup
- White sugar - 0.25 cup
- All-purpose flour (sifted) - 2 tbsp
- Butter (unsalted, cold) - 2 tbsp
- Cinnamon (ground) - 0.25 tsp

Nutritional Information (for 2 servings):
calories 280 kcal, protein 2g, carbohydrates 36g, fat 14g, fiber 2g, cholesterol 30mg, sodium 40mg, potassium 90mg

Directions:
1. Preheat sous vide water bath to 185°F / 85°C
2. Combine blueberries, sugar, and flour; transfer to jars (stir well to coat berries evenly)
3. Mix butter, sugar, flour, and cinnamon into a crumble (use cold butter for best texture)
4. Top jars with crumble and seal tightly (leave space for steam expansion)
5. Sous vide for 90 minutes. Cool slightly before serving.

Cooking Temperature Range:
Optimal 185°F / 85°C (permissible range 185°F / 85°C to 190°F / 88°C).

Bread Pudding with Whiskey Sauce

Yield: 2 servings | Prep time: 15 minutes | Cook time: 1 hour 30 minutes

Indulge in the ultimate comfort of our Sous Vide Bread Pudding with Whiskey Sauce! Moist, tender bread pudding is infused with warm spices and topped with a rich, buttery whiskey sauce. Sous vide precision ensures perfect texture and bold, decadent flavors, making every bite an irresistible treat.

Ingredients:
- Brioche bread (cubed) - 2 cups
- Whole milk - 1 cup
- White sugar - 0.25 cup
- Egg (large) - 1 piece
- Butter (unsalted, melted) - 1 tbsp
- Whiskey - 1 tbsp

Nutritional Information (for 2 servings):
calories 400 kcal, protein 8g, carbohydrates 50g, fat 16g, fiber 2g, cholesterol 75mg, sodium 150mg, potassium 160mg

Directions:
1. Preheat sous vide water bath to 180°F / 82°C
2. Mix milk, sugar, egg, and melted butter in a bowl (use a whisk for a smooth consistency)
3. Soak bread cubes in the mixture for 5 minutes (ensure bread is fully coated)
4. Divide into jars, seal, and sous vide for 90 minutes (jars should be airtight)
5. Heat whiskey, sugar, and butter for sauce; pour over pudding (stir constantly to avoid burning)

Cooking Temperature Range:
Optimal 180°F / 82°C (permissible range 179°F / 81°C to 185°F / 85°C).

Brownies

Yield: 2 servings | Prep time: 15 minutes | Cook time: 1 hour 30 minutes

Dive into chocolate heaven with our Sous Vide Brownies! These rich, fudgy delights feature a perfectly dense center and a delicate, crackly top. Sous vide precision ensures consistent baking and an intense chocolate flavor, making every bite an indulgent masterpiece for brownie lovers.

Ingredients:
- Butter (unsalted, melted) - 0.5 cup
- White sugar - 0.5 cup
- Dark chocolate chips (melted) - 0.5 cup
- Egg (large) - 1 piece
- All-purpose flour (sifted) - 0.25 cup
- Salt - 1 pinch

Nutritional Information (for 2 servings):
calories 450 kcal, protein 5g, carbohydrates 52g, fat 28g, fiber 2g, cholesterol 85mg, sodium 160mg, potassium 90mg

Directions:
1. Preheat sous vide water bath to 185°F / 85°C
2. Whisk butter, sugar, and melted chocolate until smooth (mix thoroughly for a consistent texture)
3. Add egg, flour, and salt; mix until combined (do not overmix the batter)
4. Pour batter into jars, seal, and sous vide for 90 mins (use airtight jars for even cooking)
5. Cool and serve from jars or cut into squares (allow to cool slightly before serving)

Cooking Temperature Range:
Optimal 185°F / 85°C (permissible range 185°F / 85°C to 190°F / 88°C).

Cheesecake

Yield: 2 servings | Prep time: 10 minutes | Cook time: 1 hour 30 minutes

Indulge in the creamy perfection of our Sous Vide Cheesecake! This velvety dessert features a rich, smooth filling atop a buttery crust with a delicate balance of sweetness and tang. Sous vide precision ensures an even, silky texture, making every bite a luxurious treat that melts in your mouth.

Ingredients:
- Cream cheese (softened) - 8 oz
- White sugar - 0.25 cup
- Egg (large) - 1 piece
- Vanilla extract - 1 tsp
- Sour cream - 2 tbsp
- Graham crackers (crushed, topping) - 2 pieces

Nutritional Information (for 2 servings):
calories 400 kcal, protein 6g, carbohydrates 30g, fat 30g, fiber 0g, cholesterol 110mg, sodium 180mg, potassium 90mg

Directions:
1. Preheat sous vide water bath to 176°F / 80°C
2. Blend cream cheese, sugar, egg, vanilla, and sour cream (ensure mixture is smooth)
3. Divide the mixture into mason jars and seal them tightly (use 6 oz jars for even cooking)
4. Submerge jars in sous vide water bath and cook (make sure jars are fully submerged)
5. Cool to room temperature, chill, and top with graham crackers (refrigerate for at least 1 hour)

Cooking Temperature Range:
Optimal 176°F / 80°C (permissible range 175°F / 79°C to 180°F / 82°C).

INTRODUCTION TO PREPARING JELLIES AND GELS USING SOUS VIDE TECHNOLOGY

Jellies and gels are delightful desserts known for their smooth textures and versatility. Preparing them using sous vide technology requires precision, creativity, and consistency, making it accessible even to beginners.

GENERAL PRINCIPLES AND FEATURES OF SOUS VIDE JELLIES AND GELS

Sous vide technology is particularly well-suited for jellies and gels due to its precise temperature control and ability to maintain consistent heat over time. This ensures that gelling agents like gelatin or agar-agar activate correctly without the risk of overcooking or uneven texture.

Key features and benefits include:

Temperature Precision: Sous vide allows exact control of temperatures, which is essential for activating gelling agents without breaking down their structure.

Consistent Heating: The water bath provides uniform heat distribution, resulting in perfectly smooth and evenly set gels.

Infusion of Flavors: Sous vide enhances flavor infusion by sealing ingredients in vacuum bags or jars, making jellies and gels more vibrant and aromatic.

Hands-Free Cooking: Sous vide simplifies the process by maintaining consistent temperatures, allowing you to focus on other tasks.

HOW TO PACK JELLIES AND GELS CORRECTLY

Proper packing ensures that your jellies and gels are set properly and achieve the desired texture and shape.

Choose the Right Containers:
- Use small, heat-resistant jars for individual servings or layering gels.
- For sheet or molded jellies, use vacuum-sealed bags or silicone molds that can withstand sous vide temperatures.

Prepare the Mixture:
- Dissolve the gelling agent (e.g., gelatin, agar-agar, or pectin) in the liquid base before packing. Strain the mixture through a fine-mesh sieve to remove any lumps or bubbles.

Fill Containers Evenly:
- Pour the mixture into jars, molds, or bags, leaving a small gap at the top to allow for expansion if necessary.
- Let each layer set partially before adding the next to prevent mixing for layered jellies.

Seal Properly:
- For jars, screw the lids on loosely to allow air to escape. Tighten them after cooling.
- Vacuum-seal bags with minimal air to ensure even heat transfer.

SHAPING JELLIES AND GELS FOR PRESENTATION

Sous vide allows you to create stunning presentations for your jellies and gels:

Layered Desserts:
- Alternate layers of different flavors or colors in jars or molds. Each layer can be set individually to achieve clean, defined lines.

Molded Shapes:
- Use silicone molds to create decorative shapes. Sous vide ensures an even setting, making intricate designs possible.

Cut-Out Shapes:
- For sheet jellies, use cookie cutters to create geometric or themed shapes.

Suspended Ingredients:
- Add fruit pieces, herbs, or edible flowers to the mixture before setting. Sous vide helps suspend these elements evenly within the gel.

STORING JELLIES AND GELS BEFORE AND AFTER COOKING

Before Cooking:

Refrigeration: Prepared jelly mixtures can be stored in the refrigerator for up to 24 hours before cooking.

Freezing: Mixtures with high water content generally do not freeze well, as ice crystals can damage the gel's structure. However, concentrated bases can be frozen.

After Cooking:

Cooling: Immediately cool cooked jellies and gels in an ice bath to stop cooking and set the texture.

Refrigeration: Store fully set jellies and gels in the refrigerator for up to 5 days. Keep them covered or sealed to prevent them from drying out.

Freezing: If freezing, ensure the jelly or gel has a high sugar content to prevent texture degradation. Wrap tightly in plastic wrap and freeze for up to 1 month.

PREPARING THE FINISHED DISH FOR SERVING

Unmolding with Care:
- For molded jellies, dip the mold in warm water for a few seconds to loosen the gel before inverting it onto a plate.

Cutting and Plating:
- Use a sharp knife dipped in warm water to cut sheet jellies into clean shapes. Arrange them neatly on the plate.

Garnishing:
- Add garnishes like whipped cream, fresh fruit, edible flowers, or a syrup drizzle.

Pairing with Complementary Flavors:
- To create a balanced dessert, serve jellies and gels with complementary sauces, creams, or sorbets.

COMMON MISTAKES AND HOW TO AVOID THEM

Incorrect Gelatin Activation:
  Mistake: Using water that is too hot or too cold can prevent the proper activation of gelatin.
  Solution: Dissolve gelatin in warm (not boiling) liquid, typically around 120°F (49°C).

Overheating Agar-Agar:
  Mistake: Cooking agar-agar for too long can weaken its gelling properties.
  Solution: Heat just until dissolved, typically between 185°F–190°F (85°C–88°C).

Air Bubbles in Gels:
  Mistake: Air bubbles can form during mixing, creating an uneven texture.
  Solution: Gently strain the mixture before packing and gently tap the containers to release the trapped air.

Improper Setting Time:
  Mistake: Rushing the setting process can result in weak or uneven gels.
  Solution: Allow sufficient time for the gel to set completely, typically 2–4 hours in the refrigerator.

Flavor Dilution:
  Mistake: Using too much water or not balancing the sugar and acid can dilute flavors.
  Solution: Concentrate flavors and taste the mixture before setting to ensure balance.

CONCLUSION

Sous vide technology elevates the preparation of jellies and gels by providing precise temperature control and consistent results. Whether creating simple fruit jellies or intricately layered gels, sous vide makes the process easy and foolproof. By following proper packing techniques, storage guidelines, and serving tips, you can craft desserts that are as beautiful as they are delicious.

Which shape molds to use?

The choice of molds for sous vide jellies and gels depends on the presentation and purpose of your dessert. Here are some common and creative options:

THE CHOICE OF MOLDS FOR SOUS VIDE JELLIES AND GELS

1. Classic Circular Molds
  Best For: Traditional jellies, flans, or panna cottas.
  Description: Silicone molds or ramekins with smooth, rounded edges.
  Advantages: Simple and elegant, great for individual servings.

2. Square or Rectangular Molds
Best For: Sheet jellies or layered desserts.
Description: Use shallow trays or silicone molds with straight edges.
Advantages: Easy to cut into clean, uniform shapes (e.g., cubes or bars).

3. Decorative Silicone Molds
Best For: Themed or decorative desserts.
Description: Silicone molds in shapes like flowers, stars, hearts, or seasonal designs.
Advantages: It adds a fun or sophisticated touch to your dessert. Perfect for special occasions.

4. Dome or Hemisphere Molds
Best For: Modern, elegant presentations.
Description: Dome-shaped molds create a sleek, professional look.
Advantages: Can be paired with flat bases or garnishes for visual appeal.

5. Geometric Molds
Best For: High-end or artistic presentations.
Description: Molds with sharp, geometric shapes like hexagons or diamonds.
Advantages: It adds a contemporary, structured look to your dessert.

6. Mini Bundt or Donut Molds
Best For: Jellies served as centerpieces or with fillings.
Description: Molds with a hollow center, resembling mini Bundt cakes or donuts.
Advantages: Great for filling with sauces or garnishes.

7. Ice Cube Trays
Best For: Bite-sized jellies or cocktail garnishes.
Description: Silicone or plastic ice cube trays in fun shapes.
Advantages: Convenient for small portions or creative drink additions.

8. Ring Molds
Best For: Layered or suspended ingredient jellies.
Description: Metal or silicone ring molds with open centers.
Advantages: Allows for precise layering and visual appeal.

9. Flexible Silicone Sheets
Best For: Thin sheet jellies for rolling or cutting.
Description: Flat, flexible silicone sheets are used to create thin layers.
Advantages: It is perfect for creating rolls, spirals, or decorative cutouts.

10. Customizable Molds
Best For: Unique or personalized desserts.
Description: Custom molds made from silicone for specific designs.
Advantages: Tailored to fit your theme or branding.

Pro Tips for Choosing and Using Molds:
- **Material**: Silicone molds are ideal because they are nonstick, flexible, and easy to clean.
- **Size**: Choose molds appropriate for your portion size or serving style.
- **Ease of Unmolding:** Flexible molds make it easier to release delicate gels without breaking them.
- **Temperature Compatibility**: Ensure the molds can withstand sous vide cooking temperatures (usually up to 200°F/93°C).

- **Layering**: Use molds to build layers if creating multi-flavored desserts.

Do you have any tips for perfect layers?

Creating perfect layers in jellies and gels requires attention to detail and a few key techniques. Here are some tips to achieve flawless, visually striking layers:

SOME TIPS TO ACHIEVE FLAWLESS, VISUALLY STRIKING LAYERS

1. Use Transparent Containers or Molds

Why: Transparent jars or molds help you see the layers as you build them, ensuring even distribution.

How: Glass jars or clear silicone molds work best for monitoring progress.

2. Ensure the First Layer Sets Properly

Why: The first layer should be firm enough to support the next one without mixing.

How: Allow each layer to cool and partially set in the refrigerator for 20 to 30 minutes before adding the next layer. The surface should be slightly tacky, not fully hardened.

3. Pour Layers Gently

Why: Pouring too quickly can disturb the previous layer.

How: Use a spoon or ladle to slowly pour the next layer over the back of a spoon, reducing the impact on the surface below.

4. Match Temperatures Between Layers

Why: If the new layer is too warm, it can melt the layer below, causing colors and flavors to mix.

How: Let the new layer cool to room temperature before adding it to the partially set layer.

5. Use Precise Measurements

Why: Even layers require consistent proportions of each mixture.

How: To ensure uniformity, measure each layer's quantity using a scale or measuring cup.

6. Refrigerate Between Layers

Why: Cooling each layer prevents blending and creates a clean separation.

How: After adding each layer, place the mold or container in the refrigerator and cover it with plastic wrap to prevent condensation.

7. Plan Your Colors and Flavors

Why: Contrasting colors and complementary flavors create a visually appealing and harmonious dessert.

How: Alternate light and dark colors and balance sweet and tart flavors.

8. Work Quickly with Gelling Agents

Why: Some gelling agents, like gelatin or agar-agar, set quickly as they cool.

How: Prepare and pour each layer promptly while ensuring the temperature is appropriate for layering.

9. Use a Level Surface

Why: Uneven molds can cause layers to slant.

How: Place the mold flat in the refrigerator or water bath to maintain even layers.

10. Be Patient

Why: Rushing can lead to uneven or mixed layers.

How: Allow sufficient time for each layer to set before proceeding to the next.

Bonus Tip: Test on a Small Scale

- If you're trying a new recipe or layering technique, create a small test batch to refine your process before making a full dessert.

Apple Cider Gelée

Yield: 2 servings | Prep time: 10 minutes | Cook time: 30 minutes

This cozy gelée captures the comforting flavors of spiced apple cider. Infused with cinnamon and a hint of lemon, the sous vide method creates a perfectly smooth texture while preserving the warmth and richness of the ingredients, making it a delightful dessert for fall or winter gatherings.

Ingredients:
- Apple cider (fresh or store-bought cider) - 1 cup
- Sugar - 2 tbsp
- Gelatin (unflavored) - 1 tbsp
- Water - 2 tbsp
- Lemon juice (freshly squeezed) - 1 tsp
- Cinnamon (ground) - 0.25 tsp

Nutritional Information (for 2 servings):

calories 120 kcal, protein 2g, carbohydrates 26g, fat 0g, fiber 0g, cholesterol 0mg, sodium 5mg, potassium 100mg

Directions:
1. Bloom gelatin with cold water (ensure gelatin is fully hydrated before combining with liquids)
2. Mix apple cider, sugar, lemon juice, and cinnamon. Stir in bloomed gelatin (combine thoroughly to dissolve gelatin evenly)
3. Cook in a water bath at 140°F / 60°C for 30 minutes
4. Remove carefully, pour into molds, then chill until set, about 2 minutes (refrigerate thoroughly for a firm and sliceable texture)

Cooking Temperature Range:

Optimal 140°F / 60°C (permissible range 135°F / 57°C to 145°F / 63°C).

Blueberry Lavender Jelly

Yield: 2 servings | Prep time: 10 minutes | Cook time: 30 minutes

This aromatic jelly combines the natural sweetness of blueberries and the delicate floral notes of lavender. Using the sous vide method ensures a perfectly smooth texture while preserving the fresh berry flavor and subtle lavender aroma, making it an elegant dessert for any occasion.

Ingredients:
- Blueberries (rinse and remove stems) - 8 oz
- Water - 0.25 cup
- Sugar - 2 tbsp
- Gelatin (unflavored) - 1 tbsp
- Culinary Lavender (dried) - 0.5 tsp
- Lemon juice (freshly squeezed) - 1 tsp

Nutritional Information (for 2 servings):

calories 110 kcal, protein 2g, carbohydrates 22g, fat 0g, fiber 3g, cholesterol 0mg, sodium 5mg, potassium 100mg

Directions:
1. Bloom gelatin with cold water (ensure gelatin is fully hydrated before combining with liquids)
2. Puree blueberries and strain seeds if desired (straining is optional for a smoother jelly)
3. Mix puree, sugar, lavender, lemon juice, and bloomed gelatin (stir well to dissolve gelatin evenly)
4. Cook in a water bath at 140°F / 60°C for 30 minutes
5. Remove carefully, pour into molds, then chill until set, about 2 minutes pour and time for chill (refrigerate thoroughly for a firm and sliceable texture)

Cooking Temperature Range:

Optimal 140°F / 60°C (permissible range 135°F / 57°C to 145°F / 63°C).

Cherry Amaretto Gelée

Yield: 2 servings | Prep time: 10 minutes | Cook time: 30 minutes

This delightful Cherry Amaretto Gelée combines the sweet and tart notes of cherries with the subtle almond essence of amaretto. The sous vide method ensures a perfectly smooth texture and preserves the vibrant flavors, making it a perfect dessert for any occasion.

Ingredients:
- Cherry juice (unsweetened) - 0.5 cup
- Amaretto liqueur - 2 tbsp
- Sugar - 2 tbsp
- Gelatin (unflavored) - 1 tbsp
- Water - 2 tbsp

Nutritional Information (for 2 servings):
calories 130 kcal, protein 1g, carbohydrates 25g, fat 0g, fiber 0g, cholesterol 0mg, sodium 5mg, potassium 100mg

Directions:
1. Bloom gelatin with cold water (ensure gelatin is fully hydrated before combining with liquids)
2. Mix cherry juice, amaretto, and sugar. Stir in bloomed gelatin (combine thoroughly to dissolve gelatin evenly)
3. Cook in a water bath at 140°F / 60°C for 30 minutes
4. Remove carefully, pour into molds, then chill until set, about 2 minutes (chill fully for the best texture and flavor)

Cooking Temperature Range:
Optimal 140°F / 60°C (permissible range 135°F / 57°C to 145°F / 63°C).

Classic Fruit Jelly

Yield: 2 servings | Prep time: 10 minutes | Cook time: 20 minutes

This Classic Fruit Jelly uses a sous vide approach to gently set fresh juices, preserving their vibrant colors and natural aromas. The gelatin dissolves seamlessly by cooking at a low, steady temperature, creating a smooth, light, and refreshing texture. A perfect dessert for warm days or special occasions.

Ingredients:
- Fruit juice (strained juice, no pulp) - 1 cup
- Gelatin (unflavored) - 1 tbsp
- Sugar - 2 tbsp
- Lemon juice (fresh-squeezed. optional) - 1 tsp
- Salt - 1 pinch

Nutritional Information (for 2 servings):
calories 120 kcal, protein 3g, carbohydrates 28g, fat 0g, fiber 0g, cholesterol 0mg, sodium 20mg, potassium 60mg

Directions:
1. Bloom gelatin in cold fruit juice (make sure gelatin is fully hydrated before heating)
2. Add sugar, lemon juice, and salt; seal the mixture in a bag or jar (remove excess air if using a bag)
3. Cook in the water bath at 140°F / 60°C for 20 minutes
4. Remove carefully, pour into molds/ramekins, then chill until set, about 3 minutes (refrigeration helps jelly achieve a firm, sliceable set)

Cooking Temperature Range:
Optimal 140°F / 60°C (permissible range 135°F / 57°C to 145°F / 63°C).

Coconut Lime Gelée

Yield: 2 servings | Prep time: 10 minutes | Cook time: 30 minutes

This tropical-inspired gelée combines creamy coconut milk with zesty lime, creating a silky and refreshing dessert. The sous vide method ensures a smooth texture while locking in the bright citrus and creamy coconut flavors. A delightful, light treat for any occasion.

Ingredients:
- Coconut milk (full-fat, canned) - 1 cup
- Lime juice (freshly squeezed) - 0.25 cup
- Sugar - 2 tbsp
- Gelatin (unflavored) - 1 tbsp
- Water - 2 tbsp
- Lime zest (grated) - 1 tsp

Nutritional Information (for 2 servings):
calories 140 kcal, protein 2g, carbohydrates 15g, fat 8g, fiber 1g, cholesterol 0mg, sodium 15mg, potassium 100mg

Directions:
1. Bloom gelatin with cold water (ensure gelatin is fully hydrated before combining with liquid)
2. Mix coconut milk, lime juice, sugar, and lime zest. Stir in bloomed gelatin (combine thoroughly to dissolve gelatin evenly)
3. Cook in a water bath at 140°F / 60°C for 30 minutes (maintain consistent temperature for a smooth gelée texture)
4. Remove carefully, pour into molds, then chill until set, about 2 minutes pour and time for chill (refrigerate thoroughly for a firm and sliceable gelée texture)

Cooking Temperature Range:
Optimal 140°F / 60°C (permissible range 135°F / 57°C to 145°F / 63°C).

Cranberry Orange Gelatin

Yield: 2 servings | Prep time: 10 minutes | Cook time: 30 minutes

This vibrant gelatin combines the tartness of cranberries with the sweet, citrusy flavor of orange. Sous vide cooking preserves the bright colors and flavors while creating a silky texture. Perfect for a festive dessert or a refreshing treat on any occasion.

Ingredients:
- Cranberry juice (use 100% juice, no added sugar) - 0.5 cup
- Orange juice (freshly squeezed) - 0.5 cup
- Sugar - 2 tbsp
- Gelatin (unflavored) - 1 tbsp
- Orange zest (grated) - 1 tsp
- Water - 2 tbsp

Nutritional Information (for 2 servings):
calories 130 kcal, protein 2g, carbohydrates 30g, fat 0g, fiber 1g, cholesterol 0mg, sodium 10mg, potassium 80mg

Directions:
1. Bloom gelatin with cold water (ensure gelatin is fully hydrated before combining with liquids)
2. Mix cranberry juice, orange juice, sugar, and zest. Stir in bloomed gelatin (combine thoroughly to dissolve gelatin evenly)
3. Cook in a water bath at 140°F / 60°C for 30 minutes
4. Remove carefully, pour into molds, then chill until set, about 2 minutes pour and time for chill (refrigerate thoroughly for a firm and sliceable texture)

Cooking Temperature Range:
Optimal 140°F / 60°C (permissible range 135°F / 57°C to 145°F / 63°C).

Elderflower and Pear Jelly

Yield: 2 servings | Prep time: 10 minutes | Cook time: 30 minutes

This delicate jelly combines the floral notes of elderflower with the natural sweetness of pear, creating a refined dessert that is perfect for special occasions. The sous vide method enhances the flavors and ensures a smooth, velvety texture, making it an exquisite treat.

Ingredients:
- Pear juice (fresh or 100% pear juice) - 1 cup
- Elderflower Syrup - 2 tbsp
- Gelatin (unflavored) - 1 tbsp
- Water - 2 tbsp
- Lemon juice (freshly squeezed) - 1 tsp

Nutritional Information (for 2 servings):
calories 110 kcal, protein 2g, carbohydrates 25g, fat 0g, fiber 0g, cholesterol 0mg, sodium 5mg, potassium 120mg

Directions:
1. Bloom gelatin with cold water (ensure gelatin is fully hydrated before combining with liquids)
2. Mix pear juice, elderflower syrup, and lemon juice. Stir in bloomed gelatin (combine thoroughly to dissolve gelatin evenly)
3. Cook in a water bath at 140°F / 60°C for 30 minutes
4. Remove carefully, pour into molds, then chill until set, about 2 minutes (refrigerate for a firm yet delicate texture)

Cooking Temperature Range:
Optimal 140°F / 60°C (permissible range 135°F / 57°C to 145°F / 63°C).

Grapefruit Campari Jelly

Yield: 2 servings | Prep time: 10 minutes | Cook time: 30 minutes

This sophisticated jelly pairs grapefruit's tangy sweetness with Campari's herbal bitterness. The sous vide method ensures a silky texture and captures the vibrant flavors, making it an elegant dessert or a palate-cleansing treat for special occasions.

Ingredients:
- Grapefruit juice (freshly squeezed) - 0.5 cup
- Campari - 2 tbsp
- Sugar - 2 tbsp
- Gelatin (unflavored) - 1 tbsp
- Water - 2 tbsp

Nutritional Information (for 2 servings):
calories 110 kcal, protein 1g, carbohydrates 24g, fat 0g, fiber 0g, cholesterol 0mg, sodium 5mg, potassium 90mg

Directions:
1. Bloom gelatin with cold water (ensure gelatin is fully hydrated before combining with liquids)
2. Mix grapefruit juice, Campari, and sugar. Stir in bloomed gelatin (combine thoroughly to dissolve gelatin evenly)
3. Cook in a water bath at 140°F / 60°C for 30 minutes
4. Remove carefully, pour into molds, then chill until set, about 2 minutes (chill fully for the best texture and flavor)

Cooking Temperature Range:
Optimal 140°F / 60°C (permissible range 135°F / 57°C to 145°F / 63°C).

Honey Lemon Gelée

Yield: 2 servings | Prep time: 10 minutes | Cook time: 30 minutes

This delightful gelée pairs the floral sweetness of honey with the bright tang of lemon. The sous vide method ensures a perfectly smooth texture and preserves vibrant flavors, making this dessert both refreshing and indulgent—a perfect way to elevate your culinary creations.

Ingredients:
- Lemon juice (freshly squeezed) - 0.25 cup
- Honey - 2 tbsp
- Gelatin (unflavored) - 1 tbsp
- Water - 0.5 cup

Nutritional Information (for 2 servings):
calories 90 kcal, protein 1g, carbohydrates 23g, fat 0g, fiber 0g, cholesterol 0mg, sodium 10mg, potassium 60mg

Directions:
1. Bloom gelatin with cold water (ensure gelatin is fully hydrated before combining with liquids)
2. Mix lemon juice, honey, and remaining water. Stir in bloomed gelatin (combine thoroughly to dissolve gelatin evenly)
3. Cook in a water bath at 140°F / 60°C for 30 minutes
4. Remove carefully, pour into molds, then chill until set, about 2 minutes (refrigerate for a refreshing and delicate texture)

Cooking Temperature Range:
Optimal 140°F / 60°C (permissible range 135°F / 57°C to 145°F / 63°C).

Kiwi Lime Jelly

Yield: 2 servings | Prep time: 10 minutes | Cook time: 30 minutes

Brighten your taste buds with our Sous Vide Kiwi Lime Jelly! This vibrant, tangy treat blends the sweet juiciness of kiwi with the zesty kick of lime, creating a refreshing and flavorful jelly. Sous vide precision ensures a perfectly smooth texture and bold, natural flavors in every delightful bite.

Ingredients:
- Kiwi puree (strained to remove seeds) - 0.5 cup
- Lime juice (freshly squeezed) - 1 tbsp
- Sugar - 2 tbsp
- Gelatin (unflavored) - 1 tbsp
- Water - 2 tbsp

Nutritional Information (for 2 servings):
calories 120 kcal, protein 1g, carbohydrates 24g, fat 0g, fiber 1g, cholesterol 0mg, sodium 10mg, potassium 150mg

Directions:
1. Bloom gelatin with cold water (ensure gelatin is fully hydrated before combining with liquids)
2. Mix kiwi puree, lime juice, and sugar. Stir in bloomed gelatin (combine thoroughly to dissolve gelatin evenly)
3. Cook in a water bath at 140°F / 60°C for 30 minutes
4. Remove carefully, pour into molds, then chill until set, about 2 minutes (chill fully for the best texture and flavor)

Cooking Temperature Range:
Optimal 140°F / 60°C (permissible range 135°F / 57°C to 145°F / 63°C).

Lemon Gelatin Squares

Yield: 2 servings | Prep time: 10 minutes | Cook time: 30 minutes

This refreshing dessert features tangy lemon flavor in a smooth gelatin square, gently cooked sous vide to lock in its bright taste. By precisely controlling the temperature, you ensure a flawless, tender set without compromising the citrus aroma or color. Perfect for a light summer treat.

Ingredients:
- Lemon juice (freshly squeezed) - 0.5 cup
- Water - 0.25 cup
- Sugar - 2 tbsp
- Gelatin (unflavored) - 1 tbsp
- Lemon zest (grated) - 1 tsp
- Salt - 1 pinch

Nutritional Information (for 2 servings):
calories 120 kcal, protein 3g, carbohydrates 25g, fat 0g, fiber 1g, cholesterol 0mg, sodium 40mg, potassium 50mg

Directions:
1. Bloom gelatin with 2 tbsp of cold water (ensure gelatin is fully hydrated before adding it to the mixture)
2. Whisk lemon juice, water, sugar, zest, and salt. Stir in bloomed gelatin (combine thoroughly to avoid clumps)
3. Cook the sealed mixture in a water bath at 140°F / 60°C for 30 minutes
4. Remove, pour into tray or molds, and chill until set, about 2 mins pour and time for chill (refrigerate thoroughly for a firm, sliceable texture)

Cooking Temperature Range:
Optimal 140°F / 60°C (permissible range 135°F / 57°C to 145°F / 63°C).

Mango Passionfruit Jelly

Yield: 2 servings | Prep time: 10 minutes | Cook time: 25 minutes

Enjoy the tropical fusion of sweet mango and bright passionfruit in this delicate jelly, expertly prepared sous vide to capture every nuance of flavor. The controlled temperature ensures color and aroma remain at their peak, resulting in a silky, tangy treat perfect for any summery occasion.

Ingredients:
- Mango puree (ripe, blend until smooth) - 1 cup
- Passionfruit pulp (strain seeds if preferred) - 0.5 cup
- Water - 0.25 cup
- Gelatin (unflavored) - 1 tbsp
- Sugar - 2 tbsp
- Salt - 1 pinch

Nutritional Information (for 2 servings):
calories 110 kcal, protein 2g, carbohydrates 25g, fat 0g, fiber 2g, cholesterol 0mg, sodium 20mg, potassium 120mg

Directions:
1. Bloom gelatin with 2 tbsp of cold water (make sure gelatin is fully hydrated before adding to fruit mixture)
2. Mix mango puree, passionfruit pulp, water, sugar, and salt, then stir in bloomed gelatin (ensure thorough mixing for consistent texture)
3. Cook in the water bath at 140°F / 60°C for 25 minutes
4. Remove, pour into molds, and chill until set, about 2 minutes to pour, add extra time to chill (allow enough refrigeration time for a firm, sliceable jelly)

Cooking Temperature Range:
Optimal 140°F / 60°C (permissible range 135°F / 57°C to 145°F / 63°C).

Peach Bellini Gelée

Yield: 2 servings | Prep time: 10 minutes | Cook time: 30 minutes

This elegant gelée captures the essence of a classic Peach Bellini, blending sweet peaches with sparkling prosecco. The sous vide method preserves the vibrant flavors and ensures a smooth, delicate texture, making it an ideal dessert for celebrations or summer evenings.

Ingredients:
- Peach puree (fresh, ripe, blended smooth) - 1 cup
- Prosecco (dry) - 0.5 cup
- Sugar - 2 tbsp
- Gelatin (unflavored) - 1 tbsp
- Lemon juice (freshly squeezed) - 1 tsp
- Water - 2 tbsp

Nutritional Information (for 2 servings):
calories 140 kcal, protein 2g, carbohydrates 30g, fat 0g, fiber 1g, cholesterol 0mg, sodium 10mg, potassium 150mg

Directions:
1. Bloom gelatin with cold water (ensure gelatin is fully hydrated before combining with liquids)
2. Mix peach puree, prosecco, sugar, and lemon juice. Stir in bloomed gelatin (combine thoroughly to dissolve gelatin evenly)
3. Cook in a water bath at 140°F / 60°C for 30 minutes
4. Remove carefully, pour into molds, then chill until fully set, about 2 minutes (refrigerate thoroughly for a firm and sliceable gelée texture)

Cooking Temperature Range:
Optimal 140°F / 60°C (permissible range 135°F / 57°C to 145°F / 63°C).

Pineapple Ginger Jelly

Yield: 2 servings | Prep time: 10 minutes | Cook time: 30 minutes

This tropical-inspired jelly combines the tangy sweetness of pineapple with the warm spice of ginger. The sous vide method ensures a silky texture and preserves vibrant flavors, making this dessert a refreshing and elegant treat perfect for any occasion.

Ingredients:
- Pineapple juice (fresh or 100% juice, no sugar added) - 1 cup
- Sugar - 2 tbsp
- Gelatin (unflavored) - 1 tbsp
- Water - 2 tbsp
- Ginger (fresh, grated) - 1 inch

Nutritional Information (for 2 servings):
calories 110 kcal, protein 2g, carbohydrates 25g, fat 0g, fiber 0g, cholesterol 0mg, sodium 10mg, potassium 120mg

Directions:
1. Bloom gelatin with cold water (ensure gelatin is fully hydrated before combining with liquids)
2. Mix pineapple juice, sugar, and grated ginger. Stir in bloomed gelatin (combine thoroughly to dissolve gelatin evenly)
3. Cook in a water bath at 140°F / 60°C for 30 minutes
4. Remove carefully, strain, pour into molds, then chill until set, about 2 minutes (strain ginger pieces for a clean jelly texture)

Cooking Temperature Range:
Optimal 140°F / 60°C (permissible range 135°F / 57°C to 145°F / 63°C).

Raspberry Gelée

Yield: 2 servings | Prep time: 10 minutes | Cook time: 25 minutes

Experience fresh raspberries' vibrant color and tangy taste in this silky gelée, gently prepared sous vide to preserve the fruit's natural flavor and aroma. The gelatin dissolves seamlessly by maintaining a precise temperature, ensuring a delicate set that highlights the fruit's sweetness. Serve this elegant dessert chilled for a refreshing finish to any meal.

Ingredients:

- Raspberries (rinsed, with removed any leaves or stems) - 8 oz
- Water - 0.5 cup
- Sugar - 2 tbsp
- Gelatin (unflavored) - 1 tbsp
- Lemon juice (fresh-squeezed. optional) - 1 tsp
- Salt - 1 pinch

Nutritional Information (for 2 servings):

calories 100 kcal, protein 2g, carbohydrates 23g, fat 0g, fiber 3g, cholesterol 0mg, sodium 10mg, potassium 120mg

Directions:

1. Bloom gelatin with 2 tbsp of cold water (make sure gelatin is fully hydrated before combining with puree)
2. Puree raspberries, remaining water, sugar, lemon juice, and salt. Combine with bloomed gelatin (a blender or food processor helps achieve a smooth mixture)
3. Transfer to a sealed bag or jar. Sous vide at 140°F / 60°C for 25 minutes
4. Remove carefully, pour into molds or cups, then chill until set, about 2 minutes to pour, plus chilling time (allow enough time in the fridge for a firm gelée texture)

Cooking Temperature Range:

Optimal 140°F / 60°C (permissible range 135°F / 57°C to 145°F / 63°C).

Strawberry Champagne Jelly

Yield: 2 servings | Prep time: 10 minutes | Cook time: 25 minutes

This elegant dessert combines strawberries' sweet freshness with champagne's bubbly lightness, transformed into silky jelly squares through sous vide cooking. The gentle heat preserves the fruit's natural flavor and the champagne's effervescence, making it a perfect treat for special occasions.

Ingredients:

- Strawberries (rinse, hull, and puree) - 8 oz
- Champagne (dry or semi-dry) - 0.5 cup
- Sugar - 2 tbsp
- Gelatin (unflavored) - 1 tbsp
- Water - 2 tbsp
- Lemon juice (freshly squeezed) - 1 tsp

Nutritional Information (for 2 servings):

calories 120 kcal, protein 2g, carbohydrates 25g, fat 0g, fiber 2g, cholesterol 0mg, sodium 10mg, potassium 150mg

Directions:

1. Puree strawberries and strain seeds if desired (straining is optional for a smoother texture)
2. Bloom gelatin in cold water (ensure gelatin is fully hydrated)
3. Mix puree, champagne, sugar, lemon juice, and bloomed gelatin (stir well to dissolve gelatin evenly)
4. Cook in water bath at 140°F / 60°C for 25 minutes
5. Remove and pour into molds, then chill until set, about 2 minutes to pour and time for chill (chill for at least 2 hours for a firm texture)

Cooking Temperature Range:

Optimal 140°F / 60°C (permissible range 135°F / 57°C to 145°F / 63°C).

Vanilla Bean Gelatin

Yield: 2 servings | Prep time: 10 minutes | Cook time: 30 minutes

This silky and aromatic vanilla bean gelatin perfectly blends simplicity and elegance. The sous vide technique ensures a smooth, melt-in-your-mouth texture while preserving vanilla's natural flavor. A delightful dessert for any occasion.

Ingredients:
- Whole milk (fresh milk or plant-based alternatives) - 1 cup
- Vanilla bean (split and scrape seeds) - 1 piece
- Sugar - 2 tbsp
- Gelatin (unflavored) - 1 tbsp
- Water - 2 tbsp

Nutritional Information (for 2 servings):
calories 120 kcal, protein 5g, carbohydrates 20g, fat 2g, fiber 0g, cholesterol 10mg, sodium 30mg, potassium 150mg

Directions:
1. Bloom gelatin with cold water (ensure gelatin is fully hydrated before combining with liquids)
2. Heat milk, sugar, and vanilla bean until warm (do not let the milk boil to preserve its flavor)
3. Stir in bloomed gelatin and transfer to a heat-safe bag (mix thoroughly to dissolve gelatin evenly)
4. Cook in a water bath at 140°F / 60°C for 30 minutes
5. Remove carefully, strain out the vanilla pod, pour into molds, and chill for about 2 minutes (chill fully for the best texture and flavor)

Cooking Temperature Range:
Optimal 140°F / 60°C (permissible range 135°F / 57°C to 145°F / 63°C).

Watermelon Mint Jelly

Yield: 2 servings | Prep time: 10 minutes | Cook time: 30 minutes

This refreshing jelly blends the sweet juiciness of watermelon with a hint of cool mint, creating a perfectly balanced dessert. The sous vide method ensures a smooth texture and preserves the vibrant color and flavors, making it an ideal treat for warm days.

Ingredients:
- Watermelon juice (freshly juiced) - 1 cup
- Sugar - 2 tbsp
- Gelatin (unflavored) - 1 tbsp
- Water - 2 tbsp
- Mint leaves (finely chopped) - 4 leaves

Nutritional Information (for 2 servings):
calories 90 kcal, protein 2g, carbohydrates 20g, fat 0g, fiber 0g, cholesterol 0mg, sodium 10mg, potassium 120mg

Directions:
1. Bloom gelatin with cold water (ensure gelatin is fully hydrated before combining with liquids)
2. Mix watermelon juice, sugar, and mint leaves. Stir in bloomed gelatin (combine thoroughly to dissolve gelatin evenly)
3. Cook in a water bath at 140°F / 60°C for 30 minutes
4. Remove carefully, strain, pour into molds, then chill until set, about 2 minutes (strain to remove mint leaves for a clean jelly texture)

Cooking Temperature Range:
Optimal 140°F / 60°C (permissible range 135°F / 57°C to 145°F / 63°C).

INTRODUCTION TO PREPARING CHOCOLATE TREATS USING SOUS VIDE TECHNOLOGY

Chocolate desserts hold a special place in the world of sweets, offering a rich, luxurious flavor that's hard to resist. Using sous vide technology, you can create chocolate treats with unmatched precision and consistency. From velvety ganaches to molten lava cakes, sous vide ensures a perfect balance of texture and flavor, making it easier than ever for home cooks to achieve professional results.

GENERAL PRINCIPLES AND FEATURES OF SOUS VIDE CHOCOLATE DESSERTS

Sous vide cooking is particularly suited for chocolate-based desserts. It allows for gentle and precise heating, which is crucial for chocolate's delicate composition.

Here are some of the key features and benefits:

Temperature Precision: Chocolate is sensitive to temperature changes, and sous vide ensures exact control, preventing issues like curdling or seizing.

Even Cooking: The water bath provides uniform heat distribution, ensuring consistent results across all portions.

Moisture Retention: The sealed cooking environment preserves moisture, resulting in fudgy cakes and creamy ganaches.

Hands-Free Simplicity: Once packed, chocolate desserts require minimal intervention, making sous vide a convenient choice.

HOW TO PACK CHOCOLATE DESSERTS CORRECTLY

Proper packing is essential for achieving your chocolate treats' desired texture and appearance. Here's how to do it:

Choose the Right Containers:
- Use small heat-resistant jars or ramekins for molten lava cakes, brownies, or puddings.
- For sauces, ganaches, or custards, vacuum-sealed bags or silicone pouches work best.

Prepare the Containers:
- Grease jars or ramekins lightly with butter or cooking spray to prevent sticking.
- If using bags, ensure they are food-safe and designed for sous vide cooking.

Portion Carefully:
- Fill jars or ramekins evenly, leaving about ½ inch of space at the top to allow for expansion during cooking.
- Avoid overfilling bags to prevent uneven cooking.

Seal Properly:
- If using jars, screw the lids on loosely to allow air to escape. Tighten them after cooking.
- For vacuum-sealed bags, ensure all air is removed for optimal heat transfer.

SHAPING CHOCOLATE TREATS FOR PRESENTATION

Sous vide allows for the creative shaping and plating of chocolate desserts:

Individual Servings:
- Use small jars or molds for single-portion desserts like chocolate pots de crème or mousse.

Layered Desserts:
- Prepare components like mousse, cake, and ganache separately, then assemble layers for an elegant presentation.

Decorative Molds:
- Use silicone molds with intricate designs to create visually stunning treats. Sous vide ensures even cooking, even with complex shapes.

Garnishes:
- Add powdered sugar, fresh berries, edible flowers, or a drizzle of caramel for a polished look.

STORING CHOCOLATE TREATS BEFORE AND AFTER COOKING

Before Cooking:

Refrigeration: Store batter or ganache in jars, molds, or bags in the refrigerator for up to 24 hours before cooking.

Freezing: For long-term storage, freeze the prepared mixture in sealed containers. Thaw it in the refrigerator before cooking.

After Cooking:

Cooling: Place cooked desserts in an ice bath to halt cooking and set their texture.

Refrigeration: Cool desserts can be stored in the refrigerator for 5 days. To maintain their freshness, keep them tightly sealed.

Freezing: Dense desserts like brownies or ganache can be frozen for up to two months. Wrap them tightly in plastic wrap or store them in airtight containers.

PREPARING THE FINISHED DISH FOR SERVING

Serve Warm or Chilled:
- Warm desserts like lava cakes can be reheated in a sous vide water bath or oven. For the best molten center, serve immediately.
- Custards, mousses, or ganaches are often served chilled. Remove from the refrigerator 15 minutes before serving for the best flavor.

Unmold with Care:
- Run a knife along the edge for ramekins or jars and invert the dessert onto a plate. Tap gently to release.

Add Finishing Touches:
- Dust with cocoa powder, sprinkle with sea salt, or top with a dollop of whipped cream for extra flavor and presentation.

Pair with Complementary Flavors:
- Serve with a side of fresh fruit, a scoop of ice cream, or a drizzle of flavored sauce for a complete dessert.

COMMON MISTAKES AND HOW TO AVOID THEM

Overcooking Chocolate:
  Mistake: Chocolate can seize or burn at high temperatures.
  Solution: Stick to recommended temperatures, typically between 175°F–185°F (79°C–85°C).

Overfilling Containers:
  Mistake: Overfilled jars or molds can result in uneven cooking.
  Solution: Leave enough space for expansion and even heat distribution.

Skipping the Ice Bath:
  Mistake: Failing to cool desserts quickly can lead to texture issues.
  Solution: Always cool food in an ice bath immediately after cooking.

Incorrect Sealing:
  Mistake: Air in the bag or overtightened jar lids can affect cooking consistency.
  Solution: Use vacuum-sealed bags or finger-tight jar lids for optimal results.

Using Poor-Quality Chocolate:
  Mistake: Cheap chocolate can result in grainy or overly sweet desserts.
  Solution: Invest in high-quality chocolate with a high cocoa content (60% or more).

CONCLUSION

Sous vide technology elevates chocolate desserts to new heights, offering precision, convenience, and versatility. By mastering the basics of packing, temperature control, and storage, you can create a wide array of chocolate treats that are as delicious as they are impressive. With sous vide, your chocolate creations will delight and amaze every time.

Which toppings enhance chocolate textures?

The right toppings can enhance chocolate desserts by contrasting and complementing their rich, velvety texture. Here are some excellent topping ideas to elevate the texture of your chocolate creations:

SOME TOPPING IDEAS FOR YOUR CHOCOLATE CREATIONS

1. Crunchy Toppings
  Toasted Nuts: Almonds, hazelnuts, pecans, or pistachios add a satisfying crunch.
  Cookie Crumbs: Crushed cookies (e.g., Oreos, biscotti, or graham crackers) provide a crumbly texture.
  Candied Nuts or Seeds: Add a sweet, crispy layer with candied almonds, sunflower seeds, or pepitas.

Chocolate Shards: Create texture by scattering tempered or broken chocolate pieces.

Cacao Nibs: Their bitter crunch complements the sweetness of chocolate desserts.

2. Creamy Toppings

Whipped Cream: Light and airy, it contrasts beautifully with dense chocolate.

Mascarpone or Cream Cheese: Adds a velvety richness and tangy balance.

Ganache: A smooth layer of chocolate ganache creates a luscious, glossy finish.

Soft Cheese: Try a dollop of ricotta or goat cheese for a sophisticated pairing.

3. Fruity Toppings

Fresh Berries: Raspberries, strawberries, or blackberries provide a juicy burst of flavor.

Citrus Segments: Orange or grapefruit slices add brightness and acidity.

Dried Fruits: Dried cherries, apricots, or cranberries offer a chewy contrast.

Candied Orange Peel: Combines sweetness with a slight bitterness for depth.

4. Spiced and Sweet Elements

Caramel Drizzle: Adds a smooth, buttery texture and sweetness.

Salted Caramel Chips: Enhance contrast with pockets of chewy saltiness.

Spiced Sugar Dusting: Cinnamon, nutmeg, or chili-infused sugar adds a subtle kick.

Honeycomb Pieces: Crispy, light, and slightly sweet, they complement chocolate perfectly.

5. Ice Cream or Sorbet

Creamy Ice Cream: Vanilla, coffee, or hazelnut ice cream pairs wonderfully with chocolate's richness.

Fruit Sorbet: Raspberry or passionfruit sorbet adds a refreshing, tangy contrast.

Frozen Yogurt: For a lighter, tangy topping that cuts through the richness.

6. Elegant Finishing Touches

Gold or Silver Leaf: Adds a luxurious and striking visual element.

Powdered Sugar or Cocoa: A simple dusting enhances both flavor and presentation.

Edible Flowers: Flowers like violets or pansies add a delicate and colorful accent.

Chocolate Curls or Shavings: Thin, elegant chocolate pieces enhance texture and appearance.

7. Decadent Additions

Marshmallows: Torch them slightly for a gooey, toasty finish.

Peanut Butter Swirls: Adds creaminess with a salty-sweet contrast.

Chopped Toffee: A sweet, crunchy topping that adds a buttery flavor.

Popcorn: Drizzle with chocolate or caramel for a playful, crunchy element.

Pro Tips:

- **Balance Textures:** Combine contrasting textures (e.g., creamy with crunchy) for a more dynamic eating experience.
- **Keep Portions Appropriate:** Avoid overwhelming the chocolate by using toppings sparingly.
- **Focus on Flavor Harmony**: Ensure the toppings enhance the chocolate's natural richness rather than overpower it.

> Are any sweet-salty combos recommended?

> Sweet-salty combinations can elevate chocolate desserts by adding depth and contrast, balancing richness with a savory touch. Here are some delicious sweet-salty combos that work beautifully with chocolate

SOME SWEET-SALTY COMBOS FOR CHOCOLATE

1. Salted Caramel and Chocolate
Why: Caramel's buttery sweetness pairs perfectly with chocolate, and a sprinkle of sea salt enhances the flavor's complexity.
How: Drizzle salted caramel sauce over chocolate cake, mousse, or ice cream, or use salted caramel chips in brownies.

2. Pretzels and Chocolate
Why: Pretzels provide a salty crunch, contrasting with chocolate's rich texture.
How: Top chocolate bark with pretzel pieces, dip pretzel rods in melted chocolate, or add pretzel crumbs to a chocolate tart crust.

3. Sea Salt and Dark Chocolate
Why: A simple sprinkle of flaky sea salt enhances the deep, bitter-sweetness of dark chocolate.
How: For a sophisticated finish, garnish chocolate truffles, brownies, or ganache with Maldon or fleur de sel.

4. Chocolate and Peanut Butter
Why: Peanut butter's salty nuttiness pairs beautifully with chocolate's richness.
How: Swirl peanut butter into chocolate cheesecake, layer it in brownies, or garnish with peanut butter cups.

5. Chocolate-Covered Potato Chips
Why: The salty crunch of potato chips creates an addictive contrast with creamy, sweet chocolate.
How: Dip potato chips halfway into melted chocolate or crumble chips onto chocolate desserts for texture.

6. Chocolate and Bacon
Why: Bacon's savory, smoky saltiness unexpectedly and deliciously complements chocolate's sweetness.
How: Sprinkle candied bacon pieces over chocolate brownies or ice cream or incorporate it into chocolate bark.

7. Chocolate and Salted Nuts
Why: The saltiness of roasted nuts, such as almonds, cashews, or pistachios, balances the chocolate's sweetness while adding crunch.

How: Crushed salted nuts can be added to chocolate bars, cakes, or cookies or used in clusters or brittle.

8. Chocolate and Cheese
Why: Creamy, salty cheeses like brie or mascarpone offer a rich contrast to chocolate's sweetness.
How: Pair chocolate fondue with cheese slices or layer chocolate and mascarpone in desserts like trifles.

9. Chocolate and Salted Caramel Popcorn
Why: Popcorn's light, crispy texture and salty caramel coating are delightful with chocolate.
How: Add caramel popcorn to chocolate cakes or brownies, or create a sweet-salty chocolate popcorn mix.

10. Chocolate and Salted Honey
Why: Honey's floral sweetness is amplified by a touch of salt, enhancing the chocolate's richness.
How: Drizzle salted honey over chocolate pudding, mousse, or ice cream.

11. Chocolate and Pretzel-Crusted Cheesecake
Why: A salty pretzel crust adds crunch and flavor depth to creamy, sweet chocolate cheesecake.
How: Crushed pretzels with butter can be used as the crust base for a baked or no-bake chocolate cheesecake.

12. Chocolate and Salted Pistachios
Why: Pistachios bring a buttery, slightly salty flavor and vibrant green color.
How: Use salted pistachios as a topping for chocolate bark, gelato, or cookies.

13. Dark Chocolate and Sea Salt Toffee
Why: Sea salt enhances the rich, buttery toffee, creating a satisfying crunch and sweetness.
How: Break salted toffee into pieces and add to chocolate bark or sprinkle over cakes.

14. Chocolate and Salty Graham Crackers
Why: A slightly salty graham cracker base balances chocolate's richness, especially in s'mores or pies.
How: Use salted graham crackers in crusts, s'mores bars, or topping for chocolate mousse.

15. Chocolate and Salted Coconut
Why: Coconut's natural sweetness with a hint of salt enhances chocolate's tropical side.
How: Sprinkle salted coconut flakes over chocolate cake, brownies, or frozen treats.

Pro Tips for Sweet-Salty Combos:
- **Start Lightly:** Begin with a small amount of salt or savory toppings to avoid overpowering the sweetness.
- **Balance the Flavors:** Ensure the salt enhances rather than dominates the chocolate's flavor.
- **Use High-Quality Salt:** Flaky sea salts like Maldon or Fleur de Sel provide bursts of flavor without being harsh.

Chocolate Brownies

Yield: 2 servings | Prep time: 15 minutes | Cook time: 1 hour 30 minutes

Indulge in the ultimate decadence with our Sous Vide Chocolate Brownies! These brownies are Fudgy, rich, and intensely chocolaty and have a perfectly moist center and slightly crisp edges. Sous vide precision ensures a consistently luscious texture, making every chocolate bite bliss.

Ingredients:
- White sugar - 0.5 cup
- Butter (unsalted, melted) - 0.25 cup
- Cocoa powder (unsweetened, sifted) - 0.25 cup
- Egg (large) - 2 pieces
- All-purpose flour (sifted) - 0.25 cup
- Salt - 1 pinch

Nutritional Information (for 2 servings):
calories 320 kcal, protein 4g, carbohydrates 45g, fat 15g, fiber 2g, cholesterol 65mg, sodium 70mg, potassium 80mg

Directions:
1. Preheat sous vide water bath to 185°F / 85°C
2. Mix sugar, melted butter, and cocoa powder. Add egg and mix (ensure the mixture is smooth)
3. Stir in flour and salt until just combined (avoid overmixing the batter)
4. Pour batter into mason jars, seal, and submerge in the bath (ensure jars are fully submerged)
5. Remove, cool, and serve from jars or transfer to a plate (cool for best texture)

Cooking Temperature Range:
Optimal 185°F / 85°C (permissible range 183°F / 84°C to 190°F / 88°C).

Chocolate Cake

Yield: 2 servings | Prep time: 20 minutes | Cook time: 1 hour 30 minutes

Delight in the rich decadence of our Sous Vide Chocolate Cake! This luscious dessert boasts an irresistibly moist and velvety texture, with a deep, bold chocolate flavor in every bite. Sous vide precision ensures perfect baking, creating a show-stopping treat for chocolate lovers everywhere.

Ingredients:
- White sugar - 0.5 cup
- Butter (unsalted, melted) - 0.25 cup
- Cocoa powder (unsweetened, sifted) - 0.25 cup
- Egg (large) - 2 pieces
- All-purpose flour (sifted) - 0.33 cup
- Vanilla extract - 0.5 tsp

Nutritional Information (for 2 servings):
calories 360 kcal, protein 5g, carbohydrates 50g, fat 15g, fiber 3g, cholesterol 65mg, sodium 75mg, potassium 90mg

Directions:
1. Preheat sous vide water bath to 185°F / 85°C
2. Whisk sugar, butter, and cocoa powder until smooth. Add egg (ensure the mixture is lump-free)
3. Gradually fold in flour and vanilla extract until combined (avoid overmixing to keep batter light)
4. Pour batter into mason jars, seal, and submerge in bath (ensure jars are airtight)
5. Remove, cool, and serve from jars or unmold onto plates (cool completely for best texture)

Cooking Temperature Range:
Optimal 185°F / 85°C (permissible range 183°F / 84°C to 190°F / 88°C).

Chocolate Cheesecake

Yield: 2 servings | Prep time: 20 minutes | Cook time: 1 hour

Indulge in the ultimate decadence with our Sous Vide Chocolate Cheesecake! This velvety dessert blends chocolate's rich, bold flavor with the creamy smoothness of cheesecake, all atop a buttery crust. Sous vide precision ensures a flawless texture and intense chocolate bliss in every bite.

Ingredients:
- Cream cheese (softened) - 4 oz
- Dark chocolate (melted) - 2 oz
- White sugar - 0.25 cup
- Heavy cream - 0.25 cup
- Egg (large) - 2 pieces
- Vanilla extract - 0.5 tsp

Nutritional Information (for 2 servings):
calories 520 kcal, protein 9g, carbohydrates 30g, fat 40g, fiber 0g, cholesterol 140mg, sodium 80mg, potassium 150mg

Directions:
1. Prepare the ingredients by softening the cream cheese and melting the chocolate (ensure the chocolate cools before mixing)
2. Blend all ingredients until smooth (avoid overmixing)
3. Cook at 176°F / 80°C for 60 minutes (ensure jars are sealed properly)
4. Chill for 2 hours before serving (garnish if desired)

Cooking Temperature Range:
Optimal 176°F / 80°C (permissible range 172°F / 78°C to 180°F / 82°C).

Chocolate Chip Cookies

Yield: 2 servings | Prep time: 15 minutes | Cook time: 45 minutes

Indulge in the ultimate comfort with our Sous Vide Chocolate Chip Cookies! Crispy on the edges, chewy in the center, and studded with gooey, melted chocolate chips, these cookies are pure perfection. Sous vide precision ensures evenly baked, irresistibly delicious treats in every bite.

Ingredients:
- All-purpose flour (sifted) - 0.5 cup
- Butter (unsalted, softened) - 0.25 cup
- Brown sugar - 0.25 cup
- White sugar - 2 tbsp
- Egg yolk (large) - 1 piece
- Chocolate chips - 0.25 cup

Nutritional Information (for 2 servings):
calories 300 kcal, protein 4g, carbohydrates 40g, fat 15g, fiber 1g, cholesterol 50mg, sodium 90mg, potassium 100mg

Directions:
1. Preheat sous vide water bath to 180°F / 82°C
2. Mix butter, sugars, and egg yolk. Gradually fold in flour and chips (do not overmix the dough)
3. Shape the dough into balls and seal them in a vacuum bag or jar (leave space for dough expansion)
4. Submerge in the water bath and cook for 45 minutes (keep bag fully submerged)
5. Cool slightly and serve warm (enjoy immediately for best results)

Cooking Temperature Range:
Optimal 180°F / 82°C (permissible range 179°F / 81°C to 185°F / 85°C).

Chocolate Coconut Custard

Yield: 2 servings | Prep time: 10 minutes | Cook time: 40 minutes

Discover a luscious and indulgent dessert that melds the richness of chocolate with the creaminess of coconut. Sous vide cooking gently sets the custard, locking in flavors and ensuring a silky, melt-in-your-mouth texture. A perfect ending to any meal, warm or chilled.

Ingredients:
- Coconut milk (unsweetened) - 1 cup
- Semi-sweet chocolate chips (chopped) - 4 oz
- Egg (large. room temperature) - 2 pieces
- Sugar - 2 tbsp

Nutritional Information (for 2 servings):
calories 450 kcal, protein 9g, carbohydrates 35g, fat 30g, fiber 4g, cholesterol 120mg, sodium 80mg, potassium 200mg

Directions:
1. Whisk coconut milk, chocolate chips, eggs, and sugar together (make sure the mixture is smooth and no lumps remain)
2. Transfer into jars or bags and seal tightly (remove excess air if using bags)
3. Cook in a water bath at 176°F / 80°C for 40 minutes
4. Remove carefully, let cool slightly, then enjoy warm or chilled (custard will thicken more as it cools)

Cooking Temperature Range:
Optimal 176°F / 80°C (permissible range 174°F / 79°C to 179°F / 81°C).

Chocolate Espresso Custard

Yield: 2 servings | Prep time: 10 minutes | Cook time: 1 hour

Awaken your senses with our Sous Vide Chocolate Espresso Custard! This silky, decadent dessert combines the bold intensity of espresso with the rich, velvety smoothness of chocolate. Sous vide precision ensures a flawlessly creamy texture, making every spoonful a luxurious blend of energy and indulgence.

Ingredients:
- Dark chocolate (chopped) - 2 oz
- Heavy cream - 0.5 cup
- White sugar - 0.25 cup
- Egg (large. room temperature) - 2 pieces
- Espresso powder (dissolved) - 1 tsp

Nutritional Information (for 2 servings):
calories 410 kcal, protein 6g, carbohydrates 35g, fat 30g, fiber 1g, cholesterol 100mg, sodium 40mg, potassium 140mg

Directions:
1. Prepare the ingredients and heat the cream (do not boil the cream)
2. Combine hot cream, chocolate, and espresso (stir constantly for smoothness)
3. Mix custard base with sugar and egg (add chocolate mixture slowly)
4. Portion custard into jars and seal (leave space for expansion)
5. Cook at 185°F / 85°C for 60 minutes. Chill custard before serving (garnish as desired)

Cooking Temperature Range:
Optimal 185°F / 85°C (permissible range 180°F / 82°C to 190°F / 88°C).

Chocolate Fudge Brownies

Yield: 2 servings | Prep time: 20 minutes | Cook time: 1 hour

Dive into pure decadence with our Sous Vide Chocolate Fudge Brownies! These brownies are ultra-rich and irresistibly fudgy, with an intense chocolate flavor and a dense, gooey center. Sous vide precision ensures perfect consistency, making every bite a heavenly indulgence for chocolate lovers.

Ingredients:
- All-purpose flour (sifted) - 0.5 cup
- Butter (unsalted, melted) - 0.25 cup
- White sugar - 0.33 cup
- Cocoa powder (unsweetened, sifted) - 0.25 cup
- Egg (large) - 1 piece
- Vanilla extract - 0.25 tsp

Nutritional Information (for 2 servings):
calories 320 kcal, protein 5g, carbohydrates 45g, fat 15g, fiber 2g, cholesterol 50mg, sodium 80mg, potassium 110mg

Directions:
1. Preheat sous vide water bath to 185°F / 85°C
2. Whisk butter, sugar, cocoa powder, and vanilla until smooth (combine ingredients thoroughly)
3. Add egg and fold in the flour. Pour batter into a bag or jar (do not overmix the batter)
4. Submerge in a water bath and cook for 60 minutes (use weights to keep the bag submerged)
5. Cool slightly before serving (serve warm or at room temperature)

Cooking Temperature Range:
Optimal 185°F / 85°C (permissible range 183°F / 84°C to 190°F / 88°C).

Chocolate Ganache Tart

Yield: 2 servings | Prep time: 20 minutes | Cook time: 1 hour

Savor the decadence of our Sous Vide Chocolate Ganache Tart! A crisp, buttery crust cradles a luxuriously smooth chocolate ganache filling that melts in your mouth. Sous vide precision ensures a flawless texture and deep, rich flavor, making this dessert a show-stopping treat for any occasion.

Ingredients:
- Premade tart shell - 1 piece
- Heavy cream - 0.5 cup
- Dark chocolate (chopped) - 3 oz
- Butter (unsalted, softened) - 1 tbsp
- Vanilla extract - 1 tsp
- Sea salt - 1 pinch

Nutritional Information (for 2 servings):
calories 420 kcal, protein 6g, carbohydrates 28g, fat 32g, fiber 2g, cholesterol 40mg, sodium 120mg, potassium 150mg

Directions:
1. Prepare tart shells and check for cracks (ensure shells are intact)
2. Mix ganache ingredients in a bowl (use room-temperature ingredients)
3. Cook ganache at 180°F / 82°C for 60 minutes (fully submerge the bag in water)
4. Pipe ganache into tart shells (avoid overfilling)
5. Chill and serve (refrigerate for a firm texture)

Cooking Temperature Range:
Optimal 180°F / 82°C (permissible range 175°F / 80°C to 185°F / 85°C).

Chocolate Gelatin Mousse

Yield: 2 servings | Prep time: 10 minutes | Cook time: 30 minutes

This rich and creamy chocolate mousse is made effortlessly with a sous vide technique for a smooth and luxurious texture. Combining dark chocolate and gelatin creates a perfectly balanced, light yet indulgent dessert, ideal for special occasions or everyday treats.

Ingredients:
- Dark chocolate (70% cocoa) - 4 oz
- Heavy cream - 1 cup
- Sugar - 2 tbsp
- Gelatin (unflavored) - 1 tbsp
- Water - 2 tbsp

Nutritional Information (for 2 servings):
calories 340 kcal, protein 5g, carbohydrates 30g, fat 25g, fiber 2g, cholesterol 30mg, sodium 40mg, potassium 150mg

Directions:
1. Bloom gelatin with cold water (ensure gelatin is fully hydrated before combining with liquids)
2. Heat cream and sugar; mix with chocolate until smooth (do not overheat the cream to prevent curdling)
3. Add bloomed gelatin to the mixture and stir until dissolved (mix thoroughly for an even texture)
4. Cook in a water bath at 140°F / 60°C for 30 minutes
5. Remove carefully, pour into serving glasses, then chill until set, about 2 minutes (refrigerate for a firm yet creamy texture)

Cooking Temperature Range:
Optimal 140°F / 60°C (permissible range 135°F / 57°C to 145°F / 63°C).

Chocolate Hazelnut Cheesecake

Yield: 2 servings | Prep time: 15 minutes | Cook time: 1 hour 30 minutes

Indulge in pure decadence with our Sous Vide Chocolate Hazelnut Cheesecake! This rich, velvety dessert blends deep chocolate flavor with the nutty sweetness of hazelnuts atop a buttery crust. Sous vide precision ensures a luxuriously creamy texture, making every bite a truly indulgent experience.

Ingredients:
- Cream cheese (softened) - 8 oz
- White sugar - 0.25 cup
- Egg (large) - 1 piece
- Cocoa powder (unsweetened, sifted) - 2 tbsp
- Hazelnut spread - 2 tbsp
- Vanilla extract - 0.25 tsp

Nutritional Information (for 2 servings):
calories 410 kcal, protein 7g, carbohydrates 25g, fat 32g, fiber 2g, cholesterol 90mg, sodium 100mg, potassium 150mg

Directions:
1. Preheat sous vide water bath to 176°F / 80°C
2. Beat cream cheese and sugar until smooth. Add remaining ingredients (mix the batter until smooth and well combined)
3. Pour batter into jars, leaving ½ inch space. Seal jars tightly (avoid overfilling jars)
4. Submerge jars and cook for 90 minutes (use weights if jars float)
5. Cool at room temperature, then refrigerate (serve chilled for best texture)

Cooking Temperature Range:
Optimal 176°F / 80°C (permissible range 175°F / 79°C to 179°F / 81°C).

Chocolate Lava Cake

Yield: 2 servings | Prep time: 15 minutes | Cook time: 1 hour

Experience molten magic with our Sous Vide Chocolate Lava Cake! This decadent dessert boasts a tender, rich outer shell that gives way to a luscious, gooey chocolate center. Sous vide precision ensures perfect baking, delivering a flawless blend of textures and deep chocolate indulgence in every bite.

Ingredients:
- Dark chocolate (chopped) - 3 oz
- Butter (unsalted, softened) - 3 tbsp
- White sugar - 2 tbsp
- Egg (large) - 1 piece
- All-purpose flour (sifted) - 2 tbsp
- Vanilla extract - 0.25 tsp

Nutritional Information (for 2 servings):
calories 380 kcal, protein 5g, carbohydrates 27g, fat 30g, fiber 2g, cholesterol 85mg, sodium 70mg, potassium 150mg

Directions:
1. Preheat sous vide water bath to 185°F / 85°C
2. Melt chocolate and butter; whisk until smooth. Add remaining ingredients (mix until fully combined)
3. Pour batter into the greased jars, leaving ½ ½-inch space. Seal tightly (use greased jars for easy removal)
4. Submerge jars and cook for 60 minutes (use weights if jars float)
5. Cool slightly before serving warm for the molten center (serve immediately for the best texture)

Cooking Temperature Range:
Optimal 185°F / 85°C (permissible range 183°F / 84°C to 190°F / 88°C).

Chocolate Mousse

Yield: 2 servings | Prep time: 15 minutes | Cook time: 1 hour

Dive into the luxurious decadence of our Sous Vide Chocolate Mousse! This creamy, airy delight melts in your mouth, delivering a perfect balance of rich chocolate flavor and velvety smooth texture. Sous vide precision ensures flawless consistency, making every spoonful a heavenly indulgence.

Ingredients:
- Dark chocolate (chopped) - 4 oz
- Butter (unsalted, softened) - 2 tbsp
- Egg yolk (large) - 2 pieces
- White sugar - 2 tbsp
- Heavy cream - 0.5 cup

Nutritional Information (for 2 servings):
calories 450 kcal, protein 6g, carbohydrates 28g, fat 36g, fiber 2g, cholesterol 120mg, sodium 60mg, potassium 140mg

Directions:
1. Preheat sous vide water bath to 176°F / 80°C
2. Melt chocolate and butter in a heat-safe bag; seal and submerge (use a heat-safe bag for safe cooking)
3. Whisk egg yolks and sugar until pale, then add chocolate mixture (mix thoroughly for a smooth texture)
4. Whip heavy cream to soft peaks and fold into the chocolate mixture (gently fold to maintain a light texture)
5. Chill for 30 minutes before serving (serve chilled for the best flavor)

Cooking Temperature Range:
Optimal 176°F / 80°C (permissible range 175°F / 79°C to 179°F / 81°C).

Chocolate Oat Pudding

Yield: 2 servings | Prep time: 10 minutes | Cook time: 1 hour

Treat yourself to the comforting decadence of our Sous Vide Chocolate Oat Pudding! Creamy oats blend with rich, velvety chocolate to create a luscious dessert or indulgent breakfast. Sous vide precision ensures a perfectly smooth texture and deep, satisfying flavor in every spoonful.

Ingredients:
- Rolled oats - 0.5 cup
- Milk (whole) - 1 cup
- Cocoa powder (unsweetened, sifted) - 2 tbsp
- White sugar - 2 tbsp
- Vanilla extract - 0.5 tsp

Nutritional Information (for 2 servings):
calories 220 kcal, protein 7g, carbohydrates 34g, fat 6g, fiber 4g, cholesterol 10mg, sodium 50mg, potassium 150mg

Directions:
1. Preheat sous vide water bath to 185°F / 85°C
2. Combine all ingredients in a heat-safe bag or jar (seal tightly to prevent leakage)
3. Submerge in the water bath and cook for 60 minutes (ensure the bag or jar stays fully submerged)
4. Remove, stir, and serve warm or chilled (stir to mix ingredients evenly)

Cooking Temperature Range:
Optimal 185°F / 85°C (permissible range 183°F / 84°C to 190°F / 88°C).

Chocolate Peanut Butter Cheesecake

Yield: 2 servings | Prep time: 15 minutes | Cook time: 1 hour 30 minutes

Indulge in the ultimate flavor duo with our Sous Vide Chocolate Peanut Butter Cheesecake! This decadent dessert combines rich, velvety chocolate and creamy, nutty peanut butter atop a buttery crust. Sous vide precision ensures a flawlessly smooth texture, making every bite a heavenly treat for dessert lovers.

Ingredients:
- Cream cheese (softened) - 8 oz
- Peanut butter (creamy) - 2 tbsp
- White sugar - 2 tbsp
- Egg (large) - 1 piece
- Dark chocolate (melted) - 1 oz
- Vanilla extract - 0.5 tsp

Nutritional Information (for 2 servings):
calories 360 kcal, protein 9g, carbohydrates 15g, fat 30g, fiber 1g, cholesterol 105mg, sodium 160mg, potassium 130mg

Directions:
1. Preheat sous vide water bath to 176°F / 80°C
2. Blend all ingredients and transfer to mason jars (use small mason jars and seal them tightly)
3. Submerge jars in the water bath and cook for 90 minutes (make sure jars are fully submerged)
4. Remove jars, cool, and refrigerate until firm (serve chilled for best results)

Cooking Temperature Range:
Optimal 176°F / 80°C (permissible range 175°F / 79°C to 180°F / 82°C).

Chocolate Pots de Crème

Yield: 2 servings | Prep time: 15 minutes | Cook time: 1 hour

Indulge in the silky richness of our Sous Vide Chocolate Pots de Crème! This luxurious dessert delivers intense chocolate flavor in a creamy, velvety custard. Sous vide precision ensures a flawless texture, making every spoonful a decadent, melt-in-your-mouth experience.

Ingredients:
- Dark chocolate (chopped) - 4 oz
- Heavy cream - 1 cup
- Egg yolk (large) - 2 pieces
- White sugar - 2 tbsp
- Vanilla extract - 0.5 tsp

Nutritional Information (for 2 servings):
calories 430 kcal, protein 5g, carbohydrates 22g, fat 37g, fiber 1g, cholesterol 155mg, sodium 45mg, potassium 140mg

Directions:
1. Preheat sous vide water bath to 176°F / 80°C
2. Combine ingredients in a bowl and mix until smooth (use a whisk or blender for best results)
3. Pour mixture into mason jars and seal tightly (ensure jars are airtight)
4. Submerge jars in a water bath and cook for 60 minutes (keep jars fully submerged during cooking)
5. Cool jars and refrigerate before serving (chill for at least 2 hours for best texture)

Cooking Temperature Range:
Optimal 176°F / 80°C (permissible range 175°F / 79°C to 180°F / 82°C).

Chocolate Pudding

Yield: 2 servings | Prep time: 10 minutes | Cook time: 45 minutes

Delight in the creamy decadence of our Sous Vide Chocolate Pudding! This rich and velvety dessert bursts with bold chocolate flavor, perfectly balanced with silky smoothness. Sous vide precision ensures a flawless texture, making every spoonful an indulgent treat that melts in your mouth.

Ingredients:
- Dark chocolate (chopped) - 3 oz
- Whole milk - 1 cup
- White sugar - 3 tbsp
- Egg yolk (large) - 1 piece
- Vanilla extract - 0.5 tsp

Nutritional Information (for 2 servings):
calories 380 kcal, protein 7g, carbohydrates 34g, fat 22g, fiber 1g, cholesterol 150mg, sodium 55mg, potassium 210mg

Directions:
1. Preheat sous vide water bath to 176°F / 80°C
2. Mix milk, sugar, and egg yolk, then add chocolate and vanilla (whisk until fully combined)
3. Pour mixture into mason jars and seal tightly (ensure jars are airtight)
4. Submerge jars in a water bath and cook for 45 minutes (keep jars submerged during cooking)
5. Chill jars in the refrigerator for 2 hours before serving (serve chilled for best texture)

Cooking Temperature Range:
Optimal 176°F / 80°C (permissible range 175°F / 79°C to 180°F / 82°C).

Chocolate Soufflé

Yield: 2 servings | Prep time: 15 minutes | Cook time: 1 hour

Rise to the occasion with our Sous Vide Chocolate Soufflé! This decadent dessert boasts a light, airy texture with a molten, rich chocolate center. Sous vide precision ensures perfect consistency and an irresistibly indulgent flavor, making every bite a masterpiece of chocolate delight.

Ingredients:
- Dark chocolate (chopped) - 4 oz
- Butter (unsalted, softened) - 2 tbsp
- Egg (separated) - 2 pieces
- White sugar - 0.25 cup
- Salt - 1 pinch
- Vanilla extract - 0.25 tsp

Nutritional Information (for 2 servings):
calories 410 kcal, protein 7g, carbohydrates 28g, fat 30g, fiber 2g, cholesterol 215mg, sodium 50mg, potassium 140mg

Directions:
1. Prepare the ingredients by chopping the chocolate (use room-temperature eggs)
2. Melt chocolate and butter at 115°F / 46°C (stir until smooth and glossy)
3. Whip egg whites to stiff peaks and fold gently (fold gently to avoid deflating the mix)
4. Cook at 180°F / 82°C for 60 minutes (seal jars tightly to prevent water)
5. Cool slightly and serve warm (dust with powdered sugar if desired)

Cooking Temperature Range:
Optimal 180°F / 82°C (permissible range 175°F / 80°C to 185°F / 85°C).

Chocolate Tart

Yield: 2 servings | Prep time: 15 minutes | Cook time: 1 hour

Indulge in the sophisticated decadence of our Sous Vide Chocolate Tart! A buttery, crisp crust cradles a luxuriously smooth and rich chocolate filling. Sous vide precision ensures a perfectly creamy texture and deep chocolate flavor, making this dessert a stunning centerpiece for any occasion.

Ingredients:
- Dark chocolate (chopped) - 3 oz
- Heavy cream - 0.5 cup
- White sugar - 2 tbsp
- Egg yolk (large) - 1 piece
- Tart crust (small. pre-baked) - 1 piece

Nutritional Information (for 2 servings):
calories 460 kcal, protein 7g, carbohydrates 34g, fat 32g, fiber 1g, cholesterol 180mg, sodium 60mg, potassium 220mg

Directions:
1. Preheat sous vide water bath to 176°F / 80°C
2. Mix cream, sugar, and egg yolk, then add melted chocolate (whisk until smooth)
3. Pour mixture into mason jars and seal tightly (ensure jars are airtight)
4. Submerge jars in a water bath and cook for 60 minutes (keep jars submerged during cooking)
5. Pour mixture into tart crust and refrigerate for 1 hour (serve chilled for best results)

Cooking Temperature Range:
Optimal 176°F / 80°C (permissible range 175°F / 79°C to 180°F / 82°C).

Chocolate Truffle Filling

Yield: 2 servings | Prep time: 10 minutes | Cook time: 1 hour

Craft luxurious confections with our Sous Vide Chocolate Truffle Filling! This silky, rich ganache combines intense chocolate flavor with a velvety, smooth texture. Sous vide precision ensures perfect consistency, making it the ideal base for decadent truffles or a luscious dessert filling.

Ingredients:
- Dark chocolate (chopped) - 6 oz
- Heavy cream - 0.25 cup
- Butter (unsalted, softened) - 1 tbsp
- White sugar - 1 tbsp
- Salt - 1 pinch
- Vanilla extract - 0.25 tsp

Nutritional Information (for 2 servings):
calories 480 kcal, protein 4g, carbohydrates 30g, fat 38g, fiber 3g, cholesterol 20mg, sodium 30mg, potassium 150mg

Directions:
1. Prepare the ingredients by chopping the chocolate (use high-quality chocolate)
2. Combine all ingredients in a heatproof bag (seal the bag tightly)
3. Cook at 115°F / 46°C for 60 minutes (massage the bag halfway through)
4. Chill the mixture for 2 hours until firm (ready for shaping truffles)

Cooking Temperature Range:
Optimal 115°F / 46°C (permissible range 113°F / 45°C to 117°F / 47°C).

Dark Chocolate Crémeux

Yield: 2 servings | Prep time: 10 minutes | Cook time: 45 minutes

This luscious sous vide dessert blends dark chocolate's bold, slightly bitter flavor with silky cream for a melt-in-your-mouth texture. Gently cooking the mixture at a precise temperature helps preserve its velvety consistency, resulting in a smooth, decadent treat perfect for any chocolate enthusiast.

Ingredients:
- Dark chocolate (chopped) - 6 oz
- Heavy cream - 0.5 cup
- Egg yolk (large) - 3 pieces
- Sugar - 2 tbsp
- Salt - 1 pinch

Nutritional Information (for 2 servings):
calories 600 kcal, protein 8g, carbohydrates 40g, fat 40g, fiber 3g, cholesterol 180mg, sodium 80mg, potassium 250mg

Directions:
1. Whisk chocolate, cream, egg yolks, sugar, and salt until well combined (ensure the mixture is smooth with no lumps)
2. Transfer into sealed bags or jars (remove excess air if using bags)
3. Submerge in water bath at 180°F / 82°C for 45 minutes
4. Remove carefully, cool slightly, and whisk or stir before serving (the crémeux thickens as it cools; serve warm or chilled)

Cooking Temperature Range:
Optimal 180°F / 82°C (permissible range 177°F / 81°C to 182°F / 83°C).

Dark Chocolate Fondant Cake

Yield: 2 servings | Prep time: 15 minutes | Cook time: 1 hour

Delight in the decadence of our Sous Vide Dark Chocolate Fondant Cake! This dessert is pure indulgence with a rich, tender exterior and a molten, gooey dark chocolate center. Sous vide precision ensures a flawless texture and perfectly flowing middle, making every bite a luxurious chocolate experience.

Ingredients:
- Dark chocolate (70% cocoa) - 4 oz
- Butter (unsalted) - 4 tbsp
- White sugar - 0.25 cup
- Egg (large) - 1 piece
- Egg yolk (large) - 1 piece
- All-purpose flour (sifted) - 2 tbsp

Nutritional Information (for 2 servings):
calories 450 kcal, protein 6g, carbohydrates 40g, fat 30g, fiber 2g, cholesterol 120mg, sodium 50mg, potassium 120mg

Directions:
1. Preheat sous vide water bath to 185°F / 85°C
2. Melt chocolate and butter, then let cool slightly (avoid overheating the chocolate)
3. Whisk sugar, egg, yolk, and flour into the chocolate mixture (mix until smooth and lump-free)
4. Pour batter into jars or vacuum bags and seal tightly (avoid overfilling containers)
5. Cook in a water bath for 60 minutes. Cool slightly to serve (serve warm for the best texture)

Cooking Temperature Range:
Optimal 185°F / 85°C (permissible range 184°F / 84°C to 186°F / 86°C).

Dark Chocolate Mousse

Yield: 2 servings | Prep time: 15 minutes | Cook time: 1 hour

Indulge in the velvety richness of our Sous Vide Dark Chocolate Mousse! This decadent dessert combines dark chocolate's bold, intense flavor with an irresistibly creamy, airy texture. Sous vide precision ensures a flawlessly smooth mousse, making every spoonful a luxurious chocolate experience.

Ingredients:
- Dark chocolate (chopped) - 3 oz
- Heavy cream - 0.5 cup
- Egg (large. room temperature) - 1 piece
- White sugar - 2 tbsp
- Vanilla extract - 1 tsp

Nutritional Information (for 2 servings):
calories 410 kcal, protein 6g, carbohydrates 24g, fat 34g, fiber 2g, cholesterol 110mg, sodium 50mg, potassium 100mg

Directions:
1. Prepare the ingredients and ensure readiness (use fresh eggs and quality chocolate)
2. Blend ingredients until smooth (medium speed for better texture)
3. Cook at 180°F / 82°C for 60 minutes (ensure full bag submersion)
4. Cool and refrigerate for 1 hour (garnish before serving)

Cooking Temperature Range:
Optimal 180°F / 82°C (permissible range 175°F / 80°C to 185°F / 85°C).

Fudge Brownies

Yield: 2 servings | Prep time: 20 minutes | Cook time: 1 hour

Dive into the gooey decadence of our Sous Vide Fudge Brownies! These rich, chocolatey delights boast a dense, fudgy center with a slightly crisp crust. Sous vide precision ensures consistent baking and intense flavor, making every bite an indulgent treat for chocolate lovers.

Ingredients:
- Dark chocolate (chopped) - 4 oz
- Butter (unsalted, softened) - 0.25 cup
- White sugar - 0.5 cup
- Egg (large) - 2 pieces
- All-purpose flour (sifted) - 0.25 cup
- Vanilla extract - 0.25 tsp

Nutritional Information (for 2 servings):
calories 420 kcal, protein 6g, carbohydrates 45g, fat 24g, fiber 2g, cholesterol 215mg, sodium 60mg, potassium 120mg

Directions:
1. Prepare the ingredients by chopping the chocolate (use room-temperature ingredients)
2. Melt chocolate and butter at 115°F / 46°C (stir thoroughly for a smooth mixture)
3. Mix melted chocolate with sugar, eggs, and flour (do not overmix)
4. Cook batter at 180°F / 82°C for 60 minutes (ensure jars are tightly sealed)
5. Cool slightly and serve warm (enjoy with ice cream if desired)

Cooking Temperature Range:
Optimal 180°F / 82°C (permissible range 175°F / 80°C to 185°F / 85°C).

Hazelnut Chocolate Spread

Yield: 2 servings | Prep time: 10 minutes | Cook time: 45 minutes

Savor the nutty decadence of our Sous Vide Hazelnut Chocolate Spread! Creamy and luscious, this indulgent treat combines rich chocolate with roasted hazelnuts for the perfect balance of sweetness and nuttiness. Sous vide precision ensures a silky texture, making it irresistible on toast or fruit or by the spoonful.

Ingredients:
- Roasted hazelnuts - 0.5 cup
- Dark chocolate (chopped) - 3 oz
- Heavy cream - 2 tbsp
- Sugar (powdered) - 1 tbsp
- Vanilla extract - 0.25 tsp
- Salt - 1 pinch

Nutritional Information (for 2 servings):
calories 320 kcal, protein 5g, carbohydrates 20g, fat 24g, fiber 2g, cholesterol 10mg, sodium 20mg, potassium 150mg

Directions:
1. Prepare the ingredients by chopping the chocolate (use high-quality dark chocolate)
2. Melt chocolate and cream at 115°F / 46°C (stir to combine)
3. Blend all ingredients until smooth (scrape sides for even blending)
4. Cook at 140°F / 60°C for 30 minutes (stir occasionally)
5. Cool and store in a jar (refrigerate for up to two weeks)

Cooking Temperature Range:
Optimal 140°F / 60°C (permissible range 135°F / 57°C to 145°F / 63°C).

Hot Chocolate Custard

Yield: 2 servings | Prep time: 15 minutes | Cook time: 1 hour

Cozy up with our Sous Vide Hot Chocolate Custard! This creamy, velvety dessert captures hot chocolate's rich, indulgent flavor in a luxuriously smooth custard. Sous vide precision ensures perfect texture and warmth in every spoonful, making it the ultimate comfort treat.

Ingredients:
- Dark chocolate (chopped) - 4 oz
- Whole milk - 1 cup
- Heavy cream - 0.5 cup
- White sugar - 0.25 cup
- Egg yolk (large) - 2 pieces
- Vanilla extract - 0.5 tsp

Nutritional Information (for 2 servings):
calories 450 kcal, protein 8g, carbohydrates 40g, fat 30g, fiber 2g, cholesterol 150mg, sodium 50mg, potassium 200mg

Directions:
1. Prepare the ingredients by chopping the chocolate (ensure the chocolate is finely chopped)
2. Warm milk, cream, and sugar; mix in chocolate, then add yolks and vanilla (avoid cooking the eggs by cooling the mixture)
3. Cook at 176°F / 80°C for 60 minutes (seal jars tightly)
4. Chill for 2 hours before serving (garnish as desired)

Cooking Temperature Range:
Optimal 176°F / 80°C (permissible range 172°F / 78°C to 180°F / 82°C).

Mint Chocolate Mousse

Yield: 2 servings | Prep time: 15 minutes | Cook time: 45 minutes

Refresh your palate with the luxurious delight of our Sous Vide Mint Chocolate Mousse! This creamy, airy dessert pairs the cool essence of mint with the rich depth of chocolate. Sous vide precision ensures a silky texture and a perfect balance of flavors, making every spoonful a refreshing indulgence.

Ingredients:
- Dark chocolate (chopped) - 3 oz
- Heavy cream - 0.5 cup
- White sugar - 2 tbsp
- Egg yolk (large. room temperature) - 2 pieces
- Peppermint extract - 0.5 tsp

Nutritional Information (for 2 servings):
calories 400 kcal, protein 6g, carbohydrates 30g, fat 32g, fiber 1g, cholesterol 120mg, sodium 35mg, potassium 150mg

Directions:
1. Prepare the ingredients and heat the cream (stir occasionally to prevent scorching)
2. Combine chocolate, cream, and peppermint (ensure the chocolate is fully melted)
3. Mix custard base with sugar and egg yolks (temper eggs to avoid curdling)
4. Portion custard into jars and seal (leave space for expansion)
5. Cook at 176°F / 80°C for 45 minutes. Chill before serving (garnish as desired)

Cooking Temperature Range:
Optimal 176°F / 80°C (permissible range 175°F / 80°C to 180°F / 82°C).

Pomegranate Chocolate Cake

Yield: 2 servings | Prep time: 25 minutes | Cook time: 1 hour 30 minutes

Dive into decadence with our Sous Vide Pomegranate Chocolate Cake. This luxurious dessert blends rich, velvety chocolate with the vibrant tartness of pomegranate, creating a perfectly moist and indulgent cake enhanced by the precision of sous vide cooking.

Ingredients:
- Pomegranate arils (fresh) - 0.25 cup
- All-purpose flour (sifted) - 0.5 cup
- Cocoa powder (unsweetened, sifted) - 2 tbsp
- Egg (whisked) - 2 pieces
- Butter (unsalted, melted) - 2 tbsp
- Baking powder - 0.5 tsp

Nutritional Information (for 2 servings):
calories 320 kcal, protein 7g, carbohydrates 40g, fat 14g, fiber 2g, cholesterol 125mg, sodium 65mg, potassium 150mg

Directions:
1. Whisk eggs, melted butter, and cocoa powder (ensure smooth mixing)
2. Fold in flour, baking powder, and seeds (do not overmix)
3. Divide batter into greased jars (seal loosely)
4. Cook in a sous vide water bath at 185°F / 85°C for 90 minutes (ensure jars are submerged)
5. Cool and serve directly or unmold onto a plate (let cool completely)

Cooking Temperature Range:
Optimal 185°F / 85°C (permissible range 176°F / 80°C to 190°F / 88°C).

Raspberry-Infused Chocolate Ganache

Yield: 2 servings | Prep time: 15 minutes | Cook time: 1 hour

This raspberry-infused chocolate ganache is gently cooked sous vide to ensure a silky texture and preserve the brightness of the raspberries. You keep moisture in and unwanted flavors out by sealing chocolate chips, cream, and raspberry puree together. The result is a rich, velvety ganache perfect for a topping, filling, or indulgent dip.

Ingredients:
- Semi-sweet chocolate chips - 8 oz
- Heavy cream - 0.5 cup
- Raspberry puree - 0.25 cup
- Butter (unsalted) - 1 tbsp
- Salt - 1 pinch

Nutritional Information (for 2 servings):
calories 850 kcal, protein 10g, carbohydrates 60g, fat 55g, fiber 6g, cholesterol 75mg, sodium 60mg, potassium 300mg

Directions:
1. Place chocolate chips, cream, raspberry puree, and butter in a resealable bag (make sure the bag is well-sealed to avoid water ingress)
2. Remove air from the bag and seal it (use a vacuum sealer or water displacement method)
3. Submerge in water bath at 140°F / 60°C for 60 minutes
4. Remove the bag, cool the ganache slightly, then whisk until smooth (ensure the ganache is fully emulsified)

Cooking Temperature Range:
Optimal 140°F / 60°C (permissible range 135°F / 57°C to 145°F / 63°C).

Triple Chocolate Pudding Cake

Yield: 2 servings | Prep time: 15 minutes | Cook time: 1 hour

Indulge in the ultimate chocolate-lover's dream with our Sous Vide Triple Chocolate Pudding Cake! This decadent dessert layers rich chocolate cake, molten chocolate pudding, and gooey chocolate sauce. Sous vide precision ensures a perfectly moist and luscious texture, making every bite a triple dose of pure bliss.

Ingredients:
- Dark chocolate (chopped) - 2 oz
- Milk chocolate (chopped) - 2 oz
- White chocolate (chopped) - 1 oz
- All-purpose flour (sifted) - 0.25 cup
- White sugar - 0.25 cup
- Butter (unsalted, melted) - 2 tbsp
- Egg (large) - 2 pieces

Nutritional Information (for 2 servings):
calories 420 kcal, protein 6g, carbohydrates 45g, fat 24g, fiber 2g, cholesterol 75mg, sodium 30mg, potassium 160mg

Directions:
1. Prepare the ingredients by chopping the chocolates (use high-quality chocolate)
2. Mix batter with flour, sugar, egg, and butter (ensure no lumps remain)
3. Portion batter into jars and top with white chocolate (leave space for expansion)
4. Cook jars at 185°F / 85°C for 60 minutes (ensure jars are submerged)
5. Cool slightly and serve warm (garnish with whipped cream or berries)

Cooking Temperature Range:
Optimal 185°F / 85°C (permissible range 180°F / 82°C to 190°F / 88°C).

White Chocolate Panna Cotta

Yield: 2 servings | Prep time: 15 minutes | Cook time: 1 hour

Delight in the elegance of our Sous Vide White Chocolate Panna Cotta! This silky, creamy dessert is infused with the delicate sweetness of white chocolate, creating a luxurious and refined treat. Sous vide precision ensures a perfectly smooth texture, making every spoonful a heavenly indulgence.

Ingredients:
- White chocolate (chopped) - 2 oz
- Heavy cream - 1 cup
- White sugar - 1 tbsp
- Vanilla extract - 1 tsp
- Salt - 1 pinch

Nutritional Information (for 2 servings):
calories 460 kcal, protein 4g, carbohydrates 28g, fat 38g, fiber 0g, cholesterol 90mg, sodium 50mg, potassium 150mg

Directions:
1. Prepare the ingredients and chop the white chocolate (use high-quality chocolate)
2. Blend all ingredients until smooth (ensure the mixture is fully emulsified)
3. Cook at 176°F / 80°C for 60 minutes (use sealed mason jars)
4. Chill and refrigerate for 2 hours (garnish before serving)

Cooking Temperature Range:
Optimal 176°F / 80°C (permissible range 172°F / 78°C to 180°F / 82°C).

INTRODUCTION TO PREPARING FROZEN DESSERTS USING SOUS VIDE TECHNOLOGY

Frozen desserts are a favorite treat, offering a refreshing and indulgent experience. From creamy ice creams and gelatos to vibrant sorbets and semifreddos, sous vide ensures frozen desserts maintain a perfect texture and rich flavor.

GENERAL PRINCIPLES AND FEATURES OF SOUS VIDE FROZEN DESSERTS

Sous vide cooking is ideal for frozen desserts as it provides precise temperature control, which is critical for achieving the right consistency and flavor. This method ensures custard bases, fruit purees, or other mixtures are cooked gently and evenly, avoiding common issues like curdling or graininess.

Key features and benefits of using sous vide for frozen desserts include:

Temperature Precision: Sous vide allows exact control of temperatures, which is crucial for pasteurizing eggs in custard-based desserts or maintaining the integrity of delicate flavors in fruit-based desserts.

Enhanced Flavor Development: Cooking ingredients in a sealed environment intensifies flavors by preventing evaporation and preserving aromatic compounds.

Smooth Texture: Gentle heating ensures custards and creams develop a silky consistency, free from lumps or overcooking.

Consistent Results: Sous vide eliminates guesswork, ensuring each batch turns out perfect every time.

HOW TO PACK FROZEN DESSERTS CORRECTLY

Proper packing is essential for uniform cooking and optimal texture for frozen desserts. Here's how to do it:

Choose the Right Containers:
- Use vacuum-sealed bags for liquid bases like ice cream or sorbet mixtures.
- Opt for jars or silicone molds for semifreddos, frozen custards, or layered desserts.

Prepare the Containers:
- If using jars, grease lightly with butter or spray to ensure easy removal after freezing.
- For bags, ensure they are food-safe and designed for sous vide cooking.

Seal Properly:
- Vacuum-seal bags tightly to remove all air, which prevents uneven cooking.
- For jars, screw the lids on loosely to allow air to escape during cooking. Tighten them after cooling.

Portion Carefully:
- Divide the mixture evenly between the containers for consistent results. Leave about ½ inch of space at the top to allow for expansion during freezing.

SHAPING FROZEN DESSERTS FOR PRESENTATION

Sous vide provides flexibility in shaping frozen desserts, allowing you to create stunning presentations:

Molded Shapes:
- Use silicone molds for intricate designs. Sous vide ensures an even setting, making complex shapes possible.

Individual Servings:
- Prepare desserts in small jars, ramekins, or molds for single-portion servings.

Layered Creations:
- Build layers by freezing one component at a time. For a visually striking dessert, alternate layers of ice cream and fruit puree.

Cut-Out Shapes:
- Freeze desserts on a flat sheet and use cookie cutters to create geometric or themed shapes.

Whipped Shapes:
- Before freezing, use a piping bag to shape semifreddos or ice cream into elegant swirls or designs.

STORING FROZEN DESSERTS BEFORE AND AFTER COOKING

Before Cooking:

Refrigeration: Mixtures can be stored in jars or vacuum-sealed bags in the refrigerator for up to 24 hours before sous vide cooking.

Freezing: Uncooked mixtures can be frozen for up to 1 month in vacuum-sealed bags. Thaw in the refrigerator before cooking.

After Cooking:

Cooling: The cooked mixture is placed in an ice bath to stop cooking and prepare it for freezing.

Freezing: Transfer the chilled mixture to the freezer. For ice creams and sorbets, churn in an ice cream maker after chilling for the smoothest texture.

Storage: Store frozen desserts in airtight containers for up to two months to prevent freezer burn.

PREPARING THE FINISHED DISH FOR SERVING

Temper Before Serving:
- Remove frozen desserts from the freezer 5–10 minutes before serving to allow them to soften slightly for the best texture.

Unmold with Care:
- Dip the mold in warm water for molded desserts for a few seconds to release the dessert without damaging its shape.

Add Garnishes:
- Enhance presentation with fresh fruit, mint leaves, chocolate shavings, or a sauce drizzle.

Pair with Complementary Flavors:
- Serve with cookies, wafers, or a dollop of whipped cream to add contrasting textures.

Plating Techniques:
- Contrasting colors and shapes can make the dessert visually appealing. For example, bright fruit sorbets can be paired with dark chocolate sauces.

COMMON MISTAKES AND HOW TO AVOID THEM

Overheating Custard Bases:

Mistake: Cooking custards at too high a temperature can cause curdling.

Solution: Use precise sous vide temperatures, typically between 175°F–185°F (79°C–85°C), to gently cook custards.

Skipping the Ice Bath:
> **Mistake**: Not cooling mixtures quickly can result in a grainy texture.
> **Solution**: Always chill cooked bases in an ice bath before freezing.

Improper Sealing:
> **Mistake**: Air in the bag can lead to uneven cooking.
> **Solution**: Vacuum-seal bags tightly or use jars with loose-fitting lids.

Freezer Burn:
> **Mistake**: Improper storage can cause desserts to dry out in the freezer.
> **Solution**: Store in airtight containers or vacuum-sealed bags.

Overloading the Freezer:
> **Mistake**: Placing too many items in the freezer simultaneously can slow freezing and affect texture.
> **Solution**: Freeze desserts in batches, allowing adequate airflow around each item.

CONCLUSION

Sous vide technology transforms the preparation of frozen desserts, offering precision, convenience, and unparalleled results. By mastering the basics of packing, shaping, and storage, you can create an array of frozen treats that are as beautiful as they are delicious.

How to make ice cream if I don't have an ice cream maker?

Here are some methods to make ice cream without using ice cream maker:

FEW METHODS ON HOW TO MAKE ICE CREAM BY HAND WITHOUT USING AN ICE CREAM MAKER

1. The Freeze-and-Stir Method (Best for a Creamy Texture)

Chill the mixture – Pour the mixture into a shallow, freezer-safe container (like a metal or glass baking dish) and freeze for about 30 minutes.

Stir and repeat – Every 30 minutes, stir the mixture vigorously with a fork or whisk to break up the ice crystals. Repeat this process every 30 minutes for about 3 hours, or until the ice cream is smooth and fully frozen.

2. The Ziplock Bag Method (Best for Quick Results)

Create the ice bath – Fill the large ziplock bag with ice and salt, then place the smaller bag inside. Seal the large bag.

Shake it up! – Shake the bag vigorously for about 5–10 minutes, or until the ice cream firms up. (Use gloves or a towel to hold the bag, as it gets very cold.)

Tips for Success
- **Use a shallow container** for faster freezing.
- **Chill your mixture beforehand** for a smoother texture.
- **Add alcohol (like a splash of rum or vodka)** to prevent the ice cream from freezing too hard.

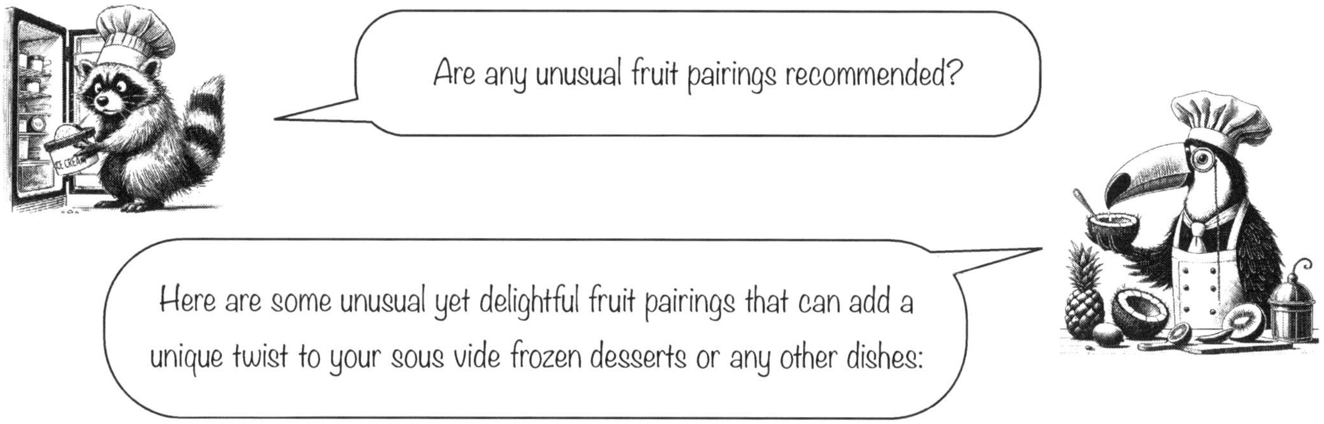

Are any unusual fruit pairings recommended?

Here are some unusual yet delightful fruit pairings that can add a unique twist to your sous vide frozen desserts or any other dishes:

SOME UNUSUAL FRUIT PAIRINGS FOR SOUS VIDE FROZEN DESSERTS

1. Pineapple and Basil
   Why: The sweetness of the pineapple is beautifully balanced by the aromatic freshness of basil.
   How: Try a pineapple-basil sorbet or use basil-infused syrup with pineapple compote.

2. Mango and Chili
   Why: Mango's tropical sweetness pairs intriguingly with the subtle heat of chili.
   How: Add a pinch of chili powder to mango sorbet or drizzle chili-infused syrup for a spicy kick.

3. Watermelon and Feta
   Why: The salty creaminess of feta complements the refreshing sweetness of watermelon.
   How: Pureed watermelon and crumbled feta make a savory-sweet gelato, or you can use this pairing in a semifreddo.

4. Strawberry and Balsamic Vinegar
   Why: The tangy depth of balsamic vinegar enhances the strawberry's natural sweetness.
   How: Make a strawberry-balsamic frozen yogurt or a balsamic reduction swirl in strawberry sorbet.

5. Orange and Black Olives
   Why: The briny umami of black olives contrasts beautifully with the citrusy brightness of orange.
   How: Use candied black olives as a topping for orange sherbet.

6. Blueberry and Lavender
   Why: The floral notes of lavender add depth to the sweet-tart profile of blueberries.
   How: Infuse lavender into a blueberry gelato base or garnish with dried lavender petals.

7. Pear and Blue Cheese

> **Why:** The creamy saltiness of blue cheese enhances the mild sweetness of pears.
>
> **How:** Make a pear and blue cheese semifreddo or a layered parfait with these flavors.

8. **Raspberry and Mint**
   > **Why:** Mint's cool freshness elevates raspberry's tartness.
   >
   > **How:** Create a raspberry-mint sorbet or use mint-infused syrup with raspberry ice cream.

9. **Banana and Cardamom**
   > **Why:** Cardamom's warm spice adds complexity to the natural creaminess of bananas.
   >
   > **How:** Add ground cardamom to banana ice cream or use it in a frozen banana pudding.

10. **Cherry and Almond**
    > **Why:** Almond's nutty sweetness complements the cherry's tart richness.
    >
    > **How:** Make a cherry-almond gelato or add toasted almond pieces to cherry sorbet.

11. **Grapefruit and Honey**
    > **Why:** The bitterness of grapefruit is mellowed by honey's floral sweetness.
    >
    > **How:** Use honey as a sweetener for grapefruit sorbet or create a grapefruit honey granita.

12. **Kiwi and Coconut**
    > **Why:** Kiwi's tangy freshness pairs well with the creamy sweetness of coconut.
    >
    > **How:** Layer kiwi puree with coconut ice cream or make a kiwi-coconut frozen parfait.

13. **Blackberry and Thyme**
    > **Why:** The earthy herbaceousness of thyme adds complexity to the blackberry's sweet-tart flavor.
    >
    > **How:** Infuse thyme into blackberry sorbet or use as a garnish for blackberry semifreddo.

14. **Fig and Lemon**
    > **Why:** The jammy sweetness of figs is brightened by the lemon's acidity.
    >
    > **How:** Make a fig-lemon frozen yogurt or a layered frozen dessert with these flavors.

15. **Plum and Star Anise**
    > **Why:** Star anise's licorice notes enhance the plum's deep sweetness.
    >
    > **How:** Infuse star anise into a plum sorbet or use it as a spice in plum gelato.

16. **Guava and Ginger**
    > **Why:** Guava's tropical sweetness is complemented by ginger's zesty warmth.
    >
    > **How:** Add freshly grated ginger to guava sorbet or drizzle ginger syrup over guava ice cream.

17. **Lemon and Lavender**
    > **Why:** Lavender's floral notes balance lemon's bright acidity.
    >
    > **How:** Infuse lavender into lemon sorbet or layer lemon-lavender semifreddo.

18. **Cantaloupe and Prosciutto**
    > **Why:** The saltiness of prosciutto contrasts with the mild sweetness of cantaloupe.
    >
    > **How:** Create a cantaloupe sorbet and top it with crispy prosciutto crumbles.

19. **Passionfruit and Coconut**
    > **Why:** The tropical tang of passionfruit pairs perfectly with creamy coconut.
    >
    > **How:** Make a passionfruit-coconut frozen parfait or swirl coconut milk into passionfruit sorbet.

20. **Apple and Rosemary**
    > **Why:** Rosemary's piney flavor complements apple's crisp sweetness.
    >
    > **How:** Infuse rosemary into apple sorbet or create a layered apple-rosemary gelato.

Vanilla Bean Ice Cream Base

Yield: 2 servings | Prep time: 10 minutes | Cook time: 1 hour

Create the ultimate homemade treat with our Sous Vide Vanilla Ice Cream Base. Infused with vanilla's pure, fragrant essence, this luxuriously creamy base is perfectly cooked for smoothness and rich flavor. Sous vide precision ensures every scoop is a velvety delight, ready to churn into perfection.

Ingredients:
- Whole milk - 1 cup
- Heavy cream - 0.5 cup
- Sugar - 0.33 cup
- Egg yolk (whisked) - 4 pieces
- Vanilla bean (split and seeds scraped) - 1 piece

Nutritional Information (for 2 servings):
calories 320 kcal, protein 6g, carbohydrates 32g, fat 18g, fiber 0g, cholesterol 200mg, sodium 50mg, potassium 160mg

Directions:
1. Whisk together milk, cream, sugar, yolks, and vanilla (ensure all ingredients are fully combined)
2. Seal the mixture in vacuum or ziplock bags (ensure bags are airtight)
3. Cook in a water bath at 176°F / 80°C for 60 minutes (maintain precise temperature)
4. Strain custard and cool to room temperature (remove vanilla pod before cooling)
5. Chill custard before churning in the ice cream maker (refrigerate for best results)

Cooking Temperature Range:
Optimal 176°F / 80°C (permissible range 176°F / 80°C to 180°F / 82°C).

Chocolate Gelato Base

Yield: 2 servings | Prep time: 10 minutes | Cook time: 45 minutes

Dive into the decadence of our Sous Vide Chocolate Gelato Base! This ultra-creamy, rich base is infused with intense chocolate flavor, creating the perfect foundation for an indulgent gelato. Sous vide precision ensures a smooth, velvety texture that will elevate every scoop to pure dessert bliss.

Ingredients:
- Whole milk - 1 cup
- Heavy cream - 0.5 cup
- Sugar - 0.25 cup
- Cocoa powder (unsweetened, sifted) - 1 tbsp
- Egg yolk (large, whisked) - 2 pieces

Nutritional Information (for 2 servings):
calories 310 kcal, protein 5g, carbohydrates 25g, fat 20g, fiber 1g, cholesterol 140mg, sodium 50mg, potassium 150mg

Directions:
1. Whisk together milk, cream, sugar, cocoa powder, and egg yolks (ensure the mixture is smooth and lump-free)
2. Transfer to a vacuum-sealed bag or zip-top bag using water displacement (use a heat-safe bag for best results)
3. Cook in a sous vide water bath at 180°F / 82°C for 45 minutes
4. Chill the mixture, then churn in an ice cream maker for about 10 minutes (follow the ice cream maker's instructions for optimal results)

Cooking Temperature Range:
Optimal 180°F / 82°C (permissible range 175°F / 79°C to 185°F / 85°C).

Strawberry Sorbet

Yield: 2 servings | Prep time: 15 minutes | Cook time: 30 minutes

Cool off with the vibrant sweetness of our Sous Vide Strawberry Sorbet! Bursting with the natural flavor of ripe strawberries, this refreshing treat is perfectly balanced with a hint of tanginess. Sous vide precision ensures a smooth, silky texture, making every scoop a delightful taste of summer.

Ingredients:
- Strawberries (hulled) - 8 oz
- Sugar - 0.25 cup
- Lemon juice (freshly squeezed) - 1 tbsp
- Water - 2 tbsp

Nutritional Information (for 2 servings):
calories 110 kcal, protein 1g, carbohydrates 28g, fat 0g, fiber 2g, cholesterol 0mg, sodium 5mg, potassium 200mg

Directions:
1. Blend strawberries, sugar, lemon juice, and water until smooth (ensure the mixture is free of lumps for a smooth texture)
2. Transfer to a vacuum-sealed bag or zip-top bag using water displacement (use a heat-safe bag for best results)
3. Cook in a sous vide water bath at 180°F / 82°C for 30 minutes
4. Chill the mixture, then churn in an ice cream maker for about 10 minutes (follow the ice cream maker's instructions for best results)

Cooking Temperature Range:
Optimal 180°F / 82°C (permissible range 175°F / 79°C to 185°F / 85°C).

Mango Coconut Ice Cream

Yield: 2 servings | Prep time: 20 minutes | Cook time: 45 minutes

Transport your taste buds to paradise with our Sous Vide Mango Coconut Ice Cream! This creamy, tropical delight combines the juicy sweetness of ripe mangoes with coconut's rich, velvety flavor. Sous vide precision ensures a smooth, luxurious texture, making every scoop a refreshing escape.

Ingredients:
- Mango (peeled, diced) - 10 oz
- Coconut milk (unsweetened) - 1 cup
- Sugar - 0.25 cup
- Egg yolk (large) - 2 pieces
- Vanilla extract (pure) - 1 tsp

Nutritional Information (for 2 servings):
calories 210 kcal, protein 4g, carbohydrates 30g, fat 8g, fiber 1g, cholesterol 85mg, sodium 15mg, potassium 180mg

Directions:
1. Blend mango, coconut milk, sugar, egg yolks, and vanilla extract until smooth (ensure the mixture is free of lumps for a creamy texture)
2. Transfer to a vacuum-sealed bag or zip-top bag using water displacement (use a heat-safe bag for best results)
3. Cook in a sous vide water bath at 180°F / 82°C for 45 minutes
4. Chill the mixture, then churn in an ice cream maker for about 15 minutes (follow the ice cream maker's instructions for best results)

Cooking Temperature Range:
Optimal 180°F / 82°C (permissible range 175°F / 79°C to 185°F / 85°C).

Matcha Green Tea Ice Cream

Yield: 2 servings | Prep time: 20 minutes | Cook time: 45 minutes

Elevate your dessert game with our Sous Vide Matcha Green Tea Ice Cream! This creamy, vibrant treat combines the earthy richness of matcha with a perfectly smooth, velvety texture. Sous vide precision locks in the bold flavor and ensures every scoop is a refreshing, indulgent balance of sweet and tea's natural depth.

Ingredients:
- Matcha green tea powder - 1.5 tsp
- Whole milk - 0.5 cup
- Heavy cream - 0.5 cup
- Sugar - 0.25 cup
- Egg yolk (large) - 2 pieces

Nutritional Information (for 2 servings):
calories 250 kcal, protein 5g, carbohydrates 22g, fat 16g, fiber 0g, cholesterol 90mg, sodium 25mg, potassium 150mg

Directions:
1. Whisk matcha with milk to make a smooth paste, then combine with all ingredients (ensure no lumps for a smooth texture)
2. Transfer the mixture to a vacuum-sealed or zip-top bag using water displacement (ensure the bag is airtight to prevent water leakage)
3. Cook in a sous vide water bath at 180°F / 82°C for 45 minutes
4. Chill in an ice bath, then churn in an ice cream maker for about 15 minutes (use an ice cream maker's guidelines for the best results)

Cooking Temperature Range:
Optimal 180°F / 82°C (permissible range 175°F / 79°C to 185°F / 85°C).

Peach Frozen Yogurt

Yield: 2 servings | Prep time: 20 minutes | Cook time: 45 minutes

Savor the sweet, tangy bliss of our Sous Vide Peach Frozen Yogurt! This creamy and refreshing treat is filled with the juicy flavor of ripe peaches, perfectly balanced by the tanginess of yogurt. Sous vide precision guarantees a silky-smooth texture, making every scoop a delightful taste of summer.

Ingredients:
- Peaches (fresh, peeled, diced) - 1 cup
- Greek yogurt (plain) - 0.5 cup
- Honey - 2 tbsp
- Lemon juice (freshly squeezed) - 1 tsp
- Vanilla extract - 0.5 tsp

Nutritional Information (for 2 servings):
calories 160 kcal, protein 4g, carbohydrates 32g, fat 2g, fiber 1g, cholesterol 5mg, sodium 20mg, potassium 300mg

Directions:
1. Blend peaches, yogurt, honey, lemon juice, and vanilla until smooth (ensure mixture is smooth to avoid lumps)
2. Transfer to a vacuum-sealed or zip-top bag using water displacement (ensure no air remains in the bag)
3. Cook in a sous vide water bath at 180°F / 82°C for 45 minutes
4. Chill in an ice bath, then churn in an ice cream maker until creamy (follow ice cream maker instructions for best results)

Cooking Temperature Range:
Optimal 180°F / 82°C (permissible range 175°F / 79°C to 185°F / 85°C).

SOUS VIDE DESSERT																																				FROZEN DESSERTS

Mint Chocolate Chip Ice Cream

Yield: 2 servings | Prep time: 25 minutes | Cook time: 1 hour

Refresh and indulge with our Sous Vide Mint Chocolate Chip Ice Cream! Creamy and velvety, this classic favorite pairs cool, refreshing mint with rich, bittersweet chocolate chips. Sous vide precision ensures a silky texture and perfectly blended flavors, making every scoop a minty, chocolatey delight.

Ingredients:

- Heavy cream - 1 cup
- Whole milk - 0.5 cup
- Sugar - 0.25 cup
- Mint leaves (finely chopped) - 0.25 cup
- Egg yolk (large) - 2 pieces
- Chocolate chips - 0.25 cup

Nutritional Information (for 2 servings):

calories 350 kcal, protein 6g, carbohydrates 30g, fat 22g, fiber 0g, cholesterol 130mg, sodium 50mg, potassium 150mg

Directions:

1. Blend cream, milk, sugar, mint leaves, and egg yolks until combined (ensure the mixture is smooth and well-blended)
2. Transfer to a vacuum-sealed or zip-top bag using water displacement (ensure no air remains in the bag for even cooking)
3. Cook in a sous vide water bath at 180°F / 82°C for 60 minutes
4. Chill in an ice bath, then churn in an ice cream maker, adding chips (follow manufacturer's instructions for best results)

Cooking Temperature Range:

Optimal 180°F / 82°C (permissible range 175°F / 79°C to 185°F / 85°C).

SOUS VIDE DESSERT																																				FROZEN DESSERTS

Salted Caramel Ice Cream Base

Yield: 2 servings | Prep time: 15 minutes | Cook time: 1 hour

This luscious Salted Caramel Ice Cream base combines creamy textures and rich flavors. Perfectly prepared using sous vide, it ensures a silky-smooth result every time. The balance of sweet caramel and a hint of salt makes it a decadent treat for any occasion.

Ingredients:

- Egg yolk (medium) - 4 pieces
- Heavy cream - 1 cup
- Whole milk - 1 cup
- Caramel sauce (preheat if homemade) - 0.5 cup
- Vanilla extract - 0.5 tsp
- Salt - 2 pinch

Nutritional Information (for 2 servings):

calories 460 kcal, protein 7g, carbohydrates 32g, fat 34g, fiber 0g, cholesterol 140mg, sodium 170mg, potassium 150mg

Directions:

1. Preheat sous vide water bath to 180°F / 82°C
2. Mix yolks, caramel, vanilla, salt, cream, and milk until smooth (mix gradually to avoid clumps)
3. Seal the mixture in a bag using water displacement and cook for 60 minutes (ensure the bag is fully sealed)
4. Cool the bag in an ice bath immediately after cooking (prevents overcooking)
5. Churn in an ice cream maker, then freeze until firm (follow ice cream maker instructions)

Cooking Temperature Range:

Optimal 180°F / 82°C (permissible range 179°F / 81°C to 185°F / 85°C).

Espresso Gelato

Yield: 2 servings | Prep time: 20 minutes | Cook time: 1 hour

Rich and creamy, this Sous Vide Espresso Gelato delivers a bold coffee flavor with a smooth, velvety texture. Perfectly crafted for espresso lovers, this dessert is an indulgent treat that's easy to make with sous vide for consistently delicious results.

Ingredients:
- Egg yolk (medium) - 4 pieces
- Heavy cream - 1 cup
- Whole milk - 0.5 cup
- White sugar - 0.33 cup
- Espresso powder - 2 tbsp
- Vanilla extract - 0.5 tsp

Nutritional Information (for 2 servings):
calories 400 kcal, protein 6g, carbohydrates 38g, fat 25g, fiber 0g, cholesterol 150mg, sodium 60mg, potassium 100mg

Directions:
1. Preheat sous vide water bath to 180°F / 82°C
2. Whisk the yolks, sugar, and espresso powder until smooth. Add cream, milk, and vanilla (mix slowly to avoid lumps)
3. Seal in a bag and cook for 60 minutes (ensure no air remains in the bag)
4. Cool the bag in an ice bath after cooking (prevents overcooking)
5. Churn in the ice cream maker, then freeze until firm (follow the machine's instructions)

Cooking Temperature Range:
Optimal 180°F / 82°C (permissible range 179°F / 81°C to 185°F / 85°C).

Raspberry Lemon Sorbet

Yield: 2 servings | Prep time: 15 minutes | Cook time: 1 hour

This refreshing Sous Vide Raspberry Lemon Sorbet combines the tangy sweetness of raspberries with a zesty hint of lemon. It's perfect for a light dessert, with a smooth texture made easy by the sous vide method, ensuring consistent and delicious results every time.

Ingredients:
- Raspberries (fresh, rinsed, dried) - 1 cup
- White sugar - 0.5 cup
- Water - 0.5 cup
- Lemon juice (freshly squeezed) - 2 tbsp
- Lemon zest (grated) - 0.5 tsp

Nutritional Information (for 2 servings):
calories 150 kcal, protein 1g, carbohydrates 38g, fat 0g, fiber 4g, cholesterol 0mg, sodium 2mg, potassium 150mg

Directions:
1. Preheat sous vide water bath to 185°F / 85°C
2. Blend raspberries, sugar, water, lemon juice, and zest until smooth (ensure all ingredients are well combined)
3. Seal the mixture in a bag and cook for 60 minutes (remove all air for even cooking)
4. Cool in an ice bath, then strain out the seeds (use a fine mesh for a smooth texture)
5. Freeze in an ice cream maker and serve (follow the machine's instructions)

Cooking Temperature Range:
Optimal 185°F / 85°C (permissible range 183°F / 84°C to 190°F / 88°C).

Pistachio Ice Cream

Yield: 2 servings | Prep time: 20 minutes | Cook time: 1 hour

This creamy Sous Vide Pistachio Ice Cream is rich in flavor with a perfect nutty sweetness. Prepared with fresh pistachios and a hint of vanilla, this dessert delivers an indulgent, silky-smooth texture made possible by the precise sous vide cooking method.

Ingredients:
- Shelled pistachios - 0.5 cup
- Whole milk - 0.5 cup
- Heavy cream - 0.5 cup
- White sugar - 0.25 cup
- Egg yolk (large, whisk until thick) - 2 pieces
- Vanilla extract - 0.5 tsp

Nutritional Information (for 2 servings):
calories 320 kcal, protein 6g, carbohydrates 25g, fat 22g, fiber 1g, cholesterol 180mg, sodium 30mg, potassium 100mg

Directions:
1. Preheat sous vide water bath to 180°F / 82°C
2. Blend pistachios, milk, and cream until smooth (use a high-speed blender for best results)
3. Whisk the sugar and yolks, then mix in the pistachio blend and vanilla (add ingredients gradually to avoid lumps)
4. Cook the mixture in the sous vide water bath for 60 minutes (seal the bag tightly for even cooking)
5. Cool, churn, and freeze before serving (use ice bath immediately for cooling)

Cooking Temperature Range:
Optimal 180°F / 82°C (permissible range 179°F / 81°C to 185°F / 85°C).

Coconut Lime Sorbet

Yield: 2 servings | Prep time: 15 minutes | Cook time: 30 minutes

This refreshing Sous Vide Coconut Lime Sorbet combines the creaminess of coconut milk with the tangy brightness of lime. The sous vide method ensures a smooth and balanced mixture for a perfectly textured frozen dessert that's easy to prepare and full of tropical flavor.

Ingredients:
- Coconut milk (unsweetened) - 1 cup
- White sugar - 0.25 cup
- Lime juice (freshly squeezed) - 2 tbsp
- Lime zest (grated) - 1 tsp
- Salt - 1 pinch

Nutritional Information (for 2 servings):
calories 210 kcal, protein 2g, carbohydrates 21g, fat 14g, fiber 1g, cholesterol 0mg, sodium 15mg, potassium 200mg

Directions:
1. Preheat sous vide water bath to 176°F / 80°C
2. Whisk coconut milk, sugar, lime juice, lime zest, and salt (whisk until fully dissolved)
3. Transfer mixture to a resealable bag and seal tightly (remove air to ensure even cooking)
4. Cook in sous vide water bath for 30 minutes (keep the bag fully submerged)
5. Cool, churn, and freeze until firm before serving (chill thoroughly for smooth texture)

Cooking Temperature Range:
Optimal 176°F / 80°C (permissible range 175°F / 79°C to 179°F / 81°C).

Cookies and Cream Ice Cream

Yield: 2 servings | Prep time: 20 minutes | Cook time: 30 minutes

This Sous Vide Cookies and Cream Ice Cream creates a velvety base enriched with crushed chocolate cookies. Perfectly pasteurized for safety and a creamy texture, this dessert blends nostalgia and innovation, delivering the ultimate treat for ice cream lovers.

Ingredients:
- Heavy cream - 1 cup
- Whole milk - 0.5 cup
- White sugar - 0.25 cup
- Egg yolk - 2 pieces
- Vanilla extract - 0.5 tsp
- Crushed chocolate cookies - 0.33 cup

Nutritional Information (for 2 servings):
calories 380 kcal, protein 6g, carbohydrates 33g, fat 25g, fiber 1g, cholesterol 120mg, sodium 60mg, potassium 200mg

Directions:
1. Preheat sous vide water bath to 185°F / 85°C
2. Whisk cream, milk, sugar, egg yolks, and vanilla until smooth (mix thoroughly to combine flavors)
3. Pour into a resealable bag, remove air, and seal (use a vacuum sealer for best results)
4. Cook in a water bath for 30 minutes (stir bag occasionally if needed)
5. Cool, churn, and fold in cookies and freeze until firm (ensure cookies are evenly mixed)

Cooking Temperature Range:
Optimal 185°F / 85°C (permissible range 183°F / 84°C to 190°F / 88°C).

Banana Peanut Butter Ice Cream

Yield: 2 servings | Prep time: 20 minutes | Cook time: 30 minutes

This Sous Vide Banana Peanut Butter Ice Cream combines ripe bananas, creamy peanut butter, and a velvety custard base. Perfectly pasteurized for safety, it delivers a decadent treat with rich flavors and a smooth, indulgent texture, making it an irresistible dessert for any occasion.

Ingredients:
- Heavy cream - 1 cup
- Whole milk - 0.5 cup
- White sugar - 0.25 cup
- Banana - 1 piece
- Peanut butter (mix in blender) - 2 tbsp
- Egg yolk - 2 pieces

Nutritional Information (for 2 servings):
calories 400 kcal, protein 7g, carbohydrates 36g, fat 28g, fiber 2g, cholesterol 120mg, sodium 75mg, potassium 300mg

Directions:
1. Preheat sous vide water bath to 185°F / 85°C
2. Blend all ingredients until smooth (use a blender for best results)
3. Seal the mixture in a bag and remove air (use a vacuum sealer for precision)
4. Cook the bag in the water bath for 30 minutes (ensure even cooking by submerging fully)
5. Cool, churn, and freeze until firm (chill in an ice bath immediately)

Cooking Temperature Range:
Optimal 185°F / 85°C (permissible range 183°F / 84°C to 190°F / 88°C).

Blueberry Cheesecake Ice Cream

Yield: 2 servings | Prep time: 20 minutes | Cook time: 30 minutes

This rich Sous Vide Blueberry Cheesecake Ice Cream features the tang of cream cheese, the sweetness of blueberries, and a silky custard base. The precision sous vide method ensures a perfectly smooth texture, making this indulgent treat both luxurious and irresistible.

Ingredients:
- Heavy cream - 0.75 cup
- Whole milk - 0.5 cup
- Cream cheese (softened) - 0.25 cup
- White sugar - 0.25 cup
- Blueberries - 0.33 cup
- Egg yolk - 2 pieces

Nutritional Information (for 2 servings):
calories 390 kcal, protein 6g, carbohydrates 35g, fat 26g, fiber 1g, cholesterol 115mg, sodium 70mg, potassium 250mg

Directions:
1. Preheat sous vide water bath to 185°F / 85°C
2. Blend all ingredients until smooth (use a blender for best results)
3. Seal the mixture in a bag and remove air (use a vacuum sealer for precision)
4. Cook the bag in the water bath for 30 minutes (ensure even cooking by submerging fully)
5. Cool, churn, and freeze until firm (chill in an ice bath immediately)

Cooking Temperature Range:
Optimal 185°F / 85°C (permissible range 183°F / 84°C to 190°F / 88°C).

Pumpkin Spice Ice Cream

Yield: 2 servings | Prep time: 20 minutes | Cook time: 30 minutes

Capture the essence of fall with our Sous Vide Pumpkin Spice Ice Cream! This creamy, velvety treat is infused with real pumpkin and warm spices like cinnamon, nutmeg, and cloves. Sous vide precision ensures a smooth texture and perfectly balanced flavor, making every scoop a cozy, spiced indulgence.

Ingredients:
- Heavy cream - 0.75 cup
- Whole milk - 0.5 cup
- Pumpkin puree - 0.33 cup
- White sugar - 0.25 cup
- Egg yolk - 2 pieces
- Pumpkin pie spice - 0.5 tsp

Nutritional Information (for 2 servings):
calories 320 kcal, protein 5g, carbohydrates 30g, fat 20g, fiber 1g, cholesterol 110mg, sodium 60mg, potassium 240mg

Directions:
1. Preheat sous vide water bath to 185°F / 85°C
2. Blend all ingredients until smooth (use a blender for best results)
3. Seal the mixture in a bag and remove air (use a vacuum sealer for precision)
4. Cook the bag in the water bath for 30 minutes (fully submerge the bag)
5. Cool, churn, and freeze until firm (chill in an ice bath immediately)

Cooking Temperature Range:
Optimal 185°F / 85°C (permissible range 183°F / 84°C to 190°F / 88°C).

Blackberry Frozen Yogurt

Yield: 2 servings | Prep time: 15 minutes | Cook time: 30 minutes

Treat yourself to the vibrant tang of our Sous Vide Blackberry Frozen Yogurt! This creamy, refreshing dessert bursts with the bold sweetness of ripe blackberries and the smooth tanginess of yogurt. Sous vide precision ensures a silky texture, making every scoop a luscious and fruity delight.

Ingredients:
- Blackberries (rinse well) - 1 cup
- Greek yogurt (plain) - 0.5 cup
- White sugar - 0.25 cup
- Lemon juice (freshly squeezed) - 1 tbsp

Nutritional Information (for 2 servings):
calories 180 kcal, protein 5g, carbohydrates 35g, fat 2g, fiber 4g, cholesterol 5mg, sodium 20mg, potassium 200mg

Directions:
1. Preheat sous vide water bath to 180°F / 82°C
2. Blend blackberries, yogurt, sugar, and lemon juice (use a high-speed blender)
3. Strain the mixture and pour into a resealable bag (remove seeds for smooth texture)
4. Cook the sealed bag in a water bath for 30 minutes (fully submerge the bag)
5. Cool, churn in the ice cream maker, and freeze until firm (at least 2 hours)

Cooking Temperature Range:
Optimal 180°F / 82°C (permissible range 179°F / 81°C to 185°F / 85°C).

Passionfruit Sorbet

Yield: 2 servings | Prep time: 15 minutes | Cook time: 30 minutes

Refresh your palate with the tropical tang of our Sous Vide Passionfruit Sorbet! Bursting with passionfruit's vibrant, tart sweetness, this silky, frozen delight is as refreshing as it is flavorful. Sous vide precision ensures a perfectly smooth texture, making every scoop a taste of paradise.

Ingredients:
- Passionfruit pulp (fresh or frozen) - 0.5 cup
- White sugar - 0.33 cup
- Water - 0.25 cup
- Lime juice (freshly squeezed) - 1 tbsp

Nutritional Information (for 2 servings):
calories 140 kcal, protein 1g, carbohydrates 35g, fat 0g, fiber 2g, cholesterol 0mg, sodium 10mg, potassium 150mg

Directions:
1. Preheat sous vide water bath to 180°F / 82°C
2. Blend passionfruit pulp, sugar, water, and lime juice (use a high-speed blender)
3. Pour mixture into a resealable bag and remove air (seal tightly to prevent leaks)
4. Cook in the sous vide bath for 30 minutes (fully submerge the bag)
5. Cool, churn in an ice cream maker, and freeze until firm (at least 2 hours)

Cooking Temperature Range:
Optimal 180°F / 82°C (permissible range 179°F / 81°C to 185°F / 85°C).

Cherry Vanilla Ice Cream

Yield: 2 servings | Prep time: 20 minutes | Cook time: 1 hour

Delight in the creamy elegance of our Sous Vide Cherry Vanilla Ice Cream! Juicy cherries blend perfectly with the fragrant sweetness of vanilla in this velvety treat. Sous vide precision ensures a silky texture and vibrant flavor, making every scoop a luxurious and refreshing indulgence.

Ingredients:
- Whole milk - 1 cup
- Heavy cream - 0.5 cup
- White sugar - 0.33 cup
- Egg yolk (medium) - 2 pieces
- Cherry puree (fresh or frozen) - 0.5 cup
- Vanilla extract (pure) - 1 tsp

Nutritional Information (for 2 servings):
calories 290 kcal, protein 5g, carbohydrates 28g, fat 18g, fiber 1g, cholesterol 150mg, sodium 40mg, potassium 150mg

Directions:
1. Preheat sous vide water bath to 180°F / 82°C
2. Blend milk, cream, sugar, egg yolks, cherry puree, and vanilla (blend until smooth)
3. Pour into a resealable bag, remove air, and seal (use water displacement method)
4. Cook in the sous vide bath for 60 minutes (fully submerge the bag)
5. Cool in an ice bath, churn in an ice cream maker, and freeze (freeze for 2 hours or more)

Cooking Temperature Range:
Optimal 180°F / 82°C (permissible range 179°F / 81°C to 185°F / 85°C).

Tropical Pineapple Coconut Sorbet

Yield: 2 servings | Prep time: 15 minutes | Cook time: 1 hour

Escape to paradise with our Sous Vide Tropical Pineapple Coconut Sorbet! Sweet, juicy pineapple pairs perfectly with the creamy richness of coconut, creating a refreshing and exotic frozen treat. Sous vide precision ensures a silky-smooth texture, giving every scoop a tropical burst of flavor.

Ingredients:
- Pineapple chunks (fresh or canned) - 1 cup
- Coconut milk (unsweetened) - 0.5 cup
- White sugar - 0.25 cup
- Lime juice (freshly squeezed) - 1 tsp
- Vanilla extract (pure) - 0.5 tsp

Nutritional Information (for 2 servings):
calories 160 kcal, protein 1g, carbohydrates 30g, fat 5g, fiber 2g, cholesterol 0mg, sodium 10mg, potassium 150mg

Directions:
1. Preheat sous vide water bath to 185°F / 85°C
2. Blend all ingredients until smooth (blend until fully pureed)
3. Transfer to a resealable bag, remove air, and seal (use water displacement method)
4. Cook in the sous vide bath for 60 minutes (fully submerge the bag)
5. Cool in an ice bath, churn in an ice cream maker, and freeze (freeze for at least 2 hours)

Cooking Temperature Range:
Optimal 185°F / 85°C (permissible range 183°F / 84°C to 190°F / 88°C).

APPENDICES

COMMON CONVERSION CHARTS

Temperature Conversion: Fahrenheit to Celsius and Vice Versa

Fahrenheit	Celsius	Usage
-0.4°F	-18°C	Store frozen foods
32°F	0°C	Store chilled foods
39.2°F	4°C	Ideal refrigeration temperature
100°F	37.8°C	Gentle preheating
104°F	40°C	Sous vide for delicate proteins
110°F	43.3°C	Starter for yogurt
113°F	45°C	Warm water for chocolate melting or yogurt culture
122°F	50°C	Sous vide vegetables
131°F	55°C	Sous vide medium-rare meats
140°F	60°C	Sous vide fish and poultry
145°F	62.8°C	Sous vide pasteurization
150°F	65.6°C	Cooking custards and eggs
155°F	68.3°C	Sous vide stews
160°F	71.1°C	Medium cooking temperature
165°F	73.9°C	Safe cooking for poultry
170°F	76.7°C	High-temperature sous vide
175°F	79.4°C	Preheat for frying
180°F	82.2°C	Cooking dense vegetables
185°F	85°C	Stewing
190°F	87.8°C	Deep stewing or braising
195°F	90.6°C	Frying
200°F	93.3°C	Baking or roasting
203°F	95°C	High-temperature stewing
212°F	100°C	Boiling water
248°F	120°C	Deep frying
300°F	149°C	High-temperature roasting
356°F	180°C	Frying at high heat
400°F	204°C	Baking pizzas or flatbreads
450°F	232°C	High-temperature grilling
500°F	260°C	Extreme searing or grilling
572°F	300°C	Maximum conventional oven temperature

Weight Conversion: US to Metric

US Weight	Metric Equivalent
1 oz	28.35 g
2 oz	56.7 g
5 oz	141.75 g
1/2 lb (8 oz)	226.8 g
1 lb (16 oz)	453.59 g
2 lb	907.18 g

Volume Conversion: US to Metric

US Volume	Metric Equivalent
1 tsp	5 ml
1 tbsp	15 ml
1/2 cup	120 ml
1 cup	240 ml
1 quart	0.95 liters
1 gallon	3.79 liters

Baking Ingredient Specific Weights

Ingredient	1 cup (US)	Weight in Grams (EU)
Sugar (granulated)	7 oz	200 g
Flour (all-purpose)	4.5 oz	125 g
Butter	8 oz	227 g

> **Key Notes:** Precision is essential for consistency when converting for sous vide recipes, especially in baking and desserts.

INGREDIENT SUBSTITUTION GUIDE

For dietary preferences or ingredient availability, here are some common substitutions:

Dairy Substitutes

Ingredient	Substitute
Heavy cream	Coconut cream
Whole milk	Almond or oat milk
Butter	Vegan butter or ghee

Sugar Substitutes

Ingredient	Substitute
Granulated sugar	Coconut sugar or honey
Brown sugar	Maple syrup or date sugar
Powdered sugar	Erythritol or stevia

Egg Substitutes

Ingredient	Substitute
1 egg	1/4 cup of mashed banana.
1 egg white	2 tbsp aquafaba

Gluten-Free Substitutes

Ingredient	Substitute
All-purpose flour	Almond flour or gluten-free blend
Bread crumbs	Crushed nuts or gluten-free panko

TROUBLESHOOTING SOUS VIDE DESSERTS

1. Custards or Puddings are Runny

Cause: The Temperature is too low, or there is insufficient cooking time.

Solution: Verify your sous vide device settings. Most custards should be cooked at 185°F (85°C). If necessary, extend the cooking time by 10-15 minutes.

2. The texture is Grainy or Curdled

Cause: The Temperature is too high, causing proteins to overcook.

Solution: Lower the temperature to the appropriate level. For delicate custards, stay at 176°F (80°C).

3. Chocolate Desserts Won't Set

Cause: Incorrect ratio of chocolate to liquid or insufficient chilling.

Solution: Adjust the recipe by adding more chocolate or chilling it in the fridge for at least 4 hours after cooking.

4. Cheesecake Cracks Upon Cooling

Cause: Sudden temperature changes.

Solution: Let the dessert cool gradually in the water bath before transferring it to the fridge.

5. Bags Leak During Cooking

Cause: Poor sealing or punctures.

Solution: Use high-quality vacuum-seal bags. Double-bag liquids and check for air bubbles before sealing.

6. Dessert Has an "Off" Taste

Cause: Reused or low-quality bags.

Solution: Always use food-safe, single-use sous vide bags for desserts.

7. Custard Did Not Set

Cause: Insufficient temperature or cooking time.

Solution: Check the temperature accuracy of your sous vide device. Cook at 176°F (80°C) for an additional 30 minutes.

8. Watery Texture in Desserts

Cause: Excess liquid in the recipe.

Solution: Strain or reduce liquid content before sealing.

9. Overly Sweet or Bland Flavor

Cause: Incorrect measurement or unbalanced recipe.

Solution: Taste and adjust sweeteners before cooking. Sous vide intensifies flavors over time.

INDEX RECIPES

All-purpose flour
Apple Crumble, p.106
Apple Spice Cake, p.94
Banana Walnut Cake, p.89
Black Forest Cake, p.91
Blackberry Sage Cake, p.88
Blueberry Cobbler, p.108
Blueberry Lemon Cake, p.94
Brownies, p.109
Cherry Clafoutis, p.50
Cherry Vanilla Cake, p.91
Chocolate Brownies, p.131
Chocolate Cake, p.131
Chocolate Chip Cookies, p.132
Chocolate Fudge Brownies, p.134
Chocolate Lava Cake, p.136
Cinnamon Rolls, p.99
Cranberry Orange Cake, p.88
Dark Chocolate Fondant Cake, p.141
Fig Honey Cake, p.86
Fudge Brownies, p.142
Gingerbread Pudding, p.101
Gooseberry Cardamom Cake, p.86
Kiwi Lime Cake, p.87
Lemon Bars, p.84
Lemon Blueberry Bundt Cake, p.90
Mango Coconut Cake, p.90
Peach Cobbler Cake, p.92
Pear Ginger Cake, p.87
Pineapple Upside-Down Cake, p.89
Pomegranate Chocolate Cake, p.144
Raspberry Almond Cake, p.92
Raspberry Lemon Bars, p.95
Sticky Toffee Pudding, p.99
Strawberry Shortcake, p.93
Tres Leches Cake, p.102
Triple Chocolate Pudding Cake, p.145

Almond butter
Almond Butter Brownies, p.106

Almond extract
Almond Custard, p.48
Chocolate Almond Yogurt, p.69
Raspberry Almond Cake, p.92

Almond flour
Apricot Almond Cake, p.85
Raspberry Almond Cake, p.92

Almond milk
Almond Custard, p.48
Almond Milk Panna Cotta, p.48
Chocolate Almond Yogurt, p.69

Amaretto liqueur
Apricots with Amaretto, p.23
Cherry Amaretto Gelée, p.117

Apple cider
Apple Cider Gelée, p.116

Apples
Apple Cinnamon Compote, p.23
Apple Cinnamon Pudding, p.104
Apple Crumble, p.106
Apple Spice Cake, p.94
Baked Apples, p.24
Cinnamon Apples, p.28
Vanilla-Infused Apples, p.41

Apricots
Apricot Almond Cake, p.85
Apricots with Amaretto, p.23

Arborio rice
Rice Pudding with Cinnamon, p.100

Banana
Banana Bread Pudding, p.107
Banana Cream Yogurt, p.67
Banana Peanut Butter Ice Cream, p.157
Banana Walnut Cake, p.89
Caramelized Bananas, p.27

Berries
Lemon Yogurt Parfait, p.55

Blackberries
Blackberry Coulis, p.26
Blackberry Frozen Yogurt, p.159
Blackberry Honey Yogurt, p.67
Blackberry Sage Cake, p.88

Blueberries
Blueberry Cheesecake, p.107
Blueberry Cheesecake Ice Cream, p.158
Blueberry Cobbler, p.108
Blueberry Lavender Jelly, p.116
Blueberry Lemon Cake, p.94
Blueberry Lemon Yogurt, p.68
Blueberry Syrup, p.26
Blueberry Yogurt, p.68
Fruit Salad, p.32
Lemon Blueberry Bundt Cake, p.90

Bourbon
Cherries with Bourbon, p.28

Bread
Apple Cinnamon Pudding, p.104
Banana Bread Pudding, p.107

Butterscotch Bread Pudding, p.102
Coconut Rum Pudding Cake, p.105
Maple Pecan Pudding Cake, p.103
Peach Cobbler Bread Pudding, p.103

Brioche bread
Bread Pudding with Whiskey Sauce, p.108
Salted Caramel Pudding Cake, p.105

Butterscotch chips
Butterscotch Bread Pudding, p.102

Campari
Grapefruit Campari Jelly, p.119

Caramel sauce
Salted Caramel Ice Cream Base, p.154
Salted Caramel Pudding Cake, p.105

Carrot puree
Carrot Cake Cheesecake, p.101

Champagne
Strawberry Champagne Jelly, p.123

Cherries
Cherries with Bourbon, p.28
Cherry Clafoutis, p.50

Cherry juice
Cherry Amaretto Gelée, p.117

Cherry puree
Cherry Vanilla Ice Cream, p.160

Chia seeds
Berry Smoothie Bowl, p.25

Chocolate chips
Chocolate Chip Cookies, p.132
Mint Chocolate Chip Ice Cream, p.154

Chocolate cookies
Cookies and Cream Ice Cream, p.157

Cloves
Poached Pears in Red Wine, p.38

Cocoa powder
Almond Butter Brownies, p.106
Black Forest Cake, p.91
Chocolate Almond Yogurt, p.69
Chocolate Brownies, p.131
Chocolate Cake, p.131
Chocolate Fudge Brownies, p.134
Chocolate Gelato Base, p.151
Chocolate Hazelnut Cheesecake, p.135
Chocolate Oat Pudding, p.137
Chocolate Yogurt, p.70
Pomegranate Chocolate Cake, p.144
Red Velvet Cheesecake, p.104

Coconut
Mango Coconut Cake, p.90
Pineapple Coconut Yogurt, p.75

Coconut flakes
Coconut Rum Pudding Cake, p.105

Coconut milk
Chocolate Coconut Custard, p.133
Coconut Custard, p.51
Coconut Lime Gelée, p.118
Coconut Lime Sorbet, p.156
Coconut Milk Yogurt, p.70
Coconut Rice Pudding, p.98
Coconut Rum Pudding Cake, p.105
Mango Coconut Cake, p.90
Mango Coconut Ice Cream, p.152
Tropical Pineapple Coconut Sorbet, p.160

Cranberries
Cranberry Orange Cake, p.88
Cranberry Sauce, p.31

Cranberry juice
Cranberry Orange Gelatin, p.118

Cream cheese
Blueberry Cheesecake, p.107
Blueberry Cheesecake Ice Cream, p.158
Carrot Cake Cheesecake, p.101
Cheesecake, p.109
Chocolate Cheesecake, p.132
Chocolate Hazelnut Cheesecake, p.135
Chocolate Peanut Butter Cheesecake, p.137
Lemon Cheesecake, p.85
Mixed Berry Cheesecake, p.93
Pumpkin Cheesecake, p.96
Red Velvet Cheesecake, p.104
Vanilla Bean Cheesecake, p.100

Dark chocolate
Chocolate Cheesecake, p.132
Chocolate Espresso Custard, p.133
Chocolate Ganache Tart, p.134
Chocolate Gelatin Mousse, p.135
Chocolate Lava Cake, p.136
Chocolate Mousse, p.136
Chocolate Peanut Butter Cheesecake, p.137
Chocolate Pots de Crème, p.138
Chocolate Pudding, p.138
Chocolate Soufflé, p.139
Chocolate Tart, p.139
Chocolate Truffle Filling, p.140
Chocolate Yogurt, p.70
Dark Chocolate Crémeux, p.140
Dark Chocolate Fondant Cake, p.141
Dark Chocolate Mousse, p.141

Fudge Brownies, p.142
Hazelnut Chocolate Spread, p.142
Hot Chocolate Custard, p.143
Mint Chocolate Mousse, p.143
Triple Chocolate Pudding Cake, p.145

Dark chocolate chips
Brownies, p.109

Dark rum
Pineapple with Rum and Brown Sugar, p.37

Dates
Sticky Toffee Pudding, p.99

Eggs
Almond Butter Brownies, p.106
Apple Cinnamon Pudding, p.104
Apricot Almond Cake, p.85
Blackberry Sage Cake, p.88
Blueberry Cheesecake, p.107
Bread Pudding with Whiskey Sauce, p.108
Brownies, p.109
Butterscotch Bread Pudding, p.102
Caramel Flan, p.49
Cheesecake, p.109
Cherry Clafoutis, p.50
Chocolate Brownies, p.131
Chocolate Cake, p.131
Chocolate Cheesecake, p.132
Chocolate Coconut Custard, p.133
Chocolate Espresso Custard, p.133
Chocolate Fudge Brownies, p.134
Chocolate Hazelnut Cheesecake, p.135
Chocolate Lava Cake, p.136
Chocolate Peanut Butter Cheesecake, p.137
Chocolate Soufflé, p.139
Coconut Custard, p.51
Coconut Rum Pudding Cake, p.105
Cranberry Orange Cake, p.88
Dark Chocolate Fondant Cake, p.141
Dark Chocolate Mousse, p.141
Eggnog Custard, p.52
Espresso Custard, p.53
Fig Honey Cake, p.86
Fudge Brownies, p.142
Gooseberry Cardamom Cake, p.86
Kiwi Lime Cake, p.87
Lemon Bars, p.84
Lemon Cheesecake, p.85
Maple Pecan Pudding Cake, p.103
Mixed Berry Cheesecake, p.93
Peach Cobbler Bread Pudding, p.103
Pear Ginger Cake, p.87
Pineapple Upside-Down Cake, p.89
Pomegranate Chocolate Cake, p.144

Pumpkin Cheesecake, p.96
Pumpkin Custard, p.58
Pumpkin Pie, p.96
Raspberry Lemon Bars, p.95
Red Velvet Cheesecake, p.104
S'mores Cake, p.95
Salted Caramel Pudding Cake, p.105
Sticky Toffee Pudding, p.99
Tres Leches Cake, p.102
Triple Chocolate Pudding Cake, p.145
Vanilla Bean Cheesecake, p.100
Vanilla Flan, p.62

Egg yolk
Almond Custard, p.48
Banana Peanut Butter Ice Cream, p.157
Blueberry Cheesecake Ice Cream, p.158
Chai Spiced Custard, p.50
Cherry Vanilla Ice Cream, p.160
Chocolate Chip Cookies, p.132
Chocolate Gelato Base, p.151
Chocolate Mousse, p.136
Chocolate Pots de Crème, p.138
Chocolate Pudding, p.138
Chocolate Tart, p.139
Coffee Crème Brûlée, p.51
Cookies and Cream Ice Cream, p.157
Crème Brûlée, p.52
Dark Chocolate Crémeux, p.140
Dark Chocolate Fondant Cake, p.141
Espresso Gelato, p.155
Fruit Tart, p.98
Hot Chocolate Custard, p.143
Key Lime Pie, p.84
Key Lime Pots de Crème, p.54
Lemon Curd, p.55
Lemon Pudding, p.97
Lemon Tart, p.97
Mango Coconut Ice Cream, p.152
Mango Custard, p.56
Maple Custard, p.56
Matcha Green Tea Custard, p.57
Matcha Green Tea Ice Cream, p.153
Mint Chocolate Chip Ice Cream, p.154
Mint Chocolate Mousse, p.143
Peanut Butter Custard, p.58
Pistachio Ice Cream, p.156
Pumpkin Spice Ice Cream, p.158
Salted Caramel Custard, p.59
Salted Caramel Ice Cream Base, p.154
Salted Caramel Pots de Crème, p.59
Tiramisu, p.61
Vanilla Bean Ice Cream Base, p.151
Vanilla Custard, p.62

Eggnog
Eggnog Custard, p.52

Elderflower syrup
Elderflower and Pear Jelly, p.119

Espresso
Coffee Crème Brûlée, p.51
Espresso Custard, p.53
Tiramisu, p.61

Espresso powder
Chocolate Espresso Custard, p.133
Espresso Gelato, p.155

Evaporated milk
Tres Leches Cake, p.102

Figs
Fig Compote, p.31
Fig Honey Cake, p.86
Poached Figs, p.37

Fruit juice
Classic Fruit Jelly, p.117
Fruits
Fruit Tart, p.98

Ginger
Gingerbread Pudding, p.101
Peach Ginger Yogurt, p.74
Pear Ginger Cake, p.87
Pineapple Ginger Jelly, p.122

Gooseberries
Gooseberry Cardamom Cake, p.86

Graham crackers
Carrot Cake Cheesecake, p.101
Cheesecake, p.109
Key Lime Pie, p.84
Lemon Cheesecake, p.85
Mixed Berry Cheesecake, p.93
Pumpkin Cheesecake, p.96
S'mores Cake, p.95
Vanilla Bean Cheesecake, p.100

Granola
Berry Parfait, p.49
Berry Smoothie Bowl, p.25
Lemon Yogurt Parfait, p.55
Strawberry Parfait, p.60

Grapefruit
Citrus Bliss Compote, p.30
Grapefruit, p.33
Grapefruit Segments in Vanilla Syrup, p.33

Grapefruit juice
Grapefruit Campari Jelly, p.119

Greek yogurt
Berry Parfait, p.49
Berry Smoothie Bowl, p.25
Blackberry Frozen Yogurt, p.159
Chocolate Yogurt, p.70
Peach Frozen Yogurt, p.153

Hazelnut spread
Chocolate Hazelnut Cheesecake, p.135

Heavy cream
Apple Cinnamon Pudding, p.104
Banana Bread Pudding, p.107
Banana Peanut Butter Ice Cream, p.157
Black Forest Cake, p.91
Blueberry Cheesecake Ice Cream, p.158
Caramel Flan, p.49
Chai Spiced Custard, p.50
Cherry Vanilla Ice Cream, p.160
Chocolate Cheesecake, p.132
Chocolate Espresso Custard, p.133
Chocolate Ganache Tart, p.134
Chocolate Gelatin Mousse, p.135
Chocolate Gelato Base, p.151
Chocolate Mousse, p.136
Chocolate Pots de Crème, p.138
Chocolate Tart, p.139
Chocolate Truffle Filling, p.140
Coffee Crème Brûlée, p.51
Cookies and Cream Ice Cream, p.157
Crème Brûlée, p.52
Dark Chocolate Crémeux, p.140
Dark Chocolate Mousse, p.141
Espresso Custard, p.53
Espresso Gelato, p.155
Fruit Tart, p.98
Greek Yogurt, p.71
Hazelnut Chocolate Spread, p.142
Honey Lavender Panna Cotta, p.53
Hot Chocolate Custard, p.143
Key Lime Pots de Crème, p.54
Lavender Panna Cotta, p.54
Lemon Pudding, p.97
Lemon Tart, p.97
Mango Custard, p.56
Maple Custard, p.56
Maple Pecan Pudding Cake, p.103
Matcha Green Tea Custard, p.57
Matcha Green Tea Ice Cream, p.153
Mint Chocolate Chip Ice Cream, p.154
Mint Chocolate Mousse, p.143
Panna Cotta, p.57

Peach Cobbler Bread Pudding, p.103
Peanut Butter Custard, p.58
Pistachio Ice Cream, p.156
Pumpkin Custard, p.58
Pumpkin Pie, p.96
Pumpkin Spice Ice Cream, p.158
Raspberry-Infused Chocolate Ganache, p.144
Rice Pudding with Cinnamon, p.100
Salted Caramel Custard, p.59
Salted Caramel Ice Cream Base, p.154
Salted Caramel Pots de Crème, p.59
Salted Caramel Pudding Cake, p.105
Strawberry Panna Cotta, p.60
Strawberry Shortcake, p.93
Tiramisu, p.61
Vanilla Bean Cheesecake, p.100
Vanilla Bean Ice Cream Base, p.151
Vanilla Bean Panna Cotta, p.61
Vanilla Custard, p.62
Vanilla Flan, p.62
White Chocolate Panna Cotta, p.145

Honey
Apricots with Amaretto, p.23
Banana Cream Yogurt, p.67
Berry Parfait, p.49
Berry Smoothie Bowl, p.25
Blackberry Honey Yogurt, p.67
Blueberry Lemon Yogurt, p.68
Chai-Spiced Yogurt, p.69
Chocolate Almond Yogurt, p.69
Chocolate Yogurt, p.70
Cinnamon-Infused Peaches, p.29
Fig Honey Cake, p.86
Fruit Salad, p.32
Grapefruit, p.33
Greek Yogurt, p.71
Honey Lavender Panna Cotta, p.53
Honey Lemon Gelée, p.120
Honey-Sweetened Yogurt, p.71
Honeyed Pears, p.34
Key Lime Yogurt, p.72
Lemon Yogurt Parfait, p.55
Mango with Lime and Chili, p.35
Matcha Green Tea Yogurt, p.73
Orange Blossom Yogurt, p.74
Orange Segments with Honey, p.35
Peach Frozen Yogurt, p.153
Peach Ginger Yogurt, p.74
Pineapple Coconut Yogurt, p.75
Poached Figs, p.37
Pumpkin Spice Yogurt, p.75
Raspberry Swirl Yogurt, p.76
Vanilla Bean and Lavender Yogurt, p.77
Watermelon Infused with Mint, p.41

Instant yeast
Cinnamon Rolls, p.99

Key lime juice
Key Lime Pie, p.84
Key Lime Pots de Crème, p.54
Key Lime Yogurt, p.72

Kiwi
Kiwi Lime Cake, p.87
Kiwi Lime Jelly, p.120

Ladyfingers
Tiramisu, p.61

Lemon
Citrus Marmalade, p.30

Lemon juice
Apple Cider Gelée, p.116
Apple Cinnamon Compote, p.23
Berry Compote, p.24
Berry Medley Compote, p.25
Blackberry Coulis, p.26
Blackberry Frozen Yogurt, p.159
Blueberry Lavender Jelly, p.116
Blueberry Syrup, p.26
Cinnamon Apples, p.28
Cinnamon Pears, p.29
Cinnamon-Infused Peaches, p.29
Classic Fruit Jelly, p.117
Elderflower and Pear Jelly, p.119
Fig Compote, p.31
Fruit Compote, p.32
Honey Lemon Gelée, p.120
Honeyed Pears, p.34
Lemon Bars, p.84
Lemon Cheesecake, p.85
Lemon Curd, p.55
Lemon Gelatin Squares, p.121
Lemon Pudding, p.97
Lemon Tart, p.97
Lemon Yogurt Parfait, p.55
Peach Bellini Gelée, p.122
Peach Compote, p.36
Peach Frozen Yogurt, p.153
Raspberry Gelée, p.123
Raspberry Lemon Bars, p.95
Raspberry Lemon Sorbet, p.155
Strawberry Champagne Jelly, p.123
Strawberry Compote, p.40
Strawberry Rhubarb Sauce, p.40
Strawberry Sorbet, p.152
Vanilla-Infused Apples, p.41

Lime juice
Coconut Lime Gelée, p.118
Coconut Lime Sorbet, p.156
Kiwi Lime Cake, p.87
Kiwi Lime Jelly, p.120
Mango with Lime and Chili, p.35
Passionfruit Sorbet, p.159
Tropical Pineapple Coconut Sorbet, p.160
Watermelon Infused with Mint, p.41

Mango
Mango Coconut Cake, p.90
Mango Coconut Ice Cream, p.152
Mango Custard, p.56
Mango Lassi Yogurt, p.72
Mango Passionfruit Compote, p.34
Mango Passionfruit Jelly, p.121
Mango with Lime and Chili, p.35

Maple syrup
Coconut Milk Yogurt, p.70
Maple Cinnamon Yogurt, p.73
Maple Custard, p.56
Maple Pecan Pudding Cake, p.103

Marshmallow fluff
S'mores Cake, p.95

Mascarpone
Tiramisu, p.61

Matcha green tea powder
Matcha Green Tea Custard, p.57
Matcha Green Tea Ice Cream, p.153
Matcha Green Tea Yogurt, p.73

Milk
Butterscotch Bread Pudding, p.102
Chocolate Oat Pudding, p.137
Cinnamon Rolls, p.99
Gingerbread Pudding, p.101

Milk chocolate
Triple Chocolate Pudding Cake, p.145

Mixed berries
Berry Compote, p.24
Berry Medley Compote, p.25
Berry Parfait, p.49
Berry Smoothie Bowl, p.25
Mixed Berry Cheesecake, p.93

Mixed fruits
Fruit Compote, p.32

Molasses
Gingerbread Pudding, p.101

Nutmeg
Eggnog Custard, p.52

Orange
Citrus Bliss Compote, p.30
Citrus Marmalade, p.30
Orange Segments with Honey, p.35

Orange Blossom Water
Orange Blossom Yogurt, p.74

Orange juice
Cranberry Orange Gelatin, p.118
Cranberry Sauce, p.31
Fruit Salad, p.32

Passionfruit pulp
Mango Passionfruit Compote, p.34
Mango Passionfruit Jelly, p.121
Passionfruit Sorbet, p.159

Peaches
Cinnamon-Infused Peaches, p.29
Peach and Cardamom Compote, p.36
Peach Bellini Gelée, p.122
Peach Cobbler Bread Pudding, p.103
Peach Cobbler Cake, p.92
Peach Compote, p.36
Peach Frozen Yogurt, p.153
Peach Ginger Yogurt, p.74

Peanut butter
Banana Peanut Butter Ice Cream, p.157
Chocolate Peanut Butter Cheesecake, p.137
Peanut Butter Custard, p.58

Pear juice
Elderflower and Pear Jelly, p.119

Pears
Cinnamon Pears, p.29
Honeyed Pears, p.34
Pear Ginger Cake, p.87
Poached Pears, p.38
Poached Pears in Red Wine, p.38

Pecans
Maple Pecan Pudding Cake, p.103

Pineapple
Caramelized Pineapple, p.27
Pineapple Coconut Yogurt, p.75
Pineapple with Rum and Brown Sugar, p.37

Pineapple chunks
Fruit Salad, p.32
Tropical Pineapple Coconut Sorbet, p.160

Pineapple juice
Pineapple Ginger Jelly, p.122

Pineapple slices
Pineapple Upside-Down Cake, p.89

Pistachios
Pistachio Ice Cream, p.156

Plain yogurt
Banana Cream Yogurt, p.67
Blackberry Honey Yogurt, p.67
Blueberry Lemon Yogurt, p.68
Chai-Spiced Yogurt, p.69
Chocolate Almond Yogurt, p.69
Coconut Milk Yogurt, p.70
Greek Yogurt, p.71
Honey-Sweetened Yogurt, p.71
Key Lime Yogurt, p.72
Lemon Yogurt Parfait, p.55
Mango Lassi Yogurt, p.72
Maple Cinnamon Yogurt, p.73
Matcha Green Tea Yogurt, p.73
Orange Blossom Yogurt, p.74
Peach Ginger Yogurt, p.74
Pineapple Coconut Yogurt, p.75
Pumpkin Spice Yogurt, p.75
Raspberry Swirl Yogurt, p.76
Vanilla Bean and Lavender Yogurt, p.77
Vanilla Yogurt, p.77

Plums
Spiced Plums, p.39

Pomegranate arils
Pomegranate Arils with Rose Water, p.39
Pomegranate Chocolate Cake, p.144

Prosecco
Peach Bellini Gelée, p.122

Pumpkin puree
Pumpkin Cheesecake, p.96
Pumpkin Custard, p.58
Pumpkin Pie, p.96
Pumpkin Spice Ice Cream, p.158
Pumpkin Spice Yogurt, p.75

R aspberries
Raspberry Almond Cake, p.92
Raspberry Gelée, p.123
Raspberry Lemon Bars, p.95
Raspberry Lemon Sorbet, p.155

Raspberry puree
Raspberry Swirl Yogurt, p.76
Raspberry-Infused Chocolate Ganache, p.144

Red wine
Poached Pears in Red Wine, p.38

Rhubarb
Strawberry Rhubarb Sauce, p.40

Roasted hazelnuts
Hazelnut Chocolate Spread, p.142

Rolled oats
Apple Crumble, p.106
Chocolate Oat Pudding, p.137

Rose water
Pomegranate Arils with Rose Water, p.39

Rum
Coconut Rum Pudding Cake, p.105

S age
Blackberry Sage Cake, p.88

Salted caramel sauce
Salted Caramel Custard, p.59

Semi-sweet chocolate chips
Chocolate Coconut Custard, p.133
Raspberry-Infused Chocolate Ganache, p.144
S'mores Cake, p.95

Sour cream
Cheesecake, p.109

Strawberries
Fruit Salad, p.32
Strawberry Champagne Jelly, p.123
Strawberry Compote, p.40
Strawberry Panna Cotta, p.60
Strawberry Parfait, p.60
Strawberry Rhubarb Sauce, p.40
Strawberry Shortcake, p.93
Strawberry Sorbet, p.152
Strawberry Yogurt, p.76

Sweet cherries
Black Forest Cake, p.91
Cherry Vanilla Cake, p.91

Sweetened condensed milk
Key Lime Pie, p.84
Tres Leches Cake, p.102

W alnuts
Baked Apples, p.24
Banana Walnut Cake, p.89

Watermelon
Watermelon Infused with Mint, p.41

Watermelon juice
Watermelon Mint Jelly, p.124

Whiskey
Bread Pudding with Whiskey Sauce, p.108

White chocolate
Triple Chocolate Pudding Cake, p.145
White Chocolate Panna Cotta, p.145

White rice
Coconut Rice Pudding, p.98

Whole milk
Banana Bread Pudding, p.107
Banana Cream Yogurt, p.67
Banana Peanut Butter Ice Cream, p.157
Blackberry Honey Yogurt, p.67
Blueberry Cheesecake Ice Cream, p.158
Blueberry Lemon Yogurt, p.68
Bread Pudding with Whiskey Sauce, p.108
Caramel Flan, p.49
Chai-Spiced Yogurt, p.69
Cherry Clafoutis, p.50
Cherry Vanilla Ice Cream, p.160
Chocolate Gelato Base, p.151
Chocolate Pudding, p.138
Cookies and Cream Ice Cream, p.157
Espresso Gelato, p.155
Greek Yogurt, p.71
Honey-Sweetened Yogurt, p.71
Hot Chocolate Custard, p.143
Key Lime Yogurt, p.72
Lemon Pudding, p.97

Mango Lassi Yogurt, p.72
Maple Cinnamon Yogurt, p.73
Matcha Green Tea Ice Cream, p.153
Matcha Green Tea Yogurt, p.73
Mint Chocolate Chip Ice Cream, p.154
Orange Blossom Yogurt, p.74
Peach Ginger Yogurt, p.74
Pineapple Coconut Yogurt, p.75
Pistachio Ice Cream, p.156
Pumpkin Spice Ice Cream, p.158
Pumpkin Spice Yogurt, p.75
Raspberry Swirl Yogurt, p.76
Rice Pudding with Cinnamon, p.100
Salted Caramel Ice Cream Base, p.154
Salted Caramel Pots de Crème, p.59
Strawberry Panna Cotta, p.60
Strawberry Parfait, p.60
Strawberry Yogurt, p.76
Vanilla Bean and Lavender Yogurt, p.77
Vanilla Bean Gelatin, p.124
Vanilla Bean Ice Cream Base, p.151
Vanilla Custard, p.62
Vanilla Flan, p.62
Vanilla Yogurt, p.77

Whole milk yogurt
Blueberry Yogurt, p.68

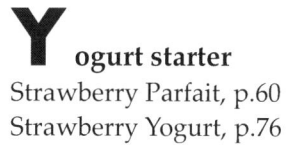

Yogurt starter
Strawberry Parfait, p.60
Strawberry Yogurt, p.76

WHY SOUS VIDE? WHY NOW?

Sous vide cooking offers precision, consistency, and unparalleled flavor development, making it ideal for home cooks and professionals alike. Whether you're crafting a perfectly creamy custard or experimenting with a bold-infused cocktail, sous vide unlocks new culinary possibilities. This series simplifies and demystifies the process for beginners while offering exciting options for seasoned cooks.

Thank you for being part of our journey. We can't wait to see what delicious creations you'll make next!

If you've enjoyed this book, now is the time to leave a review on Amazon to help others discover the joys of sous vide cooking and to let us know how to improve our books.

☆☆☆☆☆

FINAL TREAT: HEARTFELT THANKS AND AN INVITATION TO EXPLORE MORE

Thank you for choosing the *Sous Vide Cookbook for Beginners: Dessert Lover's Book, Everyday, Party, and Holiday Sweet Treat Recipes for Two Servings with Ingredients, Nutritional Information, and Clear Instructions*! We're thrilled to be part of your culinary journey. This book is designed to bring sous vide desserts to life with easy-to-follow instructions and nutritional transparency for two perfect servings.

DISCOVER MORE WITH THE "COOKBOOK FOR BEGINNERS" SERIES

"Sous Vide Cookbook for Beginners: Two Servings Recipes with Ingredients, Nutritional Information, and Clear Instructions. Includes Temperature Ranges for Joint Cooking Different Dishes".

This comprehensive guide is a must-have for anyone looking to master the sous vide cooking method. It includes:
- Step-by-step guidance tailored for beginners.
- Recipes cover a variety of dishes, from proteins to vegetables, and beyond.
- Use two-serving portions to reduce waste and make portion control simple.
- Detailed nutritional information for each recipe.
- A breakdown of temperature ranges to help you plan and cook multiple dishes simultaneously.

Whether you're a novice or looking to refine your sous vide skills, this book is the perfect kitchen companion.

Find it now on Amazon, or scan the QR code:

Happy cooking!

Made in the USA
Middletown, DE
27 March 2025